VISUAL QUICKSTART GUIDE

MAC OS X
10.2

Maria Langer

 Peachpit Press

Visual QuickStart Guide
Mac OS X 10.2
Maria Langer

Peachpit Press
1249 Eighth Street
Berkeley, CA 94710
510-524-2178 • 800-283-9444
510-524-2221 (fax)

Find us on the World Wide Web at: www.peachpit.com

To report errors, send a note to errata@peachpit.com

Peachpit Press is a division of Pearson Education

Editor: Nancy Davis
Technical Editor: Victor Gavenda
Indexer: Emily Glossbrenner
Cover Design: The Visual Group
Production: Maria Langer, Connie Jeung-Mills
DVD-Video screenshots courtesy of Sli-Fi media, www.sli-fi.com

Colophon

This book was produced with Adobe InDesign 2.0 and Adobe Photoshop 7.0 on a Power Macintosh G4. The fonts used were Utopia, Meta Plus, and PIXymbols Command. Screenshots were created using Snapz Pro X on an iMac. Screenshots reprinted by permission of Apple Computer, Inc.

Notice of Rights

Notice of Liability

Trademarks

ISBN 0-321-15801-6

9 8 7 6 5

Printed and bound in the United States of America.

Dedication

In loving memory of
Maria Soricelli
1912 - 2002

She will be sorely missed.

Thanks!

To Nancy Davis, for her ever-sharp editing skills. Nancy not only finds my grammar and typing errors, but she gently reminds me to include coverage of features that might otherwise slip through the cracks.

To Victor Gavenda, for his technical editing work. Victor picked a few nits that helped me make this book clearer and a bit more accurate.

To Connie Jeung-Mills, for yet another smooth project. I wish I could work with Connie for *all* of my books!

To the rest of the folks at Peachpit Press, for doing what they do so well.

To Grace Kvamme and Keri Walker at Apple Computer, Inc., for getting me the software, hardware, and technical support I needed to write this book. Without their help, it would be impossible for me to finish this book as quickly as I did.

To the developers at Apple, for continuing to refine the world's best operating system.

To Andrew Welch at Ambrosia Software, for developing and continuing to update Snapz Pro X. This book has over 1,000 screen shots, but with Snapz Pro, getting them was a snap (pun intended).

And to Mike, for the usual reasons.

www.marialanger.com

Table of Contents

TABLE OF CONTENTS

Author Note

You don't have to read this. It won't teach you anything about Mac OS X. But it will tell you a thing or two about the person who wrote this book.

Still reading? Well, don't say I didn't warn you.

This book, which is the eighth edition of my *Mac OS X Visual QuickStart Guide*, is also a milestone in my career as a writer: it is my *50th* title.

Not long after I began writing computer how-to books in 1991, it became clear to me that if I wanted to earn a living as a writer, I either had to write a lot of books or write a best-seller. Since bestsellers eluded me for many years (until the first edition of this book in 1997, in fact), I learned to write quickly and accurately, to produce the books my publishers (and readers) wanted on a timely basis.

To me, writing a book is like planting a seed and caring for it until it grows into a young plant. Some die before they can flower—my first PageMill book was out of date four months after it was written. Others never grow beyond a sickly sprout—I'm still trying to forget my two AOL books. But fortunately, the majority of my books either live good, long lives (if you can think of 18 to 24 months as "long") or spread like thick, healthy vines during a shorter life. These are the books that keep me working, planting new seeds.

Although it can be frustrating and tedious at times, writing and revising computer how-to books like this one is a rewarding occupation. The geek deep inside me loves playing with the latest and greatest computer hardware and software. I still get a little thrill out of seeing one of my titles on display at a bookstore. And my pulse races when some-one asks for my autograph at a computer show or other appearance. But what really makes it all worthwhile is the positive feed-back I get from readers who claim that my books have helped them.

I'm glad this book was my fiftieth. It was a lot of fun to write. Apple added a lot of great new features to Mac OS X in version 10.2 and it was a pleasure to explore them and think about how I could explain them to readers. I hope you get a lot out of this book—and my others, if you have them.

The next time you're surfing the Web, stop by for a visit. My address is (appropriately), www.marialanger.com. That's where you'll learn that there's more to me than what you see on these pages.

Maria Langer
Wickenburg, AZ
September 2002

Introduction to Mac OS X

Figure 1 The About This Mac window for Mac OS X 10.2.

Introduction

Mac OS X 10.2 (**Figure 1**) is the latest version of the computer operating system that put the phrase *graphic user interface* in everyone's vocabulary. With Mac OS, you can point, click, and drag to work with files, applications, and utilities. Because the same intuitive interface is utilized throughout the system, you'll find that a procedure that works in one program works in virtually all the others.

This Visual QuickStart Guide will help you learn Mac OS X 10.2 by providing step-by-step instructions, plenty of illustrations, and a generous helping of tips. On these pages, you'll find everything you need to know to get up and running quickly with Mac OS X—and more!

This book was designed for page flipping. Use the thumb tabs, index, or table of contents to find the topics for which you need help. If you're brand new to Mac OS, however, I recommend that you begin by reading at least the first two chapters. In them, you'll find basic information about techniques you'll use every day with your computer.

If you're interested in information about new Mac OS X features, be sure to browse through this **Introduction**. It'll give you a good idea of what you can expect to see on your computer.

✔ Tips

- The "X" in "Mac OS X" is pronounced "ten."

- When you're finished with the basics covered in this book and are ready for some more advanced information about Mac OS X, check out *Mac OS X Advanced: Visual QuickPro Guide*.

New Features in Mac OS X

Mac OS X is a major revision to the Macintosh operating system. Not only does it add and update features, but in many cases, it completely changes the way tasks are done. With a slick new look called "Aqua" (**Figure 2**) and with preemptive multitasking and protected memory that make the computer work more quickly and reliably, Mac OS X is like a breath of fresh air for Macintosh users.

Here's a look at some of the new and revised features you can expect to find in Mac OS X.

Figure 2 A look at the Aqua interface. This screenshot shows Mac OS X 10.2.

✔ Tips

■ Many of these features are covered in this book. Others are covered in *Mac OS X Advanced: Visual QuickPro Guide*.

■ *Preemptive multitasking* and *protected memory* are defined and discussed in **Chapter 5**.

■ This section discusses the new features in the original release of Mac OS X. New features in Mac OS X 10.1 and Mac OS X 10.2 are covered later in this **Introduction**.

Installer changes

◆ The Mac OS X installer automatically launches when you start from the Mac OS X install CD.

◆ The installer offers fewer customization features for installation than installers for previous versions of Mac OS.

◆ The Mac OS X Setup Assistant, which runs automatically after the installer restarts the computer, has a new look and offers several new options.

Figure 3 The System Preferences application. In Mac OS X 10.1 and Mac OS X 10.2, preferences are organized logically by function. This is how System Preferences looks in Mac OS X 10.2.

System changes

◆ System extensions and control panels no longer exist.

◆ By default, Mac OS X is set up for multiple users, making it possible for several people to set up personalized work environments on the same computer without the danger of accessing, changing, or deleting another user's files.

◆ A new Log Out command enables you to end your work session without shutting down the computer.

◆ A new System Preferences application (**Figure 3**) enables you to set options for the way the computer works.

◆ The default system font has been changed to Lucida Grande.

◆ Finder icons have a new "photo-illustrative" look (**Figure 2**).

◆ A new, customizable Dock (**Figure 2**) enables you to launch and switch applications.

NEW FEATURES IN MAC OS X

Window changes

◆ Finder windows offer a new column view (**Figure 4**). Button view is no longer available.

◆ Pop-up windows and spring-loaded folders are no longer supported. (Support for spring-loaded folders was added again in Mac OS X 10.2.)

◆ Window controls have been changed (**Figure 4**). The left end of a window's title bar now includes Close, Minimize, and Zoom buttons.

◆ *Drawers* (**Figure 5**) are subwindows that slide out the side of a window to offer more options.

◆ Document windows for different applications each reside on their own layer, making it possible for them to be intermingled. (This differs from previous versions of Mac OS which required all document windows for an application to be grouped together.)

◆ You can often activate items on an inactive window or dialog with a single click rather than clicking first to activate the window, then clicking again to activate the item.

Figure 4 A window in column view. In Mac OS X 10.2, a Search box was added to the toolbar, as shown here.

Figure 5 The Mail application utilizes the drawer interface. Mail was revised for Mac OS X 10.2, shown here.

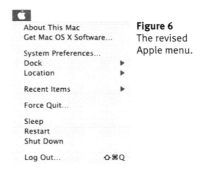

Figure 6
The revised Apple menu.

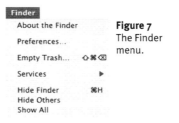

Figure 7
The Finder menu.

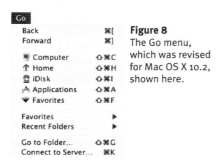

Figure 8
The Go menu, which was revised for Mac OS X 10.2, shown here.

Figure 9 A dialog sheet is attached to a window.

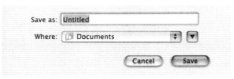

Figure 10 The Save Location dialog box collapsed to show only the bare essentials...

Figure 11 ...and expanded to show everything you need to save a file.

Menu changes

◆ Menus are now translucent so you can see underlying windows right through them.

◆ Sticky menus no longer disappear after a certain amount of time. When you click a menu's title, the menu appears and stays visible until you either click a command or click elsewhere onscreen.

◆ The Apple menu, which is no longer customizable, includes commands that work in all applications (**Figure 6**).

◆ A number of commands have been moved to the revised Apple menu (**Figure 6**) and new Finder menu (**Figure 7**). There are also new commands and new keyboard equivalents throughout the Finder.

◆ A new Go menu (**Figure 8**) makes it quick and easy to open windows for specific locations, including favorite and recent folders.

Dialog changes

◆ Dialogs can now appear as *sheets* that slide down from a window's title bar and remain part of the window (**Figure 9**). You can switch to another document or application when a dialog sheet is displayed.

◆ The Open and Save Location dialogs have been revised.

◆ The Save Location dialog can appear either collapsed (**Figure 10**) or expanded (**Figure 11**).

NEW FEATURES IN MAC OS X

Application changes

◆ Applications that are not Mac OS X compatible run in the *Classic environment*, which utilizes Mac OS 9.1 or 9.2.

◆ The list of applications and utilities that come with Mac OS has undergone extensive changes to add and remove many programs.

Help changes

◆ Balloon Help has been replaced with Help Tags (**Figure 12**).

◆ The Help Viewer offers more options for searching and following links.

◆ Guide Help is no longer available.

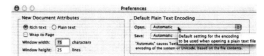

Figure 12 Help Tags replace Balloon Help.

New Features in Mac OS X 10.1

Mac OS X 10.1, the first major Mac OS X revision, which was released in Autumn of 2001, improves performance and features. Here's a quick summary of some of the changes.

✔ Tip

- Subsequent "maintenance" updates to Mac OS X 10.1 have been released. (Mac OS X 10.1.5 was the current version of Mac OS X 10.1 when I wrote this book.) These updates improve the performance, reliability, and compatibility of Mac OS, but generally do not change the way Mac OS looks or works. If you have a connection to the Internet, you can install these updates using Software Update; I explain how in *Mac OS X Advanced: Visual Quick-Pro Guide*.

Performance improvements

- ◆ Apple programmers tweaked Mac OS X to make it faster and more responsive. Improved performance is most noticeable when launching applications, resizing or moving windows, displaying menus, and choosing menu commands.

- ◆ OpenGL, which is responsible for 3D graphics, is 20 percent faster. It also has full support for the nViDIA GeForce 3 graphics card.

New Features in Mac OS X 10.1

Finder & Aqua enhancements

◆ The columns in the Finder's list views can be resized by dragging the column border (**Figure 13**).

◆ Long file names in the Finder's icon view wrap to a second line (**Figure 14**).

◆ Arrows now appear to the right of folder names in the Finder's column view (**Figure 4**). This makes it easy to distinguish between folders and files in column view.

◆ File name extensions are turned off by default. You can display the extension for a file by setting an option in its Info window (**Figure 15**) or in the Finder Preferences window (**Figure 16**).

◆ You can now customize the Dock to display it on the left, right, or bottom of the screen.

◆ The new Burn Disc command makes it quick and easy to create data CDs from within the Finder (**Figure 17**).

Figure 13 You can now change a column's width by dragging its border. This example shows a Mac OS X 10.2 window.

TextEdit Document with a very long name

Figure 14
In icon view, long document names wrap to a second line.

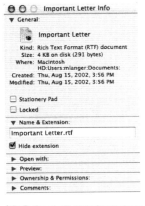

Figure 15
The Name & Extension options in a document's Info window. This is a Mac OS X 10.2 version of the Info window.

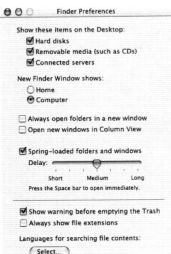

Figure 16
You can use Finder Preferences to specify whether extensions should show. This is Finder Preferences in Mac OS X 10.2.

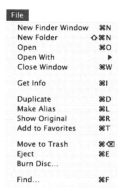

Figure 17
The Finder's File menu includes additional commands. This is the File menu in Mac OS X 10.2.

Figure 18 You can use the Desktop preferences pane to choose a background image. This is the Desktop preferences pane in Mac OS X 10.2.

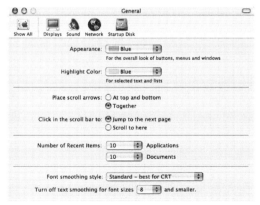

Figure 19 The General preferences pane in Mac OS X 10.2.

Figure 20 You can add menus for controlling various preferences. This example shows Modem, Displays, Sound, and Date & Time (the menu bar clock) options.

System Preferences improvements

◆ The System Preferences pane's icons are now organized logically by use (**Figure 3**).

◆ The Desktop preferences pane, which was new in Mac OS X 10.1, enables you to set a desktop picture (**Figure 18**). (This functionality was moved from Finder Preferences.)

◆ The General preferences pane now enables you to set how many recent items should appear on the Apple menu. It also enables you to set a font size threshold for the font smoothing feature (**Figure 19**).

◆ The Sound preferences pane enables you to select different settings for each output device.

◆ The Date & Time preferences pane enables you to display the menu bar clock as an analog clock.

◆ You can now display controls for a variety of System Preferences right in the menu bar (**Figure 20**). You specify whether you want to show or hide the controls in the applicable preferences pane.

NEW FEATURES IN MAC OS X 10.1

Printing improvements

◆ Mac OS X 10.1 shipped with over 200 PostScript printer description files, including files from Hewlett-Packard, Lexmark, and Xerox.

◆ In most cases, the driver for a USB printer will automatically be selected when the printer is added to the Print Center.

Networking improvements

◆ Mac OS X is now more compatible with network systems, including AppleShare, Windows NT, Windows 2000, and SAMBA.

◆ Mac OS X 10.1 now fully supports AirPort, with the AirPort Admin Utility and the AirPort Setup Assistant.

Application improvements

◆ Mac OS X 10.1 includes Java 2 for up-to-date Java compatibility.

◆ Internet Explorer 5.1 fully supports Java within the Web browser.

◆ iTunes now includes CD burning capabilities so you can create music CDs from your iTunes libraries.

◆ The new DVD Player application enables you to watch DVD movies on computers with DVD-ROM drives or SuperDrives.

◆ iDVD 2 includes many enhancements for creating your own DVD discs on Super-Drive-equipped Macs, including background encoding.

◆ AppleScript is now fully supported by Mac OS X. In fact, the Mac OS X 10.1 Finder is more scriptable than ever.

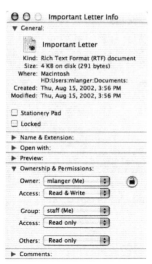

Figure 21
Any user with administrator privileges can now set ownership and permission options for a file in the file's Info window.

New Features in Mac OS X 10.2

Mac OS X 10.2, which was released in August 2002, was a major upgrade to Mac OS X. It added many new features and applications and revised some of the applications already available in previous versions of Mac OS X.

Performance enhancements

◆ Mac OS X 10.2 incorporates the features of FreeBSD 4.4 and GCC 3.1 into Mac OS X's Darwin base to enhance performance, compatibility, and usability.

◆ Quartz Extreme, the graphics processor underlying Mac OS X 10.2, increases the speed of window redraws and scrolling.

◆ The Classic environment now starts up more quickly.

Installer changes

◆ The Mac OS X 10.2 installer now comes on 2 disks, along with a third disk for installing Mac OS X 9.2.x.

◆ The Mac OS X 10.2 installer now includes a clean install option.

System improvements

◆ A user with administrator privileges now has complete control over file permissions via the Info window for a file (**Figure** 21).

◆ More information now appears in the About This Mac window (**Figure** 1).

NEW FEATURES IN MAC OS X 10.2

Finder & Aqua enhancements

◆ Simple Finder (**Figure 22**), when enabled for a user, makes the Finder easier to use, limits access, and prevents important files from being accidentally deleted.

◆ There are new alert sounds and sounds that play at certain events—for example, dragging a file to the trash.

◆ There are new system cursors, including a spinning ball that replaces the old wristwatch. (That wristwatch was getting pretty old anyway. But at least it was more modern than an hourglass.)

◆ Some folder icons are now animated.

◆ The toolbar in Finder windows now includes a Search box (**Figures 2**, **4**, and **13**), which you can use to search the window for a file by name.

◆ In icon view, you can display media-specific information for files (**Figure 23**).

◆ There are more view options in list and column views (**Figures 24** and **25**).

◆ There are additional fonts, including Roman Cochin and several Japanese and Chinese fonts.

◆ There is better support for long file names.

◆ The Info window has been modified so it can display more information at once (**Figures 15** and **21**).

Figure 22 Simple Finder is back in Mac OS X

Figure 23 In icon view, you can show information about certain files along with the file name.

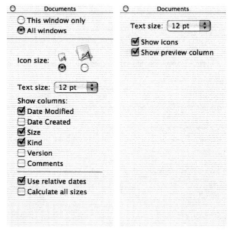

Figures 24 & 25 The View Options window for list (left) and column (right) views offer additional options.

Figure 26 The new My Account preferences pane enables you to set options for your Mac OS X account.

Figure 27 The new CDs & DVDs preferences pane enables you to set options for what should happen when you insert a CD or DVD.

Figure 28 The Sharing Preferences pane offers additional options for sharing.

System Preferences improvements

◆ The Desktop preferences pane (**Figure 18**) now enables you to change the desktop picture automatically at an interval you set.

◆ The General preferences pane (**Figure 19**) now offers additional options for font smoothing.

◆ A new My Account preferences pane (**Figure 26**) enables you to change settings for your user account.

◆ The Screen Saver preferences pane has been renamed Screen Effects. It now offers additional screen effect modules, including one that can retrieve images from a .Mac account. (Talk about a frivolous use of bandwidth!)

◆ A New CDs & DVDs preferences pane (**Figure 27**) enables you to set options for what should happen when you insert a CD or DVD.

◆ The Sharing preferences pane (**Figure 28**) offers additional networking options not available in previous versions of Mac OS.

◆ You can now set more user capability options in the Accounts preferences pane, which replaces the Users pane (**Figure 29**).

◆ The Classic preferences pane now offers more options for working with the Classic environment.

◆ Software Update has been revised to be easier to use.

◆ The Startup Disk preferences pane now enables you to start from a network disk, if one is available.

◆ News settings have been removed from the Internet preferences pane (**Figure 30**).

Printing improvements

◆ You can now save multiple custom printer settings.

◆ Mac OS X 10.2 includes new drivers for printers, including Epson and LexMark.

Device compatibility improvements

◆ Mac OS X 10.2 now supports TWAIN, Smart Card, and BlueTooth.

◆ Mac OS X 10.2 includes new drivers for Epson scanners, PC card modems, and FireWire audio.

◆ Mac OS X 10.2 includes InkWell, which enables you to use a graphics tablet with most Mac OS X applications.

Networking improvements

◆ Mac OS X 10.2 includes Rendezvous, a new technology for sharing files on a network.

◆ Administrators now have additional control over user access to applications and preferences (**Figure 29**).

◆ You can now boot from a server with NetBoot and install Mac OS over a network from Mac OS X Server.

◆ AirPort has been improved to include AirPort Network Selection and AirPort Software Base Station.

◆ You can now monitor status and set options for iDisk (**Figure 30**).

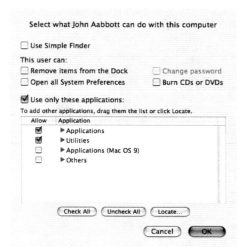

Figure 29 You can use this dialog in the Accounts preferences pane to set options for what a user can see and work with.

Figure 30 The Internet preferences pane enables you to monitor and set options for iDisk.

NEW FEATURES OF MAC OS X 10.2

Figure 31 The Calculator got a major upgrade!

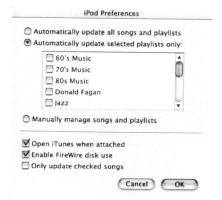

Figure 32 You can access iPod Preferences from within iTunes when an iPod is connected to your Mac.

Figure 33 QuickTime TV is gone, replaced with buttons to access content on the Web.

Application improvements

◆ Mac OS X now includes Adobe Acrobat Reader 5.

◆ Address Book has been revised with a new interface and features, including better integration with Mail and iChat.

◆ Calculator (**Figure 31**) now offers many more calculation functions and a "paper tape" feature.

◆ Mac OS X 10.2 includes iChat, which enables you to chat with AOL and .Mac users via the AOL Instant Messaging (AIM) system.

◆ Image Capture now supports scanning.

◆ iTunes, which has been upgraded to version 3.0, includes many new features, such as smart playlists and more iPod configuration options (**Figure 32**).

◆ Mail's interface was improved to make it easier to use.

◆ Preview has been revised with a modified interface and new features.

◆ QuickTime Player, which has been upgraded to version 6.0, offers a new interface for accessing Web content (**Figure 33**).

◆ TextEdit now includes a ruler and other more advanced text formatting features.

NEW FEATURES OF MAC OS X 10.2

Setting Up Mac OS X 10.2

Setting Up Mac OS X 10.2

Before you can use Mac OS X, you must install it on your computer and configure it to work the way you need it to. The steps you need to complete to do this depend on the software currently installed on your computer.

1. Use the Mac OS X 10.2 installer to do one of the following:

   ▲ Update an existing Mac OS X 10.1.x or earlier installation to Mac OS X 10.2.

   ▲ Install Mac OS X 10.2 to replace an existing Mac OS X 10.1.x or earlier installation.

   ▲ Install Mac OS X 10.2 on a computer with a Mac OS 9.x or earlier installation and no version of Mac OS X.

   Then restart your computer and use the Mac OS Setup Assistant to configure Mac OS X.

2. If Mac OS 9.2 or later is not already installed on your computer and you want to run software under the Classic environment, use the Mac OS 9.2.x installer that came with Mac OS X 10.2 to update to Mac OS 9.2.x. Then restart your computer and use the Mac OS Setup Assistant to configure Mac OS 9.2.x.

This chapter explains how to properly install and configure Mac OS X 10.2 on your computer.

✔ Tips

- I explain how to determine which versions of Mac OS are installed on your computer on the next page.

- The Classic environment, which enables you to run Mac OS 9.x applications, is discussed in **Chapter 5**.

Determining Which Mac OS Versions Are Installed

In order to know which installation and configuration steps you need to perform, you must first learn which versions of Mac OS are installed. There are several ways to do this; the easiest is to consult the Startup Disk control panel (on Mac OS 9.2.x or earlier) or the Startup Disk pane of System Preferences (on Mac OS X or later).

✔ Tips

- If your computer is brand new and you haven't started it yet, chances are you have Mac OS X 10.2 and Mac OS 9.2 (or later versions of each) installed. When you start your computer, it'll display the Mac OS Setup assistant. Skip ahead to the section titled "Configuring Mac OS X 10.2" later in this chapter.

- A quick way to tell whether your computer is currently running Mac OS 9.2 or earlier or Mac OS X or later is to consult the Apple menu icon on the far left end of the menu bar. A six-color apple appears on Mac OS 9.2 or earlier; a blue 3-D looking apple appears on Mac OS X or later.

To check the Startup Disk control panel on Mac OS 9.2 or earlier

1. Choose Apple > Control Panels > Startup Disk (**Figure 1**) to display the Startup Disk control panel.

2. If necessary, click the triangle beside the name of your hard disk to display the System folders installed on your computer (**Figures 2** and **3**). The Version column indicates which versions of Mac OS are installed.

3. Click the Startup Disk control panel's close box to dismiss it.

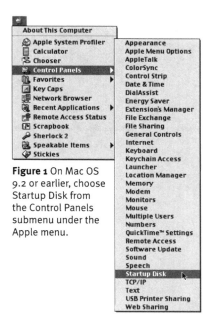

Figure 1 On Mac OS 9.2 or earlier, choose Startup Disk from the Control Panels submenu under the Apple menu.

Figure 2 Here's what the Startup Disk control panel might look like with Mac OS 9.1 and Mac OS X installed...

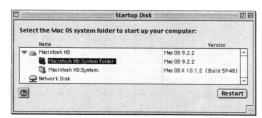

Figure 3 ... and here's what the Startup Disk control panel might look like with Mac OS 9.2.2 and Mac OS X 10.1.2 installed.

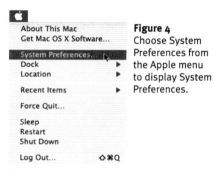

Figure 4
Choose System
Preferences from
the Apple menu
to display System
Preferences.

Figure 5 The System Preferences window looks like this in Mac OS X....

Figure 6 ... and like this in Mac OS X 10.1.

Figure 7 Here's what the Startup Disk pane might look like with Mac OS 9.1 and Mac OS X installed ...

To check the Startup Disk preferences pane on Mac OS X or later

1. Choose Apple > System Preferences (**Figure 4**) to display the System Preferences window (**Figures 5** and **6**).

2. Click the Startup Disk icon to display the Startup Disk pane (**Figures 7** and **8**). The installed versions of Mac OS appear beneath each System folder icon.

3. Choose System Prefs > Quit System Prefs (**Figure 9**), or press ⌃ ⌘Q to dismiss System Preferences.

Figure 8 ... and here's what it might look like with Mac OS 9.2.2 and Mac OS X 10.1.2 installed.

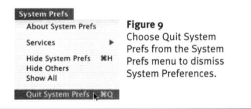

Figure 9
Choose Quit System
Prefs from the System
Prefs menu to dismiss
System Preferences.

DETERMINING THE INSTALLED MAC OS VERSION

Installing Mac OS X 10.2

Mac OS X's installer application handles all aspects of a Mac OS X installation. It restarts your computer from the Mac OS Installer CD-ROM, then displays step-by-step instructions to install Mac OS X 10.2 from its two install discs. When the installation process is finished, the installer automatically restarts your computer from your hard disk and displays the Mac OS Setup Assistant so you can configure Mac OS X 10.2 for your use.

This part of the chapter explains how to install and configure Mac OS X. Unfortunately, since there does not appear to be a way to take screen shots of the Mac OS X installation and configuration procedure, this part of the chapter won't be very "visual." Follow along closely and you'll get all the information you need to complete the installation and configuration process without any problems.

✔ Tips

- The installation instructions in this chapter assume you know basic Mac OS techniques, such as pointing, clicking, double-clicking, dragging, and selecting items from a menu. If you're brand new to the Mac and don't know any of these techniques, skip ahead to **Chapter 2**, which discusses Mac OS basics.

- You can click the Go Back button in an installer window at any time during installation to change options in a previous window.

- Remember, you can skip using the Mac OS X 10.2 installer if Mac OS X 10.2 or later is already installed on your computer. Consult the section titled "Determining Which Mac OS Versions Are Installed" earlier in this chapter to see what is installed on your computer.

Figure 10
When you insert the Mac OS X User Install disc, its icon appears on the desktop...

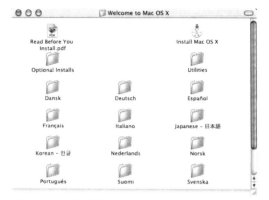

Figure 11 ...and a Welcome to Mac OS X window opens.

Figure 12 The Mac OS X installer prompts you to restart your computer.

Figure 13 If you're upgrading an existing installation of Mac OS X, you'll have to enter an administrator name and password to complete the installation.

○○○ Read Before You Install.pdf

X

Read Before You Install
Mac OS X

This document provides important information you should read before you install Mac OS X. It includes information about supported computers, system requirements, and installing Mac OS X.

For more information about Mac OS X, visit this Apple Web site:

• www.apple.com/macosx/

For the latest information about this release of Mac OS X, connect to the Internet and open Mac Help. To open Mac Help, choose Mac Help from the Help menu in the Finder.

For information about the support available for this product, see the "AppleCare Software Services and Support Guide" included with Mac OS X.

Supported computers
You can install this version of Mac OS X on any of the following computers:

• Power Mac G4
• Power Macintosh G3
• PowerBook G4
• PowerBook G3 (except the original PowerBook G3)
• iMac and eMac
• iBook

1 of 5

Figure 14 The installer comes with a file full of important information about Mac OS X 10.2 compatibility and other issues.

To launch the Mac OS X installer & select an installation language

1. Insert the Mac OS X User Install disc in your CD-ROM drive. A Mac OS X Install Disc 1 icon should appear on your desktop (**Figure 10**), along with a Welcome to Mac OS window (**Figure 11**).

2. Double-click the Install Mac OS X icon.

3. An Install Mac OS X dialog appears (**Figure 12**). Click Restart.

4. If you're using any version of Mac OS X, an authenticate dialog like the one in **Figure 13** may appear. Enter the Name and password for an administrator and click OK.

5. Wait while Mac OS X and the installer load from the CD-ROM disc.

6. In the Select Language window that appears, select the primary language you want to use with the installer and Mac OS X.

7. Click Continue.

✔ Tips

■ It's a good idea to open and read the file named Read Before You Install.pdf that's included on Mac OS X Install Disc 1 (**Figure 11**). This document (**Figure 14**) contains important information about compatibility and other installation issues.

■ The Authenticate dialog (**Figure 13**) prevents someone without administrator privileges from installing system software. This is especially important on a computer used by more than one person.

■ These instructions assume you're installing in English. Obviously, the onscreen instructions will be different if you're installing in another language!

To read important information about the installer & Mac OS X

1. Read the information in the Introduction ("Welcome to the Mac OS X Installer") window.

2. Click Continue.

3. Read the information in the Read Me ("Important Information") window.

4. Click Continue.

5. Read the information in the License ("Software License Agreement") window.

6. Click Continue.

7. Click the Agree button in the dialog sheet that appears.

✔ Tips

■ Read the information in the "Important Information" window carefully! It provides important, late-breaking news about installing Mac OS, including compatibility information and special instructions not included in this book.

■ If necessary, in step 5 you can use the pop-up menu to select a different language for the license agreement.

■ In step 7, if you click the Disagree button, you will not be able to install Mac OS X.

To select a destination disk

1. In the Select Destination ("Select a Destination") window, click to select the icon for the disk on which you want to install Mac OS X. A green arrow appears on the disk icon. The installer automatically knows if it has to upgrade an existing Mac OS X installation or install Mac OS X 10.2 from scratch.

2. To set advanced installation options, click the Options button. A dialog sheet offers up to three options, depending on what is already installed on the destination disk:

   ▲ **Upgrade Mac OS X** upgrades an existing Mac OS X installation to Mac OS X 10.2.

   ▲ **Archive and Install** moves existing Mac OS X System files to a folder named Previous System and installs Mac OS X 10.2 from scratch. You might want to use this option if you suspect there's something wrong with your Mac OS X installation and you want to force the installer to start fresh. If you select this option, you can turn on the Preserve Users and Networks Settings check box to automatically move all existing Mac OS X settings to the new installation. This also skips the Setup Assistant.

   ▲ **Erase and Install** completely erases the destination disk and installs Mac OS X 10.2 from scratch. Use this option only after backing up your data, since all data on the disk will be lost. If you select this option, choose a disk format from the "Format disk as" pop-up menu; your options are Mac OS Extended and Unix File System.

3. Click Continue.

✔ Tips

■ A note beneath the disk icons indicates how much space is available on each disk. You can see how much space a Mac OS X installation takes by looking at the bottom of the window. Make sure the disk you select has enough space for the installation.

■ Step 2 is optional. If you follow step 2 and don't know what to select, click Cancel to use the default installation option.

■ In step 2, if you select the Erase and Install option and don't know what disk format to choose from the pop-up menu, choose Mac OS Extended. (If you wanted the Unix File System option, you'd know it.)

SELECTING A DESTINATION DISK

7

To complete the installation

1. In the Installation Type ("Easy Install") window, you have two options:

   ▲ To perform a standard Mac OS X 10.2 installation, click the Install button.

   ▲ To perform a custom Mac OS X 10.2 installation, click the Customize button. In the Custom Install window that appears, toggle check marks to specify which Mac OS X components should be installed. Then click Install.

2. Wait while software from the first install disc is installed. A status area in the Install window tells you what the installer is doing and may indicate how much longer the installation will take.

3. When the installer is finished with the first install disc, it ejects the disc and prompts you to insert the second disc. Insert the disc in the drive and close the drive.

4. Wait while software from the second install disc is installed.

5. When the installer is finished, it restarts the computer and displays the first screen of the setup application.

✔ Tips

■ The Customize option is provided for Mac OS X "Power Users" and should only be utilized if you have a complete understanding of Mac OS X components and features.

■ In step 2, if the amount of time left appears in the progress window, don't believe it. In my experience, the real amount of time the installation takes is usually much shorter than the estimate.

COMPLETING THE INSTALLATION

Configuring Mac OS X 10.2

When your computer restarts after a Mac OS X installation, the Mac OS X Setup Assistant automatically appears. This program uses a simple question-and-answer process to get information about you and the way you use your computer. The information you provide is automatically entered in the various System Preferences panes of Mac OS X to configure your computer for Mac OS X.

✔ Tips

- If you just bought your Macintosh and Mac OS X is installed, the first time you start your computer, you'll see the Mac OS X Setup Assistant described here. Follow these instructions to configure your computer.

- If the Mac OS X Setup Assistant does not appear, Mac OS X is already configured. You can skip this section.

To set basic configuration options

1. In the Welcome window that appears after installing Mac OS X and restarting, select the name of the country you're in. Click Continue.

2. In the Personalize Your Settings window, select a keyboard layout. Click Continue.

3. In the Registration Information window, fill in the form. You can press Tab to move from one field to another. Click Continue.

4. In the A Few More Questions window, use the pop-up menus and radio buttons to answer a few marketing questions. Click Continue.

5. Read the information in the Thank You window and click Continue.

6. In the Create Your Account window, fill in the form to enter information to set up your Mac OS X account. Click Continue.

7. Continue following the instructions in one of the following sections:
   ▲ "To set up Mac OS X to use a new EarthLink Internet account"
   ▲ "To set up Mac OS X to use your existing Internet service"
   ▲ "To skip Internet setup"

✔ Tips

- If your country is not listed in step 1, turn on the Show All check box to display more options.

- In step 2, you can turn on the Show All check box to show additional keyboard layouts.

- In step 3, you can learn about Apple's privacy policy by clicking the Privacy button. When you're finished reading the information in the dialog sheet that appears, click OK to dismiss it and return to the Registration Information window.

- When you enter your password in step 6, it displays as bullet characters. That's why you enter it twice: so you're sure you entered what you thought you did the first time.

- Remember the password you enter in step 6! If you forget your password, you may not be able to use your computer. It's a good idea to use the Password Hint field to enter a hint that makes your password impossible to forget.

To set up Mac OS X to use a new EarthLink Internet account

1. In the Get Internet Ready window, select one of the following radio button:

   ▲ **I'd like a free trial account with EarthLink** enables you to set up a free trial account with EarthLink.

   ▲ **I have a code for a special offer from EarthLink** enables you to set up an account with EarthLink using a special offer code you already have.

2. Click Continue.

3. In the EarthLink As Your Provider window, enter your name, address, and billing information. If you have a special offer code, be sure to enter it in the appropriate box.

4. Click Continue.

5. Skip ahead to the section titled "To set .Mac options" to continue.

✔ Tip

■ EarthLink is an Internet Service Provider (ISP). I tell you more about ISPs in **Chapter 9**, which covers Internet features and software.

To set up Mac OS X to use your existing Internet service

1. In the Get Internet Ready window, select the radio button for I'll use my existing Internet service. and click Continue.

2. In the How Do You Connect window, select the radio button for your connection method. Your options are Telephone modem, Cable modem, DSL modem, Local network (Ethernet), or Local network (AirPort Wireless).

3. Click Continue.

4. Follow the instructions in one of the next four sections for your connection method.

✔ Tips

- You can only select the AirPort Wireless option if you have an AirPort card installed in your computer.

- You can get all of the information you need for setup from your ISP or network administrator.

To set up a telephone modem connection

1. In the Set Up Existing Service window, enter information about your ISP connection, including your user name, password, ISP phone number, and any dialog prefix required to get an outside line.

2. Click Continue.

3. In the Set Up Your Modem window, select your modem connection port and make and model.

4. Click Continue.

5. Skip ahead to the section titled "To set .Mac options" to continue.

To set up a cable or DSL modem connection

1. In the Your Internet Connection window, select an option from the TCP/IP Connection Type pop-up menu. The option you select will determine what fields appear beneath it.

2. Enter IP address, subnet mask, router address, DNS hosts, domain name, and proxy server information as required.

3. Click Continue.

4. Skip ahead to the section titled "To set .Mac options" to continue.

To set up a local network connection

1. The Your Local Area Network window may appear to tell you that your network configuration has been obtained from a DHCP server.

   ▲ If you want to use this information, select Yes and click Continue. You can then skip ahead to the section titled "To set .Mac options" to continue.

   ▲ If this window does not appear or you don't want to use this information, select No, change the configuration, and click Continue.

2. In the Your Internet Connection window, select an option from the TCP/IP Connection Type pop-up menu. The option you select will determine what fields appear beneath it.

3. Enter IP address, subnet mask, router address, DNS hosts, domain name, and proxy server information as required.

4. Click Continue.

5. Skip ahead to the section titled "To set .Mac options" to continue.

SETTING UP AN EXISTING INTERNET SERVICE

To skip Internet setup

1. In the Get Internet Ready window, select the radio button for "I'm not ready to connect to the Internet."

2. Click Continue.

3. In the dialog sheet that appears, click Yes to confirm that you don't want to set up an Internet connection.

4. In the Register With Apple window, select one of the options:

   ▲ **Register Now** enables you to use your Internet connection to send registration information to Apple. Click Continue.

   ▲ **Register Later** enables you to skip registration for now. Click Continue and skip ahead to the section titled "To set the time zone."

5. In the Your Phone Service window, enter your telephone number and provide other information as requested.

6. Click Continue.

7. In the Setting up your modem window, select your modem connection port and make and model.

8. Click Continue.

9. Continue following instructions in the section titled "To set .Mac options."

Skipping Internet Setup

To set .Mac options

1. In the Get .Mac window, select one of the options:

   ▲ **I'd like to set up a free .Mac trial membership** enables you to create a new trial .Mac account.

   ▲ **Use my existing .Mac membership** enables you to enter your .Mac user name and password.

   ▲ **I'll set up a .Mac membership later** enables you to skip the .Mac setup.

2. Click Continue.

3. If you indicated earlier in the setup process that you want to set up a new EarthLink account, the Your EarthLink Account window appears. Enter user name, password, and birthdate information to set up a new EarthLink account and click Continue.

4. If you indicated that you want to use an existing Internet service, continue following instructions in the section titled "To set up an e-mail account."

   or

   If you indicated that you wanted to set up an EarthLink account or not set up an Internet connection at all, continue following instructions in the section titled "To send registration information."

✔ Tips

■ You can click the Learn More button in the Get .Mac window to display a dialog with more information about .Mac. When you're finished reading about it, click the OK button to dismiss the dialog.

■ **Appendix B** provides more information about .Mac.

To send registration information

1. In the Your Phone Service window, enter your telephone number and provide other information as requested.

2. Click Continue.

3. In the Setting up your modem window, select your modem connection port and make and model.

4. Click Continue.

5. If the You're Ready to Connect window appears, read its contents and click Connect. Then wait while your computer uses its modem to connect to the Internet and exchange registration information with Apple and, if necessary, EarthLink.

6. If you indicated that you want to set up an EarthLink account earlier in the setup process, continue following the instructions in the section titled "To complete EarthLink Setup."

   or

   If you indicated that you want to set up a .Mac account, continue following the instructions in the section titled "To confirm account information."

   or

   If you're using an existing Internet account and existing .Mac membership, continue following instructions in the section titled "To set up an e-mail account."

   or

   If you indicated that you want to skip both the Internet and .Mac membership setup, continue following instructions in the section titled "To set the time zone, date, & time."

To complete an EarthLink setup

1. Read the Internet Service Plan window that appears.

2. Click Accept.

3. Read the License Agreement window that appears.

4. Click Accept.

5. In the Choose a Local Number window that appears, select a phone number.

6. Click Continue.

7. In the Choose a Number Format window that appears, choose the dialing format you want to use for the number.

8. Click Continue.

9. Continue following instructions in the section titled "To confirm account information."

To confirm account information

1. In the Account Information dialog that appears, make a note of the information it provides:

   ▲ **Your email address** is the address that's set up with your trial .Mac membership.

   ▲ **Your EarthLink email address** is the address that's set up with your trial EarthLink account.

2. Click Continue.

3. Continue following instructions in the section titled "To set the time zone, date, & time."

To set up an e-mail account

1. If the Set Up Mail window appears, use it to enter information about your e-mail account.

2. Click Continue.

✔ Tip

■ If the Set Up Mail window identifies your .Mac e-mail account and you want to add another account, select the "Add my existing e-mail account" radio button. Then enter information for your account.

To set the time zone, date, & time

1. In the Select Time Zone window, click the map to indicate your time zone.

2. If necessary, choose an option from the pop-up menu to specify the exact time zone by name.

3. Click Continue.

4. If the Set Your Date and Time window appears, use it to set your computer's date and time:

   ▲ To set the date, click today's date on the calendar. (You may have to use the arrow keys beside the name of the month and the year number to set the appropriate month and year first.)

   ▲ To set the time, click the time digits you want to change and type a new entry. Repeat this process to enter the current time, then click Save.

5. Click Continue.

6. Continue following instructions in the section titled "To finish the installation."

✔ Tip

■ In step 4, you can also change the time by dragging the clock's hands and clicking Save when the time is correct.

SETTING UP E-MAIL, SETTING THE DATE & TIME

Figure 15 At the end of the installation, the Mac OS X 10.2 desktop appears with the computer window open.

Figure 16 A Previous Systems folder appears on your hard disk if you performed a "clean" installation of Mac OS X 10.2.

To finish the installation

1. In the Thank You window that appears, click Go.

2. The Mac OS X desktop appears with the Computer window open (**Figure 15**). If necessary, eject Mac OS X Install Disc 2.

✔ Tips

- I explain how to work with the Mac OS Desktop and Finder in **Chapters 2** through **4**.

- If you chose the Archive option when you installed Mac OS X 10.2, a folder named Previous Systems appears on your hard disk (**Figure 16**). You can move items you need out of that folder and into appropriate locations on your hard disk.

FINISHING THE INSTALLATION

Installing Mac OS 9.2

To use the Classic environment with Mac OS X, you need to install a compatible version of Mac OS 9. That's why Mac OS X 10.2 comes with a Mac OS 9.2 installer disc.

Like Mac OS X, Mac OS 9.2 comes with an installer application that makes software installation easy. Simply launch the installer and follow the instructions that appear on screen to select a destination disk, learn more about the software, agree to a license agreement, and select the Mac OS 9.2 components you want installed. The installer builds the System and Finder files for your computer and copies the software you specified to your hard disk.

The Mac OS 9.2 installer can perform two types of installations:

◆ **Standard Installation** lets you select the Mac OS 9.2 components you want installed. The installer copies all standard parts of each selected component to your hard disk.

◆ **Customized Installation** lets you select the Mac OS 9.2 components you want installed and then lets you select the parts of each component to be installed.

This part of this chapter explains how to use the Mac OS 9.2 installer to perform a standard installation.

✔ Tips

- The installation instructions in this chapter assume you know basic Mac OS techniques, such as pointing, clicking, double-clicking, dragging, and selecting items from a menu. If you're brand new to the Mac and don't know any of these techniques, skip ahead to **Chapter 2**, which discusses Mac OS basics.

- A standard installation of Mac OS 9.2 includes the following components: Mac OS 9.2, AirPort, Internet Access, Apple Remote Access, Personal Web Sharing, Text-to-Speech, Mac OS Runtime for Java, ColorSync, and English Speech Recognition.

- You can click the Go Back button in an installer window at any time during installation to change options in a previous window.

- You can press ⌐Return⌐ or ⌐Enter⌐ to "click" a default button—a button with a dark border around it—such as the Continue button in **Figure 18**.

- Remember, you can skip using the Mac OS 9.2 installer if Mac OS 9.2 or later is already installed on your computer. Consult the section titled "Determining Which Mac OS Versions Are Installed" earlier in this chapter to see what is installed on your computer.

INSTALLING MAC OS 9.2

To launch the installer

1. Start your computer from the Mac OS 9.2 Install disc.

2. Locate and double-click the Mac OS Install icon (**Figure 17**).

3. After a moment, the installer's Welcome window appears (**Figure 18**). Click Continue.

✔ Tip

■ To start your computer from the Mac OS 9.2 CD-ROM, insert the disc, choose Special > Restart, and hold down Ⓒ until the "Welcome to Mac OS" message appears. This is the recommended way to start your computer when installing OS software.

Figure 17 To launch the Mac OS 9.2 installer, double-click this icon.

Figure 18 The Mac OS 9.2 installer's Welcome window appears when you launch it.

Figure 19 Use the Select Destination window to select the disk on which to install Mac OS 9.2.

Figure 20 Choose a disk from the Destination Disk pop-up menu.

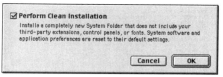

Figure 21 Turn on the Perform Clean Installation check box to create a brand new System Folder for Mac OS 9.2.

To select a destination disk

1. In the installer's Select Destination window (**Figure 19**), use the Destination Disk pop-up menu (**Figure 20**) to select the disk on which you want to install Mac OS 9.2.

2. If some version of Mac OS 9.1 or later is not already installed on the computer, click the Options button. Then turn on the check box beside Perform Clean Installation in the dialog that appears (**Figure 21**), and click OK.

3. Click Select.

✔ Tips

- Only those hard disks and removable high-capacity media (such as Zip and Jaz disks) that appear on your Desktop are listed in the Destination Disk pop-up menu (**Figure 20**).

- A status area beneath the Destination Disk pop-up menu indicates the version of Mac OS that is installed on the disk, as well as the available disk space and the amount of disk space required for a basic installation (**Figure 19**).

- You can also perform a clean installation of Mac OS 9.2 on a computer with a version of Mac OS 9.2 or earlier already installed. Follow all of the above steps, including step 2. The old System Folder is renamed "Previous Systems Folder." You should delete it after you move non-Apple control panels, extensions, and preferences files to their proper locations in the new System Folder.

SELECTING THE DESTINATION DISK

To read important information about Mac OS 9.2

1. Read the contents of the installer's Important Information window (**Figure 22**). Click the down arrow on the vertical scroll bar to scroll through the entire document.

2. When you have finished reading the information, click Continue.

✔ Tip

- Read the information in this window carefully! It provides important, late-breaking news about installing Mac OS, including compatibility information and special instructions not included in this book.

To read and agree to the Software License Agreement

1. If desired, choose a language from the pop-up menu at the top-right of the Software License Agreement window (**Figure 23**).

2. Read the contents of the window. Click the down arrow on the vertical scroll bar to scroll through the entire document.

3. When you have finished reading the agreement, click Continue.

4. A dialog appears, informing you that you must agree to the terms of the agreement you just read to continue (**Figure 24**). Click Agree.

✔ Tip

- If you click Disagree in step 4, the installer returns you to its Welcome window (**Figure 18**).

Figure 22 The Important Information window contains late-breaking news about installing Mac OS 9.2.

Figure 23 The Software License Agreement tells you exactly what you're allowed to do with Mac OS 9.2 software.

Figure 24 To complete the installation of Mac OS 9.2, you must click Agree in this dialog.

Figure 25 Use the Install Software window to select the Mac OS components you want to install.

Figure 26 You can use this dialog to set two additional installation options.

To set other installation options

1. Click the Options button in the Install Software window that appears next (**Figure 25**) to display a dialog like the one in **Figure 26**.

2. To prevent the installer from attempting to update the hard disk driver of the destination disk, turn off the Update Apple Hard Disk Drivers check box.

3. To prevent the installer from creating an installation log file, turn off the Create Installation Report check box.

4. Click OK.

✔ Tips

- As shown in **Figure 26**, both of these options are enabled by default. If you're not sure how to set these options, leave them both turned on.

- If you're not sure what to do in step 2, leave the check box turned on. The Mac OS 9.2 installer can only update the driver on an Apple-branded hard disk—one that comes with a Macintosh computer. It cannot affect a hard disk made by another manufacturer. If the installer cannot update your disk's driver, it will display a message saying so and provide additional information about updating your driver.

SETTING OTHER INSTALLATION OPTIONS

To complete the installation

1. In the Install Software window (**Figure** 25), click the Start button.

2. The installer performs some maintenance tasks, then begins installing the software you selected. A progress window like the one in **Figure** 27 appears to show you how it's doing.

3. When the installation is complete, a dialog tells you. Click Quit to dismiss it.

To restart your computer

Choose Special > Restart (**Figure 28**).

✔ Tips

■ To configure and use your newly installed Mac OS 9.2 software, you must restart your computer. This loads the new software into the computer's RAM and, if necessary, launches the Mac OS Setup Assistant.

■ Do not restart your computer by turning off power and then turning it back on! This can cause file corruption.

■ When you restart your computer, it may restart in Mac OS X. I explain how to restart with Mac OS 9.2 later in this section.

Figure 27 The Mac OS 9.2 installer displays a progress window as it works.

Figure 28
To restart your computer, choose Restart from the Special menu.

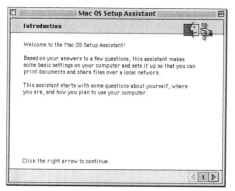

Figure 29 The Mac OS Setup Assistant offers an easy way to configure Mac OS 9.2.

The Mac OS Setup Assistant

When you restart your computer after installing Mac OS 9.2, the Mac OS Setup Assistant automatically appears (**Figure 29**). This program uses a simple question-and-answer process to get information about you and the way you use your computer. The information you provide is automatically entered into the appropriate control panels to configure Mac OS 9.2.

✔ Tip

- If the Mac OS Setup Assistant does not automatically appear at startup, you can launch it by opening the Mac OS Setup Assistant icon in the Assistants folder on your hard disk.

To use the Mac OS Setup Assistant

1. Read the information in each Mac OS Setup Assistant window. Enter information or make selections when prompted.

2. Click the right arrow button to continue.

   or

   Click the left arrow button to go back and make changes in previous windows.

✔ Tip

- The next few pages explain exactly how to enter information in each window that appears.

THE MAC OS SETUP ASSISTANT

To select regional preferences

1. If you haven't already done so, click the right arrow button in the Introduction window of the Mac OS Setup Assistant (**Figure 28**).

2. Read the information in the Regional Preferences window (**Figure 30**) to learn how Mac OS 9.2 uses your language version.

3. Click the language you prefer to select it.

4. Click the right arrow button.

✔ Tip

■ The languages that appear in this window will vary depending on the language supported by your copy of Mac OS 9.2.

To enter your name & organization

1. Read the information in the Name and Organization window (**Figure 31**) to learn how Mac OS 9.2 uses your name and company.

2. Enter your name in the What is your name? edit box.

3. Press ⌷Tab⌷ or click in the What is your company or organization? edit box to position the blinking insertion point.

4. Enter the name of your company or organization.

5. Click the right arrow button.

✔ Tip

■ You must enter a name in the What is your name? box. You may, however, leave the What is your company or organiza- tion? box empty if desired.

Figure 30 Use the Regional Preferences window to select your language version.

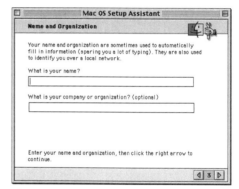

Figure 31 Enter your name and organization in these edit boxes.

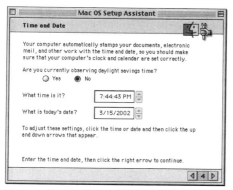

Figure 32 Use the Time and Date window to check and, if necessary, change the time or date.

Figure 33 To change the time (or date), click an incorrect number in the sequence to select it and then click the up or down arrow until the right number appears.

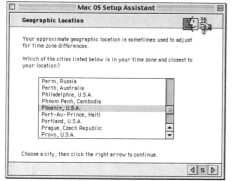

Figure 34 The Geographic Location window lists cities all over the world—including one near you.

To set the time & date

1. Read the information in the Time and Date window of the Mac OS Setup Assistant (**Figure 32**) to learn how Mac OS 9.2 uses the time and date.

2. If daylight savings time is currently in effect, click the Yes radio button to select it.

3. If the time in the What time is it? box is not correct, change it. To do this, click an incorrect number in the time sequence to select it (**Figure 33**) and either type the correct number or click the up or down arrow button beside the time until the correct number appears.

4. If the date in the What is today's date? box is not correct, change it. To do this, click an incorrect number in the date sequence to select it and either type the correct number or click the up or down arrow button beside the date until the correct number appears.

5. Click the right arrow button.

✔ Tip

■ The time and date, which are tracked by your computer's internal clock, may already be correct. If so, no changes will be necessary.

To select your geographic location

1. Read the information in the Geographic Location window of the Mac OS Setup Assistant (**Figure 34**) to learn how Mac OS 9.2 uses your location.

2. Click the up or down arrow on the scroll bar until the name of a city in your time zone (preferably near you) appears. Click it once to select it.

3. Click the right arrow button.

SETTING DATE & TIME, SELECTING LOCATION

To set Finder preferences

1. Read the information in the Finder Preferences window of the Mac OS Setup Assistant (**Figure 35**) to learn about the difference between the standard Finder and Simple Finder.

2. If you want fewer menu commands in the Finder, click the Yes radio button to select it.

3. Click the right arrow button.

To set network options

1. Read the information in the Local Network Introduction window of the Mac OS Setup Assistant (**Figure 36**) to learn more about networks.

2. Click the right arrow button.

3. Read the information in the Computer Name and Password window (**Figure 37**) to learn how Mac OS uses your computer's name and password.

4. To change the default name that the Mac OS Setup Assistant has assigned to your computer, type it in the top edit box. (The name should be selected as shown in **Figure 37**, so it is not necessary to click in the box first; simply type to overwrite the contents of the edit box.) Then press ⎯Tab⎯ or click in the bottom edit box to position the insertion point there.

   or

   To accept the default name that the Mac OS Setup Assistant has assigned to your computer, just press ⎯Tab⎯ or click in the bottom edit box to position the insertion point there.

5. In the bottom edit box, enter a password you want to use to protect your computer from unauthorized access by other network users.

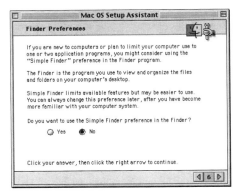

Figure 35 Use the Finder Preferences window to turn Simple Finder on or off.

Figure 36 The Local Network Introduction window tells you a little about networks.

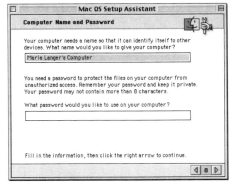

Figure 37 Use this window to enter a name for your computer and a password to protect your files from unauthorized network users.

Figure 38 Use this window to set up a shared folder—if you want one.

6. Click the right arrow button.

7. Wait while the Mac OS Setup Assistant validates the computer name and password.

8. Read the information in the Shared Folder window (**Figure 38**) to learn what a shared folder is and how it is used.

9. If you do not want a shared folder on the network, select the No radio button by clicking it. Then skip to step 11.

10. To change the default name that the Mac OS Setup Assistant has assigned to your shared folder, type it in the edit box. (The name should be selected as shown in **Figure 38**, so it is not necessary to click in the box first; simply type to overwrite the contents of the box.)

11. Click the right arrow button.

✔ Tips

■ You must go through these steps even if your computer is not connected to a network.

■ You must provide both a name and password for your computer.

To complete the setup process

1. Click the Go Ahead button in the Conclusion window of the Mac OS Setup Assistant (**Figure 39**).

2. Wait while the Mac OS Setup Assistant configures your system. The Conclusion window changes to indicate the configuration progress (**Figure 40**). When the configuration is complete, the Conclusion window tells you that the Mac OS Setup Assistant is done (**Figure 41**).

3. To stop configuring your computer, click the Quit button.

   or

   To go on to the Internet Setup Assistant, click the Continue button.

✔ Tips

- To check your settings one last time before they're written to your computer's configuration files, click the Show Details button (**Figure 39**). The Conclusion window changes to list all configuration options you entered or selected.

- If you have not installed the Internet Access component of Mac OS 9.2, the Continue button in the Conclusion window (**Figure 41**) will not appear.

- The Internet Setup Assistant is not covered in this book. You can find complete instructions for using it, excerpted from *Mac OS 9.1: Visual QuickStart Guide*, on the companion Web site to this book: www.marialanger.com/booksites/macosx.html/.

Figure 39 When the Mac OS Setup Assistant is finished asking for information, it displays this window.

Figure 40 The Conclusion window also indicates the configuration progress.

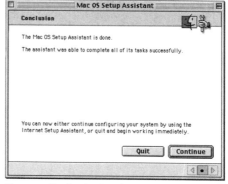

Figure 41 Finally, the Conclusion window tells you when the configuration is done.

Figure 42 Choose the folder for Mac OS X 10.2.

Choosing a Startup Disk

With two versions of Mac OS on your computer—Mac OS X 10.2 and Mac OS 9.2.x—you can choose which operating system you want to use to start.

◆ To restart with Mac OS X when Mac OS 9.x is currently running, use the Startup Disk control panel.

◆ To restart with Mac OS 9.x when Mac OS X is currently running, use the Startup Disk preferences pane.

Your computer remembers the version you selected and continues to use that version of Mac OS at startup until you tell it to do otherwise.

✔ Tip

■ In the remaining chapters of this book, I assume you have started your computer with Mac OS X 10.2. After all, that's what this book is all about!

To restart with Mac OS X 10.2

1. Choose Apple > Control Panels > Startup Disk (**Figure 1**) to display the Startup disk control panel.

2. If necessary, click the triangle beside the name of your hard disk to display the System folders installed on your computer.

3. Select the folder for Mac OS X 10.2 (**Figure 42**).

4. Click Restart. Your computer restarts with Mac OS X 10.2.

RESTARTING WITH MAC OS X 10.2

To restart with Mac OS 9.2.x

1. Choose Apple > System Preferences (**Figure** 4) to display the System Preferences window (**Figure** 43).

2. Click the Startup Disk icon to display the Startup Disk preferences pane. The installed versions of Mac OS appear beneath each System folder icon.

3. Select the Mac OS 9.2.x folder icon (**Figure** 44).

4. Click Restart. Your computer restarts with Mac OS X 9.2.x.

Figure 43 System Preferences in Mac OS X 10.2.

Figure 44 Select the Mac OS 9.2.x folder in the Startup Disk preferences pane and click Restart.

Finder Basics

2

The Finder & Desktop

The *Finder* is a program that is part of Mac OS. It launches automatically when you start your computer.

The Finder provides a graphic user interface called the *desktop* (**Figure 1**) that you can use to open, copy, delete, list, organize, and perform other operations on computer files.

This chapter provides important instructions for using the Finder and items that appear on the Mac OS X desktop. It's important that you understand how to use these basic Finder techniques, since you'll use them again and again every time you work with your computer.

✔ Tips

- You never have to manually launch the Finder; it always starts automatically.

- Under normal circumstances, you cannot quit the Finder.

- If you're new to Mac OS, don't skip this chapter. It provides the basic information you'll need to use your computer successfully.

Menu bar   Window   Desktop   Icons

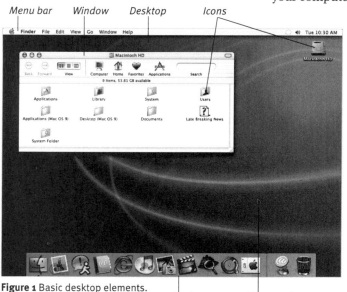

Figure 1 Basic desktop elements.

Dock   Mouse pointer

The Mouse

Mac OS, like most graphic user interface systems, uses the mouse as an input device. There are several basic mouse techniques you must know to use your computer:

◆ **Point** to a specific item onscreen.

◆ **Click** an item to select it.

◆ **Double-click** an item to open it.

◆ **Press** an item to activate it.

◆ **Drag** to move an item or select multiple items.

✔ Tip

■ Some computers use either a trackball or a trackpad instead of a mouse.

To point

1. Move the mouse on the work surface or mouse pad.

   or

   Use your fingertips to move the ball of the trackball.

   or

   Move the tip of one finger (usually your forefinger) on the surface of the trackpad.

   The mouse pointer, which usually looks like an arrow (**Figure 2**), moves on your computer screen.

2. When the tip of the mouse pointer's arrow is on the item to which you want to point (**Figure 3**), stop moving it.

✔ Tip

■ The tip of the mouse pointer is its "business end."

Figure 2 The mouse pointer usually looks like an arrow pointer when you are working in the Finder.

Figure 3 Move the mouse pointer so the arrow's tip is on the item to which you want to point.

Figure 4
Click to select
an icon...

Figure 5 ...or an item in a list.

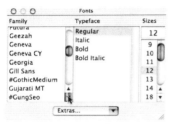

Figure 6 Press a scroll bar arrow to
activate it.

Figure 7
Drag to move items
such as folders.

To click

1. Point to the item you want to click.

2. Press (and release) the mouse button
    once. The item you clicked becomes
    selected (**Figures 4** and **5**).

To double-click

1. Point to the item you want to double-
    click.

2. Press (and release) the mouse button
    twice quickly. The item you double-
    clicked opens.

✔ Tip

■   Keep the mouse pointer still while
    double-clicking. If you move the mouse
    pointer during the double-click process,
    you may move the item instead of double-
    clicking it.

To press

1. Point to the item you want to press.

2. Press and hold the mouse button without
    moving the mouse. The item you are
    pressing is activated (**Figure 6**).

✔ Tip

■   The press technique is often used when
    working with scroll bars, as shown in
    Figure 6, where pressing is the same as
    clicking repeatedly.

To drag

1. Point to the item you want to drag.

2. Press the mouse button down.

3. While holding the mouse button down,
    move the mouse pointer. The item you
    are dragging moves (**Figure 7**).

USING THE MOUSE

Menus

The Finder—and most other Mac OS programs—offers menus full of options. There are four types of menus in Mac OS X:

◆ A **pull-down menu** appears on the menu bar at the top of the screen (**Figure 8**).

◆ A **submenu** appears when a menu option with a right-pointing triangle is selected (**Figure 9**).

◆ A **pop-up menu**, which displays a pair of triangles (or double arrow), appears within a window (**Figures 10** and **11**).

◆ A **contextual menu** appears when you hold down [Control] while clicking an item (**Figure 12**).

✔ Tips

■ A menu option followed by an ellipsis (…) (**Figure 8**) will display a dialog when chosen. Dialogs are discussed in detail in **Chapter 5**.

■ A menu option that is dimmed or gray cannot be chosen. The commands that are available vary depending on what is selected on the desktop or in a window.

■ A menu option preceded by a check mark (**Figure 8**) is enabled, or "turned on."

■ A menu option followed by a series of keyboard characters (**Figure 8**) has a keyboard equivalent. Keyboard equivalents are discussed later in this chapter.

■ Contextual menus only display options that apply to the item to which you are pointing.

■ In Mac OS X, menus are translucent. Although this makes them look cool on screen, it doesn't always look good when illustrated on paper.

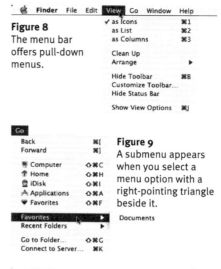

Figure 8
The menu bar offers pull-down menus.

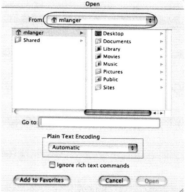

Figure 9
A submenu appears when you select a menu option with a right-pointing triangle beside it.

Figure 10 Pop-up menus can appear within dialogs.

Figure 11 To display a pop-up menu, click it.

Figure 12
A contextual menu appears when you hold down [Control] while clicking.

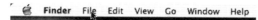

Figure 13 Point to the menu name.

Figure 14
Click (or press) to display the menu.

Figure 15
Click (or drag) to choose the menu option you want.

Figure 16
Hold down [Control] while pointing to an item.

Figure 17
A contextual menu appears when you click.

Figure 18
Click (or drag) to choose the option you want.

To use a menu

1. Point to the name of the menu (**Figure 13**).

2. Click. The menu opens, displaying its options (**Figure 14**).

3. Point to the menu option you want (**Figure 15**).

4. Click to choose the option. The menu disappears.

✔ Tips

■ Mac OS X's menus are "sticky menus"— each menu opens and stays open when you click its name.

■ To close a menu without choosing an option, click outside the menu.

■ This book uses the following notation to indicate menu commands: *Menu Name > Submenu Name* (if necessary) > *Command Name*. For example, the instructions for choosing the Documents command from the Favorites submenu under the Go menu (**Figure 9**) would be: "choose Go > Favorites > Documents."

To use a contextual menu

1. Point to the item on which you want to act.

2. Press and hold down [Control]. A tiny contextual menu icon appears beside the mouse pointer (**Figure 16**).

3. Click. A contextual menu appears at the item (**Figure 17**).

4. Click the menu option you want (**Figure 18**).

The Keyboard

The keyboard offers another way to communicate with your computer. In addition to typing text and numbers, you can also use it to choose menu commands.

There are three types of keys on a Mac OS keyboard:

◆ **Character keys**, such as letters, numbers, and symbols, are for typing information. Some character keys have special functions, as listed in **Table 1**.

◆ **Modifier keys** alter the meaning of a character key being pressed or the meaning of a mouse action. Modifier keys are listed in **Table 2**.

◆ **Function keys** perform specific functions in Mac OS or an application. Dedicated function keys, which always do the same thing, are listed in **Table 3**. Function keys labeled [F1] through [F12] or [F1] through [F15] on the keyboard can be assigned specific functions by applications.

✔ Tips

■ [⌘ ⌘] is called the *Command key* (not the Apple key).

■ Contextual menus are discussed on the previous page.

Table 1

Special Character Keys	
Key	**Function**
[Enter]	Enters information or "clicks" a default button.
[Return]	Begins a new paragraph or line or "clicks" a default button.
[Tab]	Advances to the next tab stop or the next item in a sequence.
[Delete]	Deletes a selection or the character to the left of the insertion point.
[Del]	Deletes a selection or the character to the right of the insertion point.
[Esc]	"Clicks" a Cancel button or ends the operation that is currently in progress.

Table 2

Modifier Keys	
Key	**Function**
[Shift]	Produces uppercase characters or symbols. Also works with the mouse to extend selections and to restrain movement in graphic applications.
[Option]	Produces special symbols.
[⌘ ⌘]	Accesses menu commands via keyboard equivalents.
[Control]	Modifies the functions of other keys and displays contextual menus.

Table 3

Dedicated Function Keys	
Key	**Function**
[Help]	Displays onscreen help.
[Home]	Scrolls to the beginning.
[End]	Scrolls to the end.
[Page Up]	Scrolls up one page.
[Page Down]	Scrolls down one page.
[←][→][↑][↓]	Moves the insertion point or changes the selection.

To use a keyboard equivalent

1. Hold down the modifier key(s) in the sequence. This is usually ⌘, but can be Option, Control, or Shift.

2. Press the letter, number, or symbol key in the sequence.

For example, to choose the Open command, which can be found under the File menu (**Figure 15**), hold down ⌘ and press O.

✔ Tips

■ You can learn keyboard equivalents by observing the key sequences that appear to the right of some menu commands (**Figures 8, 9,** and **14**).

■ Some commands include more than one modifier key. You must hold all modifier keys down while pressing the letter, number, or symbol key for the keyboard equivalent.

■ You can find a list of all Finder keyboard equivalents in **Appendix A**.

■ Some applications refer to keyboard equivalents as *shortcut keys*.

USING KEYBOARD EQUIVALENTS

Icons

Mac OS uses icons to graphically represent files and other items on the desktop, in the Dock, or within Finder windows:

◆ **Applications** (**Figure 19**) are programs you use to get work done. **Chapters 5** through **7** discuss working with applications.

◆ **Documents** (**Figure 20**) are the files created by applications. **Chapter 5** covers working with documents.

◆ **Folders** (**Figure 21**) are used to organize files. **Chapters 3** and **4** discuss using folders.

◆ **Disks** (**Figure 22**), including removable media, are used to store files. **Chapter 3** covers working with disks.

◆ The **Trash** (**Figure 23**), which is in the Dock, is for discarding items you no longer want and for ejecting removable media. The Trash is covered in **Chapter 3**.

✔ Tip

■ Icons can appear a number of different ways, depending on the view and view options chosen for a window. Windows are discussed later in this chapter; views are discussed in **Chapter 3**.

TextEdit   Preview   Microsoft Word

Figure 19 Application icons.

Letter   Picture.gif   Note

Figure 20 Document icons, including a TextEdit document, a Preview document, and a Word document.

Applications   System   My Stuff

Figure 21 Folder icons.

Macintosh HD   Microsoft Office X   Macintosh HD

Figure 22 Three different disk icons: hard disk, CD-ROM, and networked disk.

Figure 23 The three faces of the Trash icon in the Dock: empty, full, and while dragging removable media.

Figure 24 To select an icon, click it.

Figure 25 Hold down ⌘ or Shift while clicking other icons to add them to a multiple selection.

To select an icon

Click the icon that you want to select. The icon darkens, and its name becomes highlighted (**Figure 24**).

✔ Tip

- You can also select an icon in an active window by pressing the keyboard key for the first letter of the icon's name or by pressing Tab, Shift Tab, ←, →, ↑, or ↓ until the icon is selected.

To deselect an icon

Click anywhere in the window or on the Desktop other than on the selected icon.

✔ Tips

- If you select one icon and then click another icon, the originally selected icon is deselected and the icon you clicked becomes selected instead.

- Windows are discussed later in this chapter.

To select multiple icons by clicking

1. Click the first icon that you want to select.

2. Hold down ⌘ and click another icon that you want to select (**Figure 25**).

3. Repeat step 2 until all icons that you want to select have been selected.

✔ Tip

- Icons that are part of a multiple selection must be in the same window.

SELECTING & DESELECTING ICONS

To select multiple icons by dragging

1. Position the mouse pointer slightly above and to the left of the first icon in the group that you want to select (**Figure 26**).

2. Press the mouse button, and drag diagonally across the icons you want to select. A shaded box appears to indicate the selection area, and the items within it become selected (**Figure 27**).

3. When all the icons that you want to select are included in the selection area, release the mouse button (**Figure 28**).

✔ Tip

- To select multiple icons by dragging, the icons must be adjacent.

To select all icons in a window

Choose Edit > Select All (**Figure 29**), or press ⌃ ⌘ A.

All icons in the active window are selected.

✔ Tip

- Activating windows is covered later in this chapter.

To deselect one icon in a multiple selection

Hold down Shift or ⌃ ⌘ while clicking the icon that you want to deselect. That icon is deselected while the others remain selected.

Figure 26 Position the mouse pointer above and to the left of the first icon that you want to select.

Figure 27 Drag to draw a shaded selection box around the icons that you want to select.

Figure 28 Release the mouse button to complete the selection.

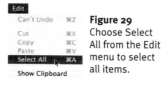

Figure 29 Choose Select All from the Edit menu to select all items.

Figure 30 Point to the icon that you want to move.

Figure 31 Drag the icon to the new location.

Figure 32 Release the mouse button to complete the move.

To move an icon

1. Position the mouse pointer on the icon that you want to move (**Figure 30**).

2. Press the mouse button, and drag the icon to the new location. As you drag, a shadowy image of the icon moves with the mouse pointer (**Figure 31**).

3. Release the mouse button when the icon is in the desired position (**Figure 32**).

✔ Tips

- You cannot drag to reposition icons within windows set to list or column view. Views are discussed in **Chapter 3**.

- You move icons to rearrange them in a window or on the Desktop, or to copy or move the items they represent to another folder or disk. Copying and moving items is discussed in **Chapter 3**.

- You can also move multiple icons at once. Simply select the icons first, then position the mouse pointer on one of the selected icons and follow steps 2 and 3 above. All selected icons move together.

- To force an icon to snap to a window's invisible grid, hold down ⌃⌘ while dragging it. The grid, which I tell you more about in **Chapter 4**, ensures consistent spacing between icons, so your window looks neat.

MOVING ICONS

To open an icon

1. Select the icon you want to open (**Figure 33**).

2. Choose File > Open (**Figure 34**), or press ⌘ ⌘ O.

or

Double-click the icon that you want to open.

✔ Tips

- Only one click is necessary when opening an item in a Finder window toolbar or the Dock. The toolbar and Dock are covered in detail later in this chapter.

- What happens when you open an icon depends on the type of icon you open. For example:
  - ▲ Opening a disk or folder icon displays the contents of the disk or folder in the same Finder window (**Figure 35**). Windows are discussed next.
  - ▲ Opening an application icon launches the application so that you can work with it. Working with applications is covered in **Chapter 5** and elsewhere in this book.
  - ▲ Opening a document icon launches the application that created that document and displays the document so you can view or edit it. Working with documents is covered in **Chapter 5**.
  - ▲ Opening the Trash displays items that will be deleted when you empty the Trash. Using and emptying the Trash is discussed in **Chapter 3**.

- To open a folder or disk in a new Finder window, hold down ⌘ while opening it.

- The File menu's Open With submenu, which is discussed in **Chapter 5**, enables you to open a document with a specific application.

Figure 33 Select the icon.

Figure 34 Choose Open from the File menu.

Figure 35 Here's the window from **Figure 33** with the Applications folder's contents displayed.

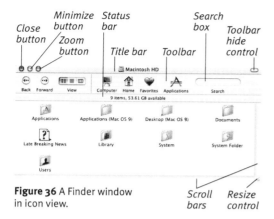

Figure 36 A Finder window in icon view.

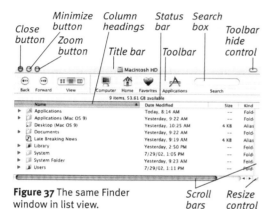

Figure 37 The same Finder window in list view.

✔ Tips

- By default, when you open a folder or disk icon, its contents appear in the active window. As discussed in **Chapter 4**, you can use Finder Preferences to tell Mac OS X to open folders in new windows, like Mac OS 9.x and earlier.

- I cover the Finder's three window views in **Chapter 3**, the toolbar later in this chapter, and the status bar and Search box in **Chapter 4**.

Windows

Mac OS makes extensive use of windows for displaying icons and other information in the Finder and documents in other applications. **Figures 36** and **37** show two different views of a Finder window.

Each window includes a variety of controls you can use to manipulate it:

- ◆ The **title bar** displays the window's icon and name and can be used to move the window.

- ◆ The **close button** closes the window.

- ◆ The **minimize button** collapses the window to an icon in the Dock.

- ◆ The **zoom button** toggles the window's size between full size and a custom size.

- ◆ The **toolbar hide control** toggles the display of the toolbar.

- ◆ The **toolbar** displays buttons and controls for working with Finder windows.

- ◆ The **Search box** enables you to search for files based on file name. (The Search box is new in Mac OS X 10.2.)

- ◆ The **status bar** provides information about items in a window and space available on disk.

- ◆ The **resize control** enables you to set a custom size for the window.

- ◆ **Scroll bars** scroll the contents of the window.

- ◆ **Column headings** (in list view only) display the names of the columns and let you quickly sort by a column. (The selected column heading is the column by which the list is sorted.)

WINDOWS

To open a new Finder window

Choose File > New Finder Window (**Figure 38**), or press ⌃⌘N. A new top-level window appears (**Figure 39**).

✔ Tip

- The top-level window is discussed in **Chapter 3**.

To open a folder or disk in a new Finder window

Hold down ⌃⌘ while opening a folder or disk icon. A new window containing the contents of the folder or disk appears.

✔ Tip

- Opening folders and disks is explained earlier in this chapter.

To close a window

Click the window's close button (**Figures 36** and **37**).

or

Choose File > Close Window (**Figure 40**), or press ⌃⌘W.

To close all open windows

Hold down Option while clicking the active window's close button (**Figures 36** and **37**).

or

Hold down Option while choosing File > Close All (**Figure 41**), or press ⌃⌘ Option W.

✔ Tip

- The Close Window/Close All commands (**Figures 40** and **41**) are examples of *dynamic menu items*—pressing a modifier key (in this case, Option) changes the menu command from Close Window (**Figure 40**) to Close All (**Figure 41**).

Figure 38
Choose New Finder Window from the File menu.

Figure 39 The active window's title bar includes color and appears atop all other windows.

Figure 40 Choose Close Window from the File menu...

Figure 41 ...or hold down Option and choose Close All from the File menu.

Figure 42 The Window menu lists all open Finder windows.

Figure 43 The Bring All to Front command brings all Finder windows to the top.

To activate a window

Click anywhere in or on the window.

or

Choose the name of the window you want to activate from the Window menu (**Figure 42**).

✔ Tips

- It's important to make sure that the window you want to work with is open and active *before* using commands that work on the active window—such as Close Window, Select All, and View menu options.

- You can distinguish between active and inactive windows by the appearance of their title bars; the active window's title bar includes color (**Figure 39**). In addition, a check mark appears beside the active window's name in the Window menu (**Figure 42**).

- When two or more windows overlap, the active window will always be on top of the stack (**Figure 39**).

To bring all Finder windows to the top

Choose Window > Bring All to Front (**Figure 43**). All open Finder windows that are not minimized are moved in front of any windows opened by other applications.

✔ Tip

- In Mac OS X, Finder windows can be intermingled with other applications' windows. The Bring All to Front command gathers the windows together in the top layers. You may find this command useful when working with many windows from several different applications.

ACTIVATING WINDOWS

To move a window

1. Position the mouse pointer on the window's title bar (**Figure 44**).

2. Press the mouse button and drag the window to a new location. As you drag, the window moves along with your mouse pointer (**Figure 45**).

3. When the outline of the window is in the desired position, release the mouse button.

To resize a window

1. Position the mouse pointer on the resize control in the lower-right corner of the window (**Figure 46**).

2. Press the mouse button and drag. As you drag, the resize control moves with the mouse pointer, changing the size and shape of the window (**Figure 47**).

3. When the window is the desired size, release the mouse button.

✔ Tips

- The larger a window is, the more you can see inside it.

- By resizing and repositioning windows, you can see inside more than one window at a time. This comes in handy when moving or copying the icons for files and folders from one window to another. Moving and copying files and folders is covered in **Chapter 3**.

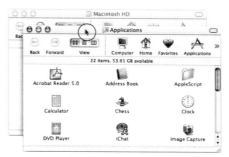

Figure 44 Position the mouse pointer on the title bar.

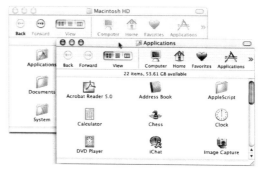

Figure 45 As you drag, the window moves.

Figure 46 Position the mouse pointer on the resize control.

Figure 47
As you drag, the window's size and shape changes.

Figure 48
The Minimize Window command minimizes the active window.

Figure 49 Minimized windows shrink down into icons in the Dock.

Figure 50
A diamond beside a window name indicates that the window has been minimized.

Figure 51
You can zoom the active window by choosing Zoom Window from the Window menu.

To minimize a window

Click the window's minimize button (**Figures 36** and **37**).

or

Choose Window > Minimize Window (**Figure 48**), or press ⌃ ⌘ M.

or

Double-click the window's title bar.

The window shrinks into an icon and slips into the Dock at the bottom of the screen (**Figure 49**).

✔ Tip

- ■ To minimize all windows, hold down Option and choose Windows > Minimize All Windows, or press Option ⌃ ⌘ M.

To redisplay a minimized window

Click the window's icon in the Dock (**Figure 49**).

or

Choose the window's name from the Window menu (**Figure 50**).

To zoom a window

Click the window's zoom button (**Figures 36** and **37**).

or

Choose Window > Zoom Window (**Figure 51**).

Each time you click the zoom button, the window's size toggles between two sizes:

- ◆ **Standard state** size is the smallest possible size that would accommodate the window's contents and still fit on your screen (**Figure 36**).

- ◆ **User state** size, which is the size you specify with the resize control (**Figure 47**).

MINIMIZING & ZOOMING WINDOWS

To scroll a window's contents

Click one of the scroll bar arrows (**Figure 52**) as follows:

◆ To scroll the window's contents up, click the down arrow on the vertical scroll bar.

◆ To scroll the window's contents down, click the up arrow on the vertical scroll bar.

◆ To scroll the window's contents to the left, click the right arrow on the horizontal scroll bar.

◆ To scroll the window's contents to the right, click the left arrow on the horizontal scroll bar.

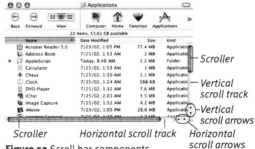

Figure 52 Scroll bar components.

✔ Tips

■ If you have trouble remembering which scroll arrow to click, think of it this way:

▲ Click down to see down.

▲ Click up to see up.

▲ Click right to see right.

▲ Click left to see left.

■ You can also scroll a window's contents by either clicking in the scroll track on either side of the scroller or by dragging the scroller to a new position on the scroll bar. Both of these techniques enable you to scroll a window's contents more quickly.

■ If all of a window's contents are displayed, you will not be able to scroll the window. A window that cannot be scrolled will have flat or empty looking scroll bars (**Figure 36**).

■ The scrollers in Mac OS X are proportional—this means that the more of a window's contents you see, the more space the scroller will take up in its scroll bar.

SCROLLING A WINDOW'S CONTENTS

Back & Forward buttons | View buttons | Folder navigation icons | Search box

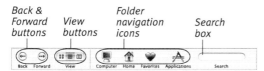

Figure 53 The toolbar.

Figure 54 When the window is narrow, some toolbar items may be hidden.

Figure 55 Click the double arrow to display a menu of hidden items.

Toolbar hide control

Figure 56 The toolbar hide control button can hide the toolbar...

Figure 57 ...or display it.

The Toolbar

The toolbar (**Figure 53**) offers navigation tools and view buttons within Finder windows:

◆ The **Back button** displays the previous window's contents.

◆ The **Forward button** displays the window that was showing before you clicked the Back button.

◆ **View buttons** enable you to change the window's view.

◆ **Folder navigation icons** open specific Finder windows.

◆ **Search box**, which is new in Mac OS X 10.2, enables you to quickly search for a file by name.

✔ Tips

■ The toolbar can be customized to show the items you use most; **Chapter 4** explains how.

■ Views and using the Search box are covered in detail in **Chapter 4**; file management and navigation is discussed in **Chapter 3**.

■ If the window is not wide enough to show all toolbar buttons, a double arrow appears on the right side of the toolbar (**Figure 54**). Click the arrow to display a menu of missing buttons (**Figure 55**), and select the button you want.

To hide or display the toolbar

Click the toolbar hide control button (**Figure 56**).

If the toolbar is displayed, it disappears (**Figure 56**); if the toolbar is not displayed, it appears (**Figure 57**).

To use a toolbar button

Click the button once.

Figure 58 The Dock displays often-used applications and documents.

The Dock

The Dock (**Figure 58**) offers easy access to often-used applications and documents, as well as minimized windows.

✔ Tip

- The Dock can be customized; **Chapter 4** explains how.

To identify items in the Dock

Point to the item. The name of the item appears above the Dock (**Figure 59**).

Figure 59 Point to an icon to see what it represents.

To identify items in the Dock that are running

Look at the Dock. A triangle appears beneath each item that is running, such as the Finder in **Figures 58**, **59**, and **60**.

Figure 60 An item's icon bounces while it is being opened.

To open an item in the Dock

Click the icon for the item you want to open. One of four things happens:

- If the icon is for an application that is running, the application becomes the active application.

- If the icon is for an application that is not running, the application launches. While the application launches, the icon in the Dock bounces (**Figure 60**) so you know something is happening.

- If the icon is for a minimized window, the window is displayed.

- If the icon is for a document that is not open, the application that created the document launches (if necessary) and the document opens.

✔ Tip

- Using applications and opening documents is discussed in greater detail in **Chapter 5**; minimizing and displaying windows is discussed earlier in this chapter.

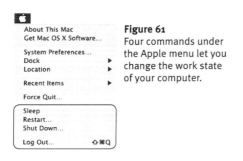

Figure 61
Four commands under the Apple menu let you change the work state of your computer.

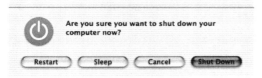

Figure 62 Pressing the power key on some Mac OS computers displays a dialog like this one.

Sleeping, Restarting, & Shutting Down

The Apple menu (**Figure 61**) offers several options that change the work state of your computer:

◆ **Sleep** puts the computer into a state where it uses very little power. The screen goes blank and the hard disk may stop spinning.

◆ **Restart** instructs the computer to shut down and immediately start back up.

◆ **Shut Down** closes all open documents and programs, clears memory, and cuts power to the computer.

◆ **Log Out** closes all open documents and programs and clears memory. Your computer remains running until you or someone else logs in.

I discuss all of these commands on the following pages.

✔ Tips

■ If your computer's keyboard includes a power key, pressing it displays a dialog with buttons for the Restart, Sleep, and Shut Down commands (**Figure 62**). This feature, however, does not work with all Mac OS–computer models.

■ Do *not* restart or shut down a computer by simply flicking off the power switch. Doing so prevents the computer from properly closing files, which may result in file corruption and related problems.

■ Mac OS X also includes a screen saver, which automatically starts up when your computer is inactive for five minutes. Don't confuse the screen saver with System or display sleep—it's different. To display the screen again, simply move the mouse or press any key. You can customize screen saver settings with the Screen Effects preferences pane, which is covered in *Mac OS X Advanced: Visual QuickPro Guide*.

Sleeping, Restarting, & Shutting Down

To put your computer to sleep

Choose Apple > Sleep (**Figure 61**).

or

1. Press the power key on the keyboard.

2. In the dialog that appears (**Figure 62**), click Sleep.

✔ Tips

■ Not all computers support sleep mode. If your computer does not support sleep mode, the Sleep command will not appear on the Apple menu.

■ When you put your computer to sleep, everything in memory is preserved. When you wake the computer, you can quickly continue working where you left off.

■ Sleep mode is an effective way to conserve the battery life of a PowerBook or iBook without turning it off.

■ By default, Mac OS X automatically puts a computer to sleep when it is inactive for 20 minutes. You can change this setting in the Energy Saver preferences pane, which is discussed in detail in *Mac OS X Advanced: Visual QuickPro Guide*.

To wake a sleeping computer

Press any keyboard key. You may have to wait several seconds for the computer to fully wake.

✔ Tips

■ It's much quicker to wake a sleeping computer than to restart a computer that has been shut down.

■ On some computer models, pressing Caps Lock or certain other keys may not wake the computer. When in doubt, press a letter key—they always work.

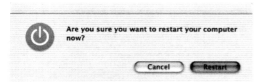

Figure 63 This dialog appears when you choose the Restart command from the Apple menu.

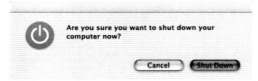

Figure 64 This dialog appears when you choose the Shut Down command from the Apple menu.

To restart your computer

1. Choose Apple > Restart (**Figure 61**).

2. In the dialog that appears (**Figure 63**), click Restart or press Return or Enter.

or

1. Press the Power key on the keyboard.

2. In the dialog that appears (**Figure 62**), click Restart.

✔ Tip

■ Restarting the computer clears memory and reloads all system files.

To shut down your computer

1. Choose Apple > Shut Down (**Figure 61**).

2. In the dialog that appears (**Figure 64**), click Shut Down or press Return or Enter.

or

1. Press the Power key on the keyboard.

2. In the dialog that appears (**Figure 62**), click Shut Down or press Return or Enter.

✔ Tip

■ On most computers, the Shut Down command will cut power to the computer as part of the shut down process. If it doesn't, a dialog will appear onscreen, telling you it's safe to turn off your computer. You can then use the power switch to cut power to the computer.

RESTARTING & SHUTTING DOWN

Logging Out & In

If your computer is shared by multiple users, you may find it more convenient to log out when you're finished working. The Log Out command under the Apple menu (**Figure 61**) closes all applications and documents and closes your account on the computer. The computer remains running, making it quick and easy for the next person to log in and get right to work.

✔ Tip

- If you are your computer's only user, you'll probably never use the Log Out command. (I hardly ever do.)

To log out

1. Choose Apple > Log Out (**Figure 61**), or press Shift ⌃ ⌘ Q.

2. A confirmation dialog like the one in **Figure 65** appears. Click Log Out or press Return or Enter.

   Your computer closes all applications and documents, then displays the Login Screen (**Figure 66** or **67**).

✔ Tip

- As the Log Out confirmation dialog in **Figure 65** explains, if you don't do anything in step 2, Mac OS X will automatically log out after two minutes.

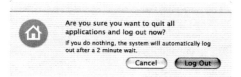

Figure 65 A dialog like this one confirms that you really do want to log out.

Figure 66 A typical Login Screen might list the computer's users...

Figure 67 ... or it might just provide text boxes for entering the Name and Password for a valid account.

Figure 68 If a Password box does not appear in the initial Login Screen (**Figure 67**), it appears when you select a user account.

To log in

1. If a Login Screen like the one in **Figure 66** appears, click the icon for your user account.

2. Enter your password in the Password box that appears (**Figure 68**).

3. Click Log In.

or

1. If a Login Screen like the one in **Figure 67** appears, enter your full or short account name in the Name box and your password in the Password box.

2. Click Log In.

Your Mac OS desktop appears, looking the same as it did when you logged out or shut down your computer.

✔ Tips

■ The appearance of the Login Screen (**Figures 66** and **67**) varies depending on how the Accounts preference pane has been configured by the system administrator. Account options is an advanced topic, which is discussed in detail in *Mac OS X Advanced: Visual QuickPro Guide*.

■ Your user name and short name are created when you use the Mac OS Setup Assistant to configure Mac OS X, as discussed in **Chapter 1**. You can use either name to log in.

LOGGING IN

File Management

File Management

In Mac OS, you use the Finder to organize and manage your files.

- ◆ View the contents of your disks in windows in a variety of ways.

- ◆ Automatically sort items by name, kind, creation date, or other criteria in ascending or descending order.

- ◆ Rename items.

- ◆ Create folders to store related items.

- ◆ Move items stored on disk to organize them so they're easy to find and back up.

- ◆ Copy items to other disks to back them up or share them with others.

- ◆ Delete items you no longer need.

- ◆ Mount and eject disks.

- ◆ Write to, or "burn," CD-ROMs.

✔ Tip

- ■ If you're brand new to Mac OS, be sure to read the information in **Chapter 2** before working with this chapter. That chapter contains information and instructions about techniques that are used throughout this chapter.

Mac OS X Disk Organization

Like previous versions of Mac OS and most other computer operating systems, Mac OS X uses a hierarchical filing system (HFS) to organize and store files, including system files, applications, and documents.

The top level of the filing system is the computer level. You can view the computer level window (**Figure 1**) by clicking the Computer icon in the toolbar of any Finder window. This level shows the computer's internal hard disk, any other disks the computer has access to, and the Network icon.

The next level down is the computer's hard disk level. You can view this level by opening the hard disk icon in the computer level window (**Figure 1**) or on the desktop. While the contents of your hard disk may differ from what's shown in **Figure 2**, some elements should be the same:

◆ **Applications** contains Mac OS X applications.

◆ **Applications (Mac OS 9)** contains applications that run under the Classic environment.

◆ **System** and **Library** contain the Mac OS X system files.

◆ **Users** (**Figure 3**) contains individual folders for each of the computer's users, as well as a Shared folder.

◆ **System Folder** contains the Mac OS 9.x system files for running the Classic environment.

◆ **Documents** contains documents you saved on your hard disk before upgrading to Mac OS X.

◆ **Desktop (Mac OS 9)** contains items that appear on the desktop when you start your computer with Mac OS 9.x.

Figure 1 The top level of your computer shows all mounted disks and a Network icon.

Figure 2 A typical hard disk window might look like this.

Figure 3 The Users folder contains a home folder for each user, as well as a Shared folder.

Figure 4 Your home folder is preconfigured with folders for storing a variety of item types.

By default, a Mac OS X hard disk is organized for multiple users. Each user has his or her own "home" folder, which is stored in the Users folder (**Figure 3**). You can view the items inside your home folder by opening the house icon with your name on it inside the Users folder (**Figure 3**) or by clicking the Home icon in the toolbar of any Finder window. Your home folder is preconfigured with folders for all kinds of items you may want to store on disk (**Figure 4**).

✔ Tips

- Applications and the Classic environment are discussed in greater detail in **Chapter 5**.

- When you install new applications on your computer, you should install Mac OS X–compatible applications in the Applications folder and Mac OS 9.x–compatible applications in the Applications (Mac OS 9) folder.

- If you upgraded from a previous version of Mac OS to Mac OS X, you may want to move the contents of the Documents folder on your hard disk (**Figure 2**) to the Documents folder inside your home folder (**Figure 4**) to keep your documents together and easier to find.

- Unless you are an administrator, you cannot access the files in any other user's home folder except those in the user's Public and Sites folders.

- If you place an item in the Shared folder inside the Users folder (**Figure 3**), it can be opened by anyone who uses the computer.

- Sharing computers and networking is beyond the scope of this book. For more information about these advanced topics, consult *Mac OS X Advanced: Visual QuickPro Guide.*

Pathnames

A *path* or *pathname* is a kind of address for a file on disk. It includes the name of the disk on which the file resides, the names of the folders the file is stored within, and the name of the file itself. For example, the pathname for a file named *Letter.rtf* in the Documents folder of the mlanger folder shown in **Figure 4** would be: Macintosh HD/Users/mlanger/Documents/Letter.rtf

When entering a pathname from a specific folder, you don't have to enter the entire pathname. Instead, enter the path as it relates to the current folder. For example, the path to the above-mentioned file from the mlanger folder would be: Documents/Letter.rtf

To indicate a specific user folder, use the tilde (~) character followed by the name of the user account. So the path to the mlanger folder (**Figure 4**) would be: ~mlanger. (You can omit the user name if you want to open your own user folder.)

To indicate the top level of your computer, use a slash (/) character. So the path to Super iMac (**Figure 1**) would be: /

When used as part of a longer pathname, the slash character indicates the *root level* of your hard disk. So /Applications/AppleScript would indicate the AppleScript folder inside the Applications folder on your hard disk.

Don't worry if this sounds confusing to you. Fortunately, you don't really need to know it to use Mac OS X. It's just a good idea to be familiar with the concept of pathnames in case you run across them while working with your computer.

✔ Tip

- As discussed in **Chapter 5**, Mac OS X's Open dialogs support pathnames in the Go to field. If you decide to take advantage of this feature, use the guidelines on this page for entering pathnames.

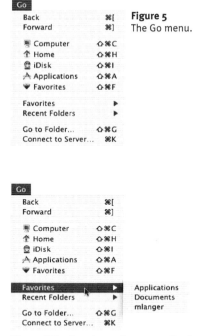

Figure 5
The Go menu.

Figure 6 The Favorites submenu on the Go menu lists your favorite locations.

Figure 7
The Recent Folders submenu lists recently opened folders.

The Go Menu

The Go menu (**Figure 5**) offers a quick way to open specific locations on your computer:

◆ **Back** (⌘[) opens the parent folder for the active window's folder. This command is only available if a window is active and if the window was used to display the contents of a folder.

◆ **Forward** (⌘]) displays the contents of the window you were viewing before you clicked the Back button. This command is only available if a window is active and if the Back button has been clicked.

◆ **Computer** (Shift ⌘C) opens the top level window for your computer (**Figure 1**).

◆ **Home** (Shift ⌘H) opens your home folder (**Figure 4**).

◆ **iDisk** (Shift ⌘I) offers access to folders stored on Apple's .Mac server via the Internet and iDisk.

◆ **Applications** (Shift ⌘A) opens the Applications folder.

◆ **Favorites** (Shift ⌘F) opens the Favorites folder, which is discussed in **Chapter 4**.

◆ **Favorites** displays a submenu of favorite locations (**Figure 6**).

◆ **Recent Folders** displays a submenu of recently opened folders (**Figure 7**).

◆ **Go to Folder** (Shift ⌘G) lets you open any folder your computer has access to.

◆ **Connect to Server** (⌘K) enables you to open a server accessible via network.

✔ Tip

■ iDisk is discussed in *Mac OS X Advanced: Visual QuickPro Guide*, and favorites are covered in **Chapter 4**.

THE GO MENU

65

To open a Go menu item

Choose the item's name from the Go menu (**Figure 5**) or one of its submenus (**Figures 6** and **7**).

To go to a folder

1. Choose Go > Go to Folder (**Figure 5**), or press Shift ⌃ ⌘ G.

2. In the Go To Folder dialog that appears (**Figure 8**), enter the pathname for the folder you want to open.

3. Click Go.

   If you entered a valid pathname, the folder opens in a Finder window.

   or

   If you did not enter a valid pathname, an error message appears in the Go To Folder dialog (**Figure 9**). Repeat steps 2 and 3 to try again or click Cancel to dismiss the dialog.

✔ Tip

■ If a window is open when you use the Go to Folder command, the Go To Folder dialog will appear as a dialog *sheet* attached to the window (**Figure 10**). The pathname you enter must be from that window's folder location on your hard disk.

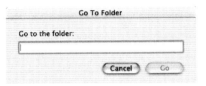

Figure 8 Use the Go To Folder dialog to enter the pathname of the folder you want to open.

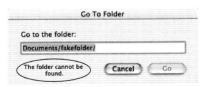

Figure 9 An error message appears in the Go To Folder window if you enter an invalid pathname.

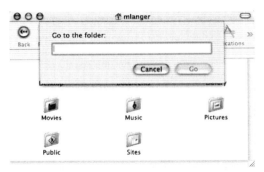

Figure 10 If a window is active when you use the Go to Folder command, the dialog appears as a sheet attached to the window.

Figure 11 The Connect to Server dialog with a server selected.

Figure 12 To connect to a server, you must provide log in information.

Figure 13 If more than one volume is available, choose the one you want to access.

Figure 14 An icon for the volume you connected to appears on your desktop and in the Volumes window.

To connect to a server

1. Choose Go > Connect to Server (**Figure 5**), or press ⌃⌘K.

2. In the Connect to Server dialog that appears (**Figure 11**), select the name of the computer you want to connect to.

3. Click Connect.

4. A log in window like the one in **Figure 12** appears. Enter your account information for the server in the appropriate boxes, and click Connect.

5. If the server has multiple volumes, a dialog like the one in **Figure 13** appears. Select the volume you want to open, and click OK.

   The icon for the server volume you connected to and the Volumes window, containing an alias icon for the volume, appear on your desktop (**Figure 14**).

✔ Tips

- A networked computer does not need to run special server software to be considered a "server" by Mac OS. For example, the computers shown in **Figure 11** are accessible via simple file sharing.

- As shown in **Figure 11**, your computer may appear in the list of available servers.

- To connect to a server using TCP/IP, enter the TCP/IP address for the server in the Address box in step 2.

- In step 5, a Mac OS X computer will display its hard disk and a separate volume for each user account you have access to.

- I tell you about aliases in **Chapter 4**.

- A more complete discussion of sharing computers and networking is beyond the scope of this book. For more information about these topics, consult *Mac OS X Advanced: Visual QuickPro Guide*.

CONNECTING TO A SERVER

Views

A Finder window's contents can be displayed using three different views:

- ◆ **Icon** displays the window's contents as small or large icons (**Figure 15**).

- ◆ **List** displays the window's contents as a sorted list (**Figure 16**).

- ◆ **Column** displays the window's contents with a multiple-column format that shows the currently selected disk or folder and the items within it (**Figure 17**).

✔ Tip

- ■ You can customize views by setting view options globally or for individual windows. I explain how in **Chapter 4**.

To change a window's view

1. If necessary, activate the window whose view you want to change.

2. Choose the view option you want from the View menu (**Figure 18**) or press the corresponding shortcut key.

   or

   Click the toolbar's view button for the view you want (**Figure 19**).

The view of the window changes.

✔ Tips

- ■ Commands on the View menu (**Figure 18**) work on the active window only.

- ■ A check mark appears on the View menu beside the name of the view applied to the active window (**Figure 18**).

- ■ You can set the view for each window individually.

Figure 15 You can display a window's contents as icons,...

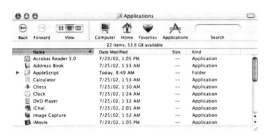

Figure 16 ...as a list,...

Figure 17 ...or as columns.

Figure 18
The View menu offers a variety of options for changing a window's view, along with three new command key equivalents for switching from one view to another.

Icon List Column
view view view

Figure 19 The view buttons in the toolbar.

Figure 20 Start with a messy window like this one...

Figure 21 ...and use the Clean Up command to put the icons in place.

Figure 22 The Arrange submenu offers several options for neatly arranging icons.

To neatly arrange icons in icon view

1. Activate the window that you want to clean up (**Figure 20**).

2. Choose View > Clean Up (**Figure 18**). The icons are neatly arranged in the window's invisible grid (**Figure 21**).

    or

    Choose one of the commands from the Arrange submenu under the View menu (**Figure 22**):

    ▲ **by Name** arranges the icons alphabetically by name (**Figure 15**).

    ▲ **by Date Modified** arranges the icons chronologically by the date they were last modified, with the most recently modified item last.

    ▲ **by Date Created** arranges the icons chronologically by the date they were created, with the most recently created item last.

    ▲ **by Size** arranges the icons in size order, with the largest item last. (Folders have a size of 0 (zero) for this option.)

    ▲ **by Kind** arranges the icons alphabetically by the kind of file.

    The icons are neatly arranged in the window's invisible grid in the order you specified (**Figure 15**).

✔ Tips

■ A window's invisible grid ensures consistent spacing between icons.

■ You can manually position an icon in the window's invisible grid by holding down ⌃⌘ while dragging it within the window.

ARRANGING ICON VIEW WINDOW CONTENTS

To sort a window's contents in list view

Click the column heading for the column you want to sort by. The list is sorted by that column (**Figure 23**).

✔ Tips

■ You can identify the column by which a list is sorted by its colored column heading (**Figures 16, 23**, and **24**).

■ You can reverse a window's sort order by clicking the sort column's heading a second time (**Figure 24**).

■ You can determine the sort direction by looking at the arrow in the sort column. When it points up, the items are sorted in ascending order (**Figure 24**); when it points down, the items are sorted in descending order (**Figure 23**).

■ To properly sort by size, you must turn on the Calculate all sizes option for the window. I explain how in **Chapter 4**.

■ You can specify which columns should appear in a window by setting View Options. I explain how in **Chapter 4**.

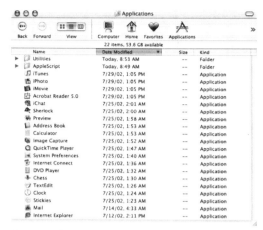

Figure 23 Click a column heading to sort by that column.

Figure 24 Click the same column heading to reverse that column's sort order.

Icon Names

Mac OS is very flexible when it comes to names for files, folders, and disks.

- ◆ A file or folder name can be up to 255 characters long. A disk name can be up to 27 characters long.

- ◆ A name can contain any character except a colon (:).

This makes it easy to give your files, folders, and disks names that make sense to you.

✔ Tips

- ■ Normally, you name documents when you save them. Saving documents is covered in **Chapter 5**.

- ■ A lengthy file name may appear truncated (or shortened) when displayed in windows and lists.

- ■ Since Mac OS 9.x and earlier cannot recognize very long file names, it's not a good idea to use them to name files you may work with in Mac OS 9. Instead, stick to file names of 31 characters or less.

- ■ No two documents in the same folder can have the same name.

- ■ Because slash characters (/) are used in pathnames, it's not a good idea to use them in names. In fact, some programs (such as Microsoft Word X) won't allow you to include a slash in a file name.

- ■ Working with and naming disks is covered later in this chapter.

ICON NAMES

To rename an icon

1. Click the icon to select it (**Figure 25**).

2. Point to the name of the icon, and click. After a brief pause, a box appears around the name and the name becomes selected (**Figure 26**).

3. Type the new name. The text you type automatically overwrites the selected text (**Figure 27**).

4. Press Return or Enter, or click anywhere else. The icon is renamed (**Figure 28**).

✔ Tips

- Not all icons can be renamed. If the edit box does not appear around an icon name (as shown in **Figure 26**), that icon cannot be renamed.

- You can also rename an icon in the Info window, which is covered in **Chapter 4**.

Figure 25
Start by selecting the icon.

Figure 26
When you click, an edit box appears around the name.

Figure 27
Type a new name for the icon.

Figure 28
When you press Return, the name changes.

Figure 29
Choose New
Folder from the
File menu.

Figure 30
A new folder
appears.

Figure 31
Enter a name for the
folder while the edit
box appears around it.

Folders

Mac OS uses folders to organize files and
other folders on disk. You can create a folder,
give it a name that makes sense to you, and
move files and other folders into it. It's a lot
like organizing paper files and folders in a file
cabinet.

✔ Tips

■ A folder can contain any number of files
and other folders.

■ It's a very good idea to use folders to
organize the files on your hard disk.
Imagine a file cabinet without file
folders—that's how your hard disk
would appear if you never used folders
to keep your files tidy.

■ As discussed earlier in this chapter, your
home folder includes folders set up for
organizing files by type. You'll find that
these folders often appear as default file
locations when saving specific types of
files from within software programs.
Saving files from within applications is
covered in **Chapter 5**.

To create a folder

1. Choose File > New Folder (**Figure 29**), or
press [Shift][⌘][N]. A new untitled folder
(**Figure 30**) appears in the active window.

2. While the edit box appears around the
new folder's name (**Figure 30**), type a
name for it (**Figure 31**) and press [Return].

✔ Tips

■ You can rename a folder the same way
you rename any other icon. Renaming
icons is discussed on the previous page.

■ Working with windows is discussed in
Chapter 2.

Moving & Copying Items

In addition to moving icons around within a window or on the desktop (see **Chapter 2**), you can move or copy items to other locations on the same disk or to other disks by dragging them:

◆ When you drag an item to a location on the same disk, the item is moved to that location.

◆ When you drag an item to a location on another disk, the item is copied to that location.

◆ When you hold down Option while dragging an item to a location on the same disk, the item is copied to that location.

The next few pages provide instructions for all of these techniques, as well as instructions for duplicating items.

✔ Tips

■ You can move or copy more than one item at a time. Begin by selecting all of the items that you want to move or copy, then drag any one of them to the destination. All items will be moved or copied.

■ You can continue working with the Finder or any other application—even start more copy jobs—while a copy job is in progress.

■ In Mac OS X, you can also copy Finder items using the Copy and Paste commands under the Finder's Edit menu. I explain how to use Copy and Paste in **Chapter 7**.

Figure 32 Drag the icon onto the icon for the folder to which you want to move it...

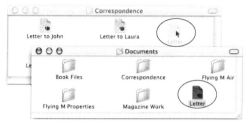

Figure 33 ...or drag the icon into the window in which you want to move it.

To move an item to another location on the same disk

1. Drag the icon for the item that you want to move as follows:

   ▲ To move the item into a specific folder on the disk, drag the icon onto the icon for the folder. The destination folder icon becomes selected when the mouse pointer moves over it (**Figure 32**).

   ▲ To move the item into a specific window on the disk, drag the icon into the window. A border appears around the inside of the destination window (**Figure 33**).

2. Release the mouse button. The item moves.

✔ Tip

■ If the destination location is on another disk, the item you drag will be copied rather than moved. You can always delete the original after the copy is made. Deleting items is discussed later in this chapter.

MOVING ITEMS TO ANOTHER DISK LOCATION

To copy an item to another disk

1. Drag the icon for the item that you want to copy as follows:

   ▲ To copy the item to the top (or *root*) level of a disk, drag the icon to the icon for the destination disk (**Figure 34**).

   ▲ To copy the item into a folder on the disk, drag the icon to the icon for the folder on the destination disk (**Figure 35**).

   ▲ To copy the item into a specific window on the disk, drag the icon into the window (**Figure 36**).

   When the item you are dragging moves on top of the destination location, a plus sign in a green circle appears beneath the mouse pointer. If the destination is an icon, the icon becomes selected.

2. Release the mouse button. A Copy window like the one in **Figure 37** appears. When it disappears, the copy is complete.

✔ Tips

- You cannot copy items to a disk that is write protected or to a folder for which you don't have write privileges. When you try, the green plus sign changes to a circle with a line through it. I tell you about write-protecting disks later in this chapter.

- If a file with the same file name already exists in the destination location, an error message appears in the Copy window (**Figure 38**). Click Stop to dismiss the window without making the copy, or click Replace to replace the existing file with the one you are copying.

- Because copying small files happens so quickly in Mac OS X, you probably won't see the Copy window (**Figure 37**) very often. It doesn't have time to appear!

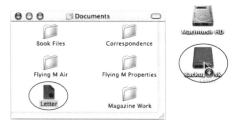

Figure 34 Drag the icon to the destination disk's icon...

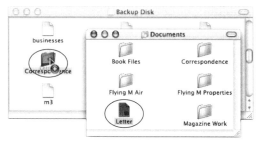

Figure 35 ...or to a folder icon in a window on the destination disk, ...

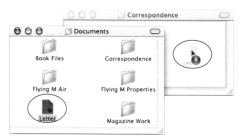

Figure 36 ...or to an open window on the destination disk.

Figure 37 A window like this indicates copy progress.

Figure 38 If a file with the same name already exists in the destination, Mac OS tells you.

COPYING ITEMS TO ANOTHER DISK

Figure 39 Hold down (Option) while dragging the item onto a folder...

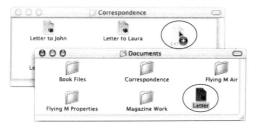

Figure 40 ...or into a window on the same disk.

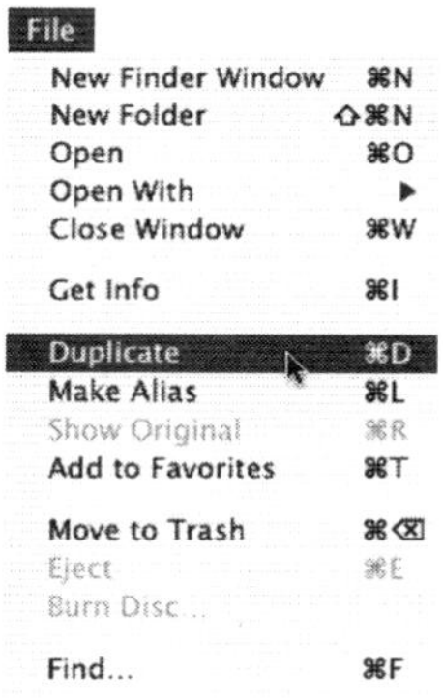

Figure 41
Choose Duplicate from the File menu.

Figure 42
A duplicate appears beneath the original.

To copy an item to another location on the same disk

1. Hold down (Option) while dragging the icon for the item that you want to copy onto a folder icon (**Figure 39**) or into a window (**Figure 40**).

   When the mouse pointer on the item you are dragging moves on top of the destination location, a plus sign in a green circle appears beneath it. If the destination is an icon, the icon becomes highlighted.

2. Release the mouse button. A Copy window like the one in **Figure 37** appears. When it disappears, the copy is complete.

✔ Tips

- When copying an item to a new location on the same disk, you *must* hold down (Option). If you don't, the item will be moved rather than copied.

- If a file with the same file name already exists in the destination location, an error message appears in the Copy window (**Figure 38**). Click Stop to dismiss the window without making the copy, or click Replace to replace the existing file with the one you are copying.

To duplicate an item

1. Select the item that you want to duplicate.

2. Choose File > Duplicate (**Figure 41**), or press ⌘ D.

or

Hold down (Option) while dragging the item that you want to duplicate to a different location in the same window.

A copy of the item you duplicated appears beside the original. The word *copy* is appended to the file name (**Figure 42**).

The Trash & Deleting Items

The Trash is a special place on your hard disk where you place items you want to delete. Items in the Trash remain there until you empty the Trash, which permanently deletes them. In Mac OS X, the Trash appears as an icon in the Dock.

To move an item to the Trash

1. Drag the icon for the item you want to delete to the Trash icon in the Dock.

2. When the mouse pointer moves over the Trash icon, the Trash icon becomes selected (**Figure 43**). Release the mouse button.

or

1. Select the item that you want to delete.

2. Choose File > Move to Trash (**Figure 44**), or press ⌃ ⌘ Delete.

✔ Tips

- The Trash icon's appearance indicates its status:

  ▲ If the Trash is empty, the Trash icon looks like an empty wire basket.

  ▲ If the Trash is not empty, the Trash icon looks like a wire basket with crumpled papers in it (**Figure 45**).

- You can delete more than one item at a time. Begin by selecting all the items you want to delete, then drag any one of them to the Trash. All items will be moved to the Trash.

- Moving a disk icon to the Trash does not delete or erase it. Instead, it *unmounts* it. Working with disks is covered a little later in this chapter.

Figure 43 To move an item to the Trash, drag it there...

Figure 44
...or select the item and choose Move to Trash from the File menu.

Figure 45
When an item has been moved to the Trash, the Trash icon looks full.

Figure 46 Opening the Trash displays the Trash window.

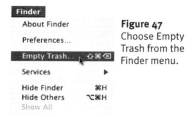

Figure 47
Choose Empty Trash from the Finder menu.

Figure 48 The Trash warning dialog asks you to confirm that you really do want to delete the items in the Trash.

Figure 49
When you point to the Trash icon in the Dock and hold the mouse button down, a menu with an Empty Trash option appears.

To move an item out of the Trash

1. Click the Trash icon in the Dock to open the Trash window (**Figure 46**).

2. Drag the item from the Trash window to the Desktop or to another window on your hard disk.

   The item is moved from the Trash to the window you dragged it to.

To empty the Trash

1. Choose Finder > Empty Trash (**Figure 47**), or press [Shift] ⌃ ⌘ [Delete].

2. A Trash warning dialog like the one in **Figure 48** appears. Click OK to permanently remove all items that are in the Trash.

or

1. Point to the Trash icon, press the mouse button, and hold it down until a menu appears (**Figure 49**).

2. Choose Empty Trash. The contents of the Trash are permanently deleted. No warning appears.

✔ Tip

■ You can disable the Trash warning dialog (**Figure 48**) in the Finder Preferences window. I explain how in **Chapter 4**.

Storage Media

A Macintosh computer can read data from, or write data to, a wide range of storage media, including:

◆ **Hard disks**—high capacity magnetic media.

◆ **CD-ROM, CD-R, DVD, and DVD-R discs**—high capacity, removable optical media.

◆ **Zip, Jaz, or other disks or cartridges**—high capacity, removable magnetic media.

◆ **Floppy disks or diskettes**—low capacity, removable magnetic media.

To use storage media, it must be:

◆ **Mounted**—inserted, attached, or otherwise accessible to your computer.

◆ **Formatted** or **initialized**—specially prepared for use with your computer.

All of these things are covered in this section.

✔ Tips

■ Don't confuse storage media with memory. The term *memory* usually refers to the amount of RAM in your computer, not disk space. RAM is discussed in **Chapter 5**.

■ At a minimum, all new Macintosh computers include a hard disk and CD-ROM drives.

■ Storage devices can be internal (inside your computer) or external (attached to your computer by a cable).

■ Some external storage devices must be properly connected and turned on *before* you start your computer or your computer may not recognize the device.

Table 1

Terminology for Storage Media Capacity		
Term	Abbreviation	Size
byte	byte	1 character
kilobyte	KB	1,024 bytes
megabyte	MB	1,024 KB
gigabyte	GB	1,024 MB

Figure 50 A write-protected icon appears in the status bar of CD-ROM discs and other write-protected media.

■ Disk storage media capacity is specified in terms of bytes, kilobytes, megabytes, and gigabytes (**Table 1**).

■ If a disk is *write-protected* or *locked*, files cannot be saved or copied to it. A pencil with a line through it appears in the status bar of write-protected or locked disks (**Figure 50**). I tell you more about the status bar in **Chapter 4**.

■ You cannot write data to a CD-ROM. But if your Mac has a CD-Recordable (CD-R) drive or SuperDrive, you can use special software to create or *burn* your own CDs.

■ Mac OS X may not recognize a built-in floppy drive on an older Mac model. It does, however, recognize most third-party USB floppy drives.

Figure 51 Here's a desktop with an internal hard disk, network volume, external hard disk, CD-ROM disc, and floppy disk mounted.

Mounting Disks

You *mount* a disk by inserting it in the disk drive so it appears on the Mac OS desktop (**Figure 51**).

✔ Tips

- You must mount a disk to use it.

- To learn how to mount disks that are not specifically covered in this book, consult the documentation that came with the disk drive.

- Mounted disks appear on the desktop as well as in the top-level window for your computer (**Figure 51**).

- You mount a network volume by using the Connect to Server command under the Go menu (**Figure 5**). I explain how earlier in this chapter.

To mount a CD or DVD disc

1. Follow the manufacturer's instructions to open the CD or DVD disc tray or eject the CD or DVD caddy.

2. Place the CD or DVD disc in the tray or caddy, label side up.

3. Gently push the tray or caddy into the drive. After a moment, the disc icon appears on the desktop. **Figure 51** shows a mounted CD-ROM (Microsoft Office X).

✔ Tip

- If your CD or DVD drive does not use a disc tray or caddy, consult its documentation for specific instructions.

To mount a Zip or Jaz disk

Insert the disk in the Zip or Jaz drive, label side up, metal side in. After a moment, the disk icon appears on the desktop.

To mount a floppy disk

Insert the disk in the floppy disk drive, label side up, metal side in. The disk's icon appears on the desktop. **Figure 51** shows a mounted Windows PC floppy disk (NO_NAME).

Ejecting Disks

When you eject a disk, the disk is physically removed from the disk drive and its icon disappears from the desktop.

✔ Tip

- When the disk's icon disappears from the desktop, it is said to be *unmounted*.

To eject a disk

1. Click the disk's icon once to select it.

2. Choose File > Eject (**Figure 52**), or press ⌃ ⌘ E.

or

1. Drag the disk's icon to the Trash (**Figure 53**). As you drag, the Trash icon turns into a rectangle with a triangle on top (**Figure 54**).

2. When the mouse pointer moves over the Trash icon, it becomes selected (**Figure 53**). Release the mouse button.

or

Press the Eject key on the keyboard.

✔ Tips

- If you try to eject a disk that contains one or more files that are in use by your computer, a dialog like the one in **Figure 55** appears. Click OK or press Return or Enter to dismiss the dialog, then quit the open application. You should then be able to eject the disk. Working with applications is covered in **Chapter 5**.

- Not all keyboards include an Eject key. On some keyboards, F12 may act as an Eject key.

Figure 52
Select the disk, and then choose Eject from the File menu to eject the disk.

Figure 53
Or drag the disk icon to the Trash.

Figure 54 When you drag a disk icon, the Trash icon transforms into an icon like this.

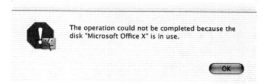

The operation could not be completed because the disk "Microsoft Office X" is in use.

Figure 55 A dialog like this appears if you try to eject a disk that contains open files.

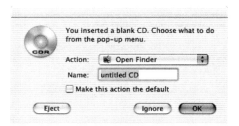

Figure 56 When you insert a blank CD-R disc, your Mac asks what you want to do.

✓ 🖥 Open Finder
🎵 Open iTunes
💾 Open Disk Copy

Open other application...

Run Script...

Figure 57
The Action pop-up menu enables you to choose the application you want to use to burn the CD.

Figure 58
An icon for the disc appears on the desktop.

Figure 59 Copy the items you want to include on the disc to the disc's window.

Burning CDs

If your Macintosh includes a CD-R drive or SuperDrive, you can write, or burn, files onto blank CD-R media. This is a great way to archive important files that you don't need on your computer's hard disk and to share files with other computer users.

✔ Tips

- This part of the chapter provides one technique for burning a CD with the Finder's Burn Disc command. You can also burn CDs or DVDs from within iTunes, iDVD, or other third party utilities, such as Roxio Toast. iTunes and iDVD are discussed in **Chapter 11**.

- Mac OS X 10.2 offers additional options for burning CDs. For example, the dialog that appears when you insert a blank CD enables you to choose the application you want to use to burn the CD (**Figure 57**) and the Burn CD command displays a dialog that enables you to select a burn speed (**Figure 62**).

To burn a CD

1. Insert a blank CD-R disc into your computer's CD-R drive or SuperDrive.

2. A dialog like the one in **Figure 56** appears. Make sure Open Finder is chosen from the Action pop-up menu (**Figure 57**). Then enter a suitable name for the disc in the edit box and click OK.

3. Wait while your computer prepares the disc. When it is finished, a CD disc icon appears on the desktop (**Figure 58**).

4. Drag the files you want to write on the disc onto the disc icon or into the open disc window (**Figure 59**).

Continued on next page...

Continued from previous page.

5. Wait while your computer copies the files.

6. Repeat steps 4 and 5 until all files you want on the disc have been copied.

7. Choose File > Burn Disc (**Figure 60**).

8. A confirmation dialog like the one in **Figure 61** appears. If desired, choose a speed from the Burn Speed pop-up menu (**Figure 62**) and then click Burn.

9. Wait while your computer prepares, burns, and verifies the disc. A Burn Disc window (**Figure 63**) reports its progress. When it disappears, the disk is ready.

✔ Tips

■ If you choose a different application from the Action pop-up menu (**Figure 57**) in step 2, Mac OS X will open that application so you can use it to burn the disc. The remaining steps do not apply.

■ In step 8, the options that appear in the Burn Speed pop-up menu (**Figure 62**) vary depending on the speed of your CD-R or DVD-R drive.

■ If you're not sure which speed to choose in step 8, choose Maximum.

Figure 60
Choose Burn Disc from the File menu.

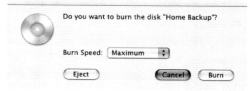

Figure 61 Your computer confirms that you want to burn the disc and enables you to choose the burn speed.

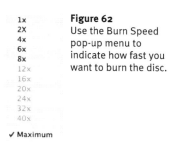

Figure 62
Use the Burn Speed pop-up menu to indicate how fast you want to burn the disc.

Figure 63 The Burn Disc window appears while the disc is being prepared, burned, and verified.

Advanced Finder Techniques

Advanced Finder Techniques

In addition to the basic Finder and file management techniques covered in **Chapters 2 and 3**, Mac OS X offers more advanced techniques you can use to customize the Finder, work with windows, and manage files:

- ◆ Customize the way the Finder and desktop look and work.

- ◆ Customize the toolbar to add buttons for the items you use most.

- ◆ Customize the Dock to add applications and documents you access often.

- ◆ Customize icon and list view windows to change the way contents are displayed.

- ◆ Use hierarchical outlines in list view windows.

- ◆ Use spring-loaded folders to access folders while copying or moving items.

- ◆ Use aliases to make frequently used files easier to access without moving them.

- ◆ Create and organize favorite items.

- ◆ Quickly reopen recently used items.

- ◆ Find files and folders on any mounted disk.

- ◆ Use the Info window to learn more about an item or set options for it.

- ◆ Undo actions you performed while working with the Finder.

This chapter covers all of these techniques.

✔ Tips

- ■ If you're brand new to Mac OS, be sure to read the information in **Chapters 2** and **3** before working with this chapter. Those chapters contain information and instructions about techniques that are used throughout this chapter.

- ■ This chapter is especially useful for experienced Mac OS users since it goes beyond the basics with new or advanced Mac OS features.

Finder Preferences

The Finder Preferences window enables you to customize several aspects of the desktop and Finder.

✔ Tip

- Mac OS X 10.2 added Finder Preferences settings for spring-loaded folders and search languages. Spring-loaded folders and finding files are discussed later in this chapter.

To set Finder Preferences

1. Choose Finder > Preferences (**Figure 1**) to display the Finder Preferences window (**Figure 2**).

2. Toggle check boxes to specify what items should appear on the desktop:

   ▲ **Hard disks** displays icons for mounted hard disks.

   ▲ **Removable media (such as CDs)** displays icons for removable media, including CDs, DVDs, Zip, Jaz, and floppy disks.

   ▲ **Connected servers** displays icons for mounted server volumes.

3. Select a radio button to determine what should appear in a new Finder window (the window that appears when you choose File > New Finder Window):

   ▲ **Home** displays the contents of your home folder (**Figure 3**).

   ▲ **Computer** displays the icons for the network and all mounted volumes (**Figure 4**).

Figure 1
Choose Preferences from the Finder menu.

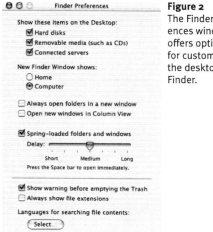

Figure 2
The Finder Preferences window offers options for customizing the desktop and Finder.

Figures 3 & 4 A new Finder window can display your Home folder (above) or the items your computer can access (below).

Figure 5 The Trash warning dialog.

Figure 6 You can set up the Finder so it always displays file extensions as part of an item's name.

Figure 7 Use the Languages dialog to indicate which languages you will use with the find by content feature.

4. Toggle check boxes to set other options:

▲ **Always open folders in a new window** opens a new window to display the contents of the folder you open. This makes Mac OS X work more like Mac OS 9.x and earlier.

▲ **Open new windows in Column View** opens all new windows in column view, regardless of which view was last used to view the window.

▲ **Spring-loaded folders and windows** enables the spring-loaded folders feature. You can use the slider to set the delay time for this feature.

▲ **Show warning before emptying the Trash** displays a confirmation dialog (**Figure 5**) each time you choose Finder > Empty Trash. Turning off this check box prevents the dialog from appearing.

▲ **Always show file extensions** displays file extensions in Finder windows (**Figure 6**).

5. To specify the languages you want to use when finding files by content, click the Select button. In the Languages dialog that appears (**Figure 7**), toggle check marks to indicate which languages are in your documents. Then click OK.

6. Click the Finder Preferences window's close button to dismiss it and save your settings.

✔ Tips

■ In step 5, choose as few languages as possible. This makes the index file used for finding files smaller and faster.

■ Spring-loaded folders and finding files are covered later in this chapter. Disks, mounting disks, and the Trash are discussed in **Chapter 3**. Views are discussed in **Chapter 3** and later in this chapter.

Customizing the Toolbar

The toolbar, which is discussed in **Chapter 2**, can be customized to include buttons and icons for a variety of commands and items.

✔ Tip

■ When you customize the toolbar, your changes affect the toolbar in all windows in which the toolbar is displayed.

To customize the toolbar

1. With any Finder window open and the toolbar displayed, choose View > Customize Toolbar (**Figure 8**). The Customize Toolbar window opens (**Figure 9**).

2. To add an item to the toolbar, drag it from the center part of the window to the position you want it to occupy in the toolbar (**Figure 10**). When you release the mouse button, the item appears on the toolbar (**Figure 11**).

3. To remove an item from the toolbar, drag it from the toolbar into the center part of the window (**Figure 12**). When you release the mouse button, the item disappears (**Figure 13**).

4. To rearrange the order of items on the toolbar, drag them into the desired position (**Figure 14**). When you release the mouse button, the items are rearranged (**Figure 15**).

5. To specify how items should appear on the toolbar, choose an option from the Show pop-up menu at the bottom of the window (**Figure 16**):

   ▲ **Icon & Text** displays both the icon and the icon's name (**Figure 15**).

   ▲ **Icon Only** displays only the icon (**Figure 18**).

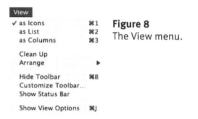

Figure 8
The View menu.

Figure 9 The Customize Toolbar window.

Figure 10 To add an item, drag it from the center part of the window to the toolbar.

Figure 11 When you release the mouse button, the item is added.

Figure 12 To remove an item, drag it from the toolbar into the center part of the window.

Figure 13 When you release the mouse button, the item is removed.

CUSTOMIZING THE TOOLBAR

Figure 14 To rearrange toolbar items, drag them around the toolbar.

Figure 15 When you release the mouse button, the items are rearranged.

✔ Icon & Text
Icon Only
Text Only

Figure 16 Show pop-up menu options.

Figures 17 & 18 You can also display the toolbar as icons only (above) or as text only (below).

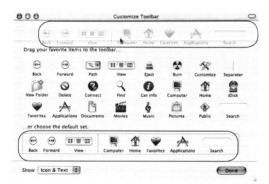

Figure 19 Drag the default set of icons to the toolbar.

▲ **Text Only** displays only the name of the icon (**Figure 17**).

6. When you are finished making changes, click Done to return to the window that was open before you displayed toolbar customization options.

✔ Tip

■ You can add *any* icon to the toolbar. For example, say you're working on a project (like a book about Mac OS), and you access its folder full of files daily. You can drag the folder's icon from the window in which it resides to the toolbar of the window. The folder appears where you placed it. You can then open the folder by simply clicking it in the toolbar of any window. To remove the icon (perhaps when the project is complete), drag it out of the toolbar. It is not necessary to display toolbar customization options to do any of this.

To restore the toolbar to its default settings

1. With any Finder window displaying the toolbar open, choose View > Customize Toolbar (**Figure 8**). The Customize Toolbar window appears (**Figure 9**).

2. Drag the group of items in a box near the bottom of the window to the toolbar (**Figure 19**). When you release the mouse button, the toolbar's default items appear (**Figure 9**).

3. Click Done to return to the window that was open before you displayed toolbar customization options.

RESTORING THE TOOLBAR

Customizing the Dock

The Dock, which is discussed in **Chapter 2**, can be customized to include icons for specific documents and applications that you use often. This makes them quick and easy to open any time you need them.

✔ Tips

- If you used the customizable Apple menu in previous versions of Mac OS, you may want to customize the Dock to include the items you previously included on the Apple menu.

- When you press the mouse button down on a Dock icon, a menu with commands or other options that apply to that icon appears (**Figure 20**). You can select a command like any other menu command.

- When you press the mouse button down on a folder in the Dock, it appears as a menu. Choose an item to open it or point to a folder within the menu to display a submenu of items within it. **Figure 21** shows an example of how you can use this feature.

Figure 20 Pressing the mouse button on a Dock item often displays a menu. In this example, pressing the Finder icon displays a menu of open Finder windows.

Figure 21 Creative use of folders in the Dock can put all your frequently used files at your fingertips—without turning the Dock into a cluttered mess.

Figure 22 Drag an icon from the window to the Dock.

Figure 23 The icon appears in the Dock.

Figure 24 Drag an icon off the Dock.

To add an icon to the Dock

1. Open the window containing the icon you want to add to the Dock.

2. Drag the icon from the window to the Dock (**Figure 22**). When you release the mouse button, the icon appears (**Figure 23**).

✔ Tips

- Dragging an icon to the Dock does not remove it from its original location.

- When dragging items to the Dock, drag applications to the left of the divider and documents and folders to the right of the divider.

To remove an icon from the Dock

Drag the item from the Dock to the desktop (**Figure 24**). When you release the mouse button, the icon disappears in a puff of "smoke" and no longer appears in the Dock.

✔ Tips

- Removing an icon from the Dock does not delete it from disk.

- If you try to remove an icon for an application that is running, the icon will not disappear from the Dock until you quit the application.

ADDING & REMOVING ICONS ON THE DOCK

91

To set basic Dock options

Choose options from the Dock submenu under the Apple menu (**Figure 25**):

◆ **Turn Magnification On** magnifies a Dock icon when you point to it (**Figure 26**). With this option enabled, the command changes to **Turn Magnification Off**, which disables magnification.

◆ **Turn Hiding On** (Option ⌥ ⌘ D) automatically hides the Dock until you point to where it should appear. This is a great way to regain screen real estate normally occupied by the Dock. With this option enabled, the command changes to **Turn Hiding Off**, which displays the Dock all the time.

◆ **Position on Left**, **Position on Bottom**, and **Position on Right** move the Dock to the left side, bottom, or right side of the screen. The option that is not available (Position on Bottom in **Figure 25**) is the one that is currently selected. When positioned on the left or right, the Dock fits vertically down the screen (**Figure 27**).

◆ **Dock Preferences** displays the Dock preferences pane, which includes a few additional options for customizing the Dock.

✔ Tips

■ To change the size of the Dock, point to the divider line. When the mouse pointer turns into a line with two arrows (**Figure 28**), press the mouse button down and drag to make the Dock bigger or smaller.

■ System Preferences, including the Dock preferences pane, is covered in detail in *Mac OS X Advanced: Visual QuickPro Guide*.

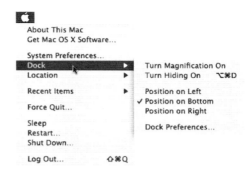

Figure 25 The Dock submenu under the Apple menu offers options for customizing the way the Dock looks and works.

Figure 26 When magnification is turned on, pointing to an icon enlarges it.

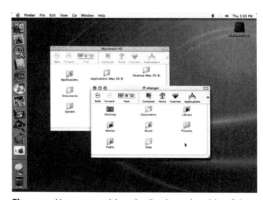

Figure 27 You can position the Dock on the side of the screen instead of the bottom.

Figure 28 You can resize the Dock by pointing to the divider line and dragging.

SETTING BASIC DOCK OPTIONS

Customizing Window & Desktop Views

As discussed in **Chapter 3**, a window's view determines how icons and other information appear within it. Mac OS X remembers a window's view settings and uses them whenever you display the window.

You can customize views a number of ways:

◆ Change the settings for the default view for icon and list views.

◆ Change the settings for an individual window's icon or list view.

◆ Change the view for the desktop.

View settings include a number of options:

◆ Icon view settings include icon size, label text size and position, display options, arrangement, and background.

◆ List view settings include icon size, text size, columns, date format, and item size calculation, as well as column width and the order in which columns appear.

◆ Column view settings include text size, icon appearance, and preview column.

◆ Desktop view settings include icon size, label text size and position, display options, and arrangement.

You can also display a status bar with disk information in any Finder window.

✔ Tip

■ The only time the Finder does not use a window's custom view is when you have the "Open new windows in Column View" option set in the Finder Preferences window (**Figure 2**). I tell you about this option and the rest of Finder Preferences earlier in this chapter.

To set icon view options

1. To set icon view options for a specific window, activate that window and make sure it is displayed in icon view.

   or

   To set default icon view options, activate any window that is displayed in icon view.

2. Choose View > Show View Options (**Figure 8**), or press ⌃⌘J to display the view options window (**Figure 29**).

3. Select the radio button for the type of option you want to set:

   ▲ **This window only** customizes the settings for the active window.

   ▲ **All windows** sets options for all icon view windows that do not have custom settings.

4. Use the Icon size slider to set the size of icons:

   ▲ Drag the slider to the left to make the icon size smaller.

   ▲ Drag the slider to the right to make the icon size larger.

5. Choose a type size from the Text size pop-up menu (**Figure 30**).

6. Select a radio button to specify where icon labels should appear:

   ▲ **Bottom** displays labels below the icons (**Figure 31**).

   ▲ **Right** displays labels to the right of the icons (**Figure 32**).

7. Toggle check boxes to specify how icons should appear:

   ▲ **Snap to grid** forces icons to snap to the window's invisible grid, thus ensuring consistent spacing between icons.

Figure 29
The view options for a Finder window in icon view.

Figure 30
The Text size pop-up menu enables you to set the size of the type for icon labels.

Figures 31 & 32 You can place icon labels beneath the icons (above), which is the default setting or to the right of icons (below), which is a brand new option in Mac OS X 10.2.

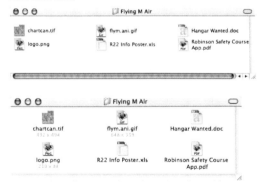

Figure 33 You can display information about an item beneath its label.

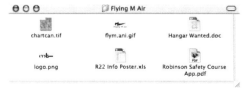

Figure 34 You can display a preview for an item instead of its icon—if a preview exists.

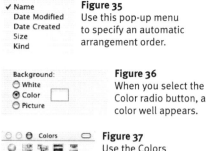

Figure 35
Use this pop-up menu to specify an automatic arrangement order.

Figure 36
When you select the Color radio button, a color well appears.

Figure 37
Use the Colors dialog to select a new background color.

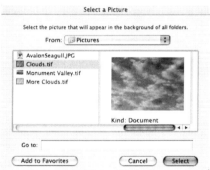

Figure 38
When you select the Picture radio button, a Select button appears.

Figure 39 Use the Select a Picture dialog to locate and select a background picture.

Figure 40 A background picture appears behind icons.

▲ **Show item info** displays information about the item beneath its name. **Figure 33** shows an example with graphic file size, in pixels, displayed.

▲ **Show icon preview** displays a document's preview, if available, in place of its standard icon. **Figure 34** shows preview icons for two graphic files.

▲ **Keep arranged by** automatically arranges icons in a certain order. If you select this option, choose a sort order from the pop-up menu beneath it (**Figure 35**).

8. Select a Background option:

   ▲ **White** makes the background white.

   ▲ **Color** enables you to select a background color for the window. If you select this option, click the color well that appears beside it (**Figure 36**), use the Colors dialog (**Figure 37**) to select a color, and click OK.

   ▲ **Picture** enables you to set a background picture for the window. If you select this option, click the Select button that appears beside it (**Figure 38**), use the Select a Picture dialog to locate and select a background picture (**Figure 39**), and click Select.

9. When you're finished setting options, click the view option window's close button to dismiss it.

✔ Tips

■ To restore the current window's options to the default settings for all icon view windows, select the All windows radio button in step 3.

■ Working with dialogs is discussed in **Chapter 5**.

■ A background picture fills the window's background behind the icons (**Figure 40**).

SETTING ICON VIEW OPTIONS

To set list view options

1. To set list view options for a specific window, activate that window and make sure it is displayed in list view.

   or

   To set default list view options, activate any window that is displayed in list view.

2. Choose View > Show View Options (**Figure 8**), or press ⌃ ⌘ J to display the view options window (**Figure 41**).

3. Select the radio button for the type of option you want to set:

   ▲ **This window only** customizes the settings for the active window.

   ▲ **All windows** sets options for all list view windows that do not have custom settings.

4. Select an Icon size option by clicking the radio button beneath the size you want.

5. Choose a type size from the Text size pop-up menu (**Figure 30**).

6. Select the columns you want to appear in list view by turning Show columns check boxes on or off:

   ▲ **Date Modified** is the date and time an item was last changed.

   ▲ **Date Created** is the date and time an item was first created.

   ▲ **Size** is the amount of disk space the item occupies.

   ▲ **Kind** is the type of item. I tell you about types of items in **Chapter 2**.

   ▲ **Version** is the item's version number.

   ▲ **Comments** is the information you entered in the Comments field of the Info window. I tell you about the Info window later in this chapter.

Figure 41
The view options for list view.

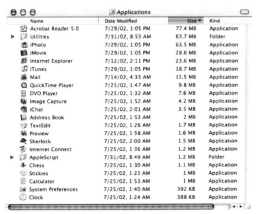

Figure 42 When you turn on the Calculate all sizes in the list view options for a window, you can sort the window's contents by size.

Figure 43
The view options for column view.

Figure 44 With the Show preview column option enabled, selecting an item that includes a preview displays the preview in the far right column.

7. To display the date in relative terms (that is, using the words "today" and "yesterday"), turn on the Use relative dates check box.

8. To display the disk space occupied by items and the contents of folders in the list, turn on the Calculate all sizes check box.

9. When you're finished setting options, click the view option window's close button to dismiss it.

✔ Tip

■ Turning on the Calculate all sizes check box in step 8 makes it possible to sort all of a window's contents by size, including folders (**Figure 42**). Sorting window contents is covered in **Chapter 3**.

To set column view options

1. Activate any window that is displayed in column view.

2. Choose View > Show View Options (**Figure 8**), or press ⌘J to display the view options window (**Figure 43**).

3. Choose a type size from the Text size pop-up menu (**Figure 30**).

4. To display icons beside item names, turn on the Show icons check box.

5. To display previews (when available) for selected items (**Figure 44**), turn on the Show preview column check box.

6. When you're finished setting options, click the view option window's close button to dismiss it.

✔ Tip

■ The ability to set view options for column view is brand new in Mac OS X 10.2.

To set desktop view options

1. Click anywhere on the desktop to activate it.

2. Choose View > Show View Options (**Figure 8**), or press ⌘⌥J to display the Desktop view options window (**Figure 45**).

3. Use the Icon size slider to set the size of icons:

   ▲ Drag the slider to the left to make the icon size smaller.

   ▲ Drag the slider to the right to make the icon size larger.

4. Choose a type size from the Text size pop-up menu (**Figure 30**).

5. Select a radio button to specify where icon labels should appear:

   ▲ **Bottom** displays labels below the icons.

   ▲ **Right** displays labels to the right of the icon.

6. Toggle check boxes to specify how icons should appear:

   ▲ **Snap to grid** forces icons to snap to the desktop's invisible grid, thus ensuring consistent spacing between icons.

   ▲ **Show item info** displays information about the item beneath its name.

   ▲ **Show icon preview** displays a document's preview, if available, in place of its standard icon.

   ▲ **Keep arranged by** automatically arranges icons in a certain order. If you select this option, choose a sort order from the pop-up menu beneath it (**Figure 35**).

7. When you're finished setting options, click the view option window's close button to dismiss it.

Figure 45
View options for the desktop.

✔ Tip

■ You can set the desktop background pattern in the Desktop preferences pane. System Preferences, including the Desktop preferences pane, are covered in *Mac OS X Advanced: Visual QuickStart Guide*.

Figure 46 Position the mouse pointer on the column border.

Figure 47 When you press the mouse button down and drag, the column's width changes.

Figure 48 Drag a column heading...

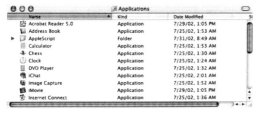

Figure 49 ...to change the column's position.

To change a column's width

1. Position the mouse pointer on the line between the heading for the column whose width you want to change and the column to its right. The mouse pointer turns into a vertical bar with two arrows (**Figure 46**).

2. Press the mouse button down and drag:
   - ▲ To make the column narrower, drag to the left (**Figure 47**).
   - ▲ To make the column wider, drag to the right.

3. When the column is displayed at the desired width, release the mouse button.

✔ Tip

- ■ If you make a column too narrow to display all of its contents, information may be truncated or condensed.

To change a column's position

1. Position the mouse pointer on the heading for the column you want to move.

2. Press the mouse button down and drag:
   - ▲ To move the column to the left, drag to the left (**Figure 48**).
   - ▲ To move the column to the right, drag to the right.

   As you drag, the other columns shift to make room for the column you're dragging.

3. When the column is in the desired position, release the mouse button. The column changes its position (**Figure 49**).

✔ Tip

- ■ You cannot change the position of the Name column.

CHANGING COLUMN WIDTH & POSITION

To display the status bar

Choose View > Show Status Bar (**Figure 8**).

The status bar appears above the window's contents (**Figure 50**).

✔ Tips

- As shown in **Figure 50**, the status bar shows the number of items in the window and the total amount of space available on the disk.

- If one or more items are selected in a window, the status bar reports how many items are selected (**Figure 51**).

- When the status bar is displayed, it appears in all Finder windows.

To hide the status bar

Choose View > Hide Status Bar (**Figure 52**).

The status bar disappears.

Status bar

Figure 50 The status bar appears above a window's content, but below the toolbar (if displayed).

Figure 51 The status bar can also report how many items are selected in a window.

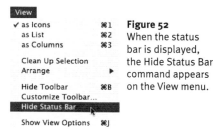

Figure 52 When the status bar is displayed, the Hide Status Bar command appears on the View menu.

Click a right-pointing triangle to expand the outline.

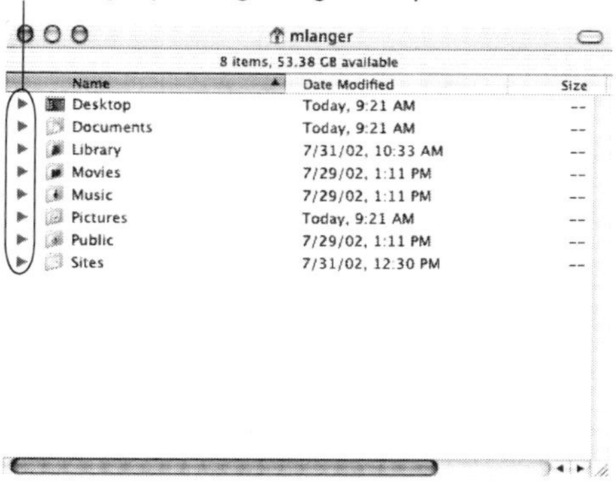

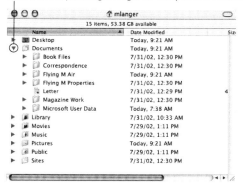

Figure 53 Right-pointing triangles indicate collapsed outlines.

Click a down-pointing triangle to collapse an outline.

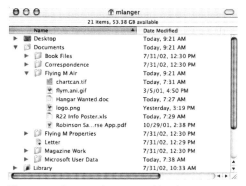

Figure 54 Folder contents can be displayed as an outline...

Figure 55 ...that can show several levels.

Outlines in List View

Windows displayed in list view have a feature not found in icon or column views: They can display the contents of folders within the window as an outline (**Figures 54** and **55**).

✔ Tip

- Views are discussed in detail in **Chapter 3** and earlier in this chapter.

To display a folder's contents

Click the right-pointing triangle beside the folder (**Figure 53**).

or

Click the folder once to select it, and press ⌃⌘→.

The items within that folder are listed below it, slightly indented (**Figure 54**).

✔ Tip

- As shown in **Figure 55**, you can use this technique to display multiple levels of folders in the same window.

To hide a folder's contents

Click the down-pointing triangle beside the folder (**Figure 54**).

or

Click the folder once to select it, and press ⌃⌘←.

The outline collapses to hide the items in the folder (**Figure 53**).

WORKING WITH LIST VIEW OUTLINES

Spring-Loaded Folders

The spring-loaded folders feature lets you move or copy items into folders deep within the file structure of a disk—without manually opening a single folder. Instead, you simply drag icons onto folders (**Figures 56** and **58**) and wait as they're automatically opened (**Figures 57** and **59**). When you drop the icon into the final window, all windows except the source and destination windows automatically close (**Figure 60**).

Figure 56 Drag an icon onto a folder and wait...

✔ Tips

- Although the spring-loaded folders feature is available in Mac OS 9.x, it was not added to Mac OS X until Mac OS X 10.2. The "click and a half" feature available in Mac OS 9.x, however, is still not available in Mac OS X.

- The spring-loaded folders feature is sometimes refered to as *spring-open folders*.

Figure 57 ...until the folder opens.

- Using the spring-loaded folders feature requires a steady hand, good mouse skills, and knowledge of the location of folders on your disk.

- To use the spring-loaded folders feature, the Spring-loaded folders and windows check box must be turned on in the Finder Preferences window (**Figure 2**). You can also set the spring-loaded folder delay length in this window. I tell you about Finder Preferences at the beginning of this chapter.

- To use the spring-loaded folders feature to move or copy more than one item at a time, select the items first, then drag any one of them.

Figure 58 Continue to drag the icon onto a folder in that window and wait...

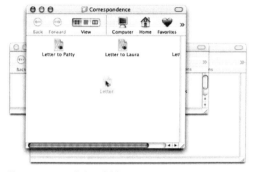

Figure 59 ...until that folder opens.

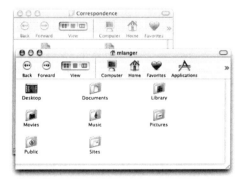

Figure 60 When you're finished, only the source window (which is active) and the destination window remain open.

To move an item using spring-loaded folders

1. Drag the item you want to move onto the folder to which you want to move it (**Figure 56**), but do not release the mouse button. After a moment, the folder blinks and opens (**Figure 57**).

2. Without releasing the mouse button, repeat step 1. The destination folder becomes selected (**Figure 58**), then blinks and opens (**Figure 59**). Do this until you reach the final destination.

3. Release the mouse button to place the item into the destination window. All windows other than the source and destination windows close; the source window remains active (**Figure 60**).

✔ Tips

■ In steps 1 and 2, to open a folder immediately, press ⎵Spacebar⎵ while dragging an item onto it.

■ To close a folder's window so you can open a different folder in the same window, drag the item away from the open window. The window closes so you can drag the item onto a different folder and open it.

To copy an item using spring-loaded folders

Hold down ⎵Option⎵ while following the above steps.

✔ Tip

■ If the destination folder is on another disk, it is not necessary to hold down ⎵Option⎵ to copy items; they're automatically copied.

USING SPRING-LOADED FOLDERS

Aliases

An *alias* (**Figure 61**) is a pointer to an item. You can make an alias of an item and place it anywhere on your computer. Then, when you need to open the item, just open its alias.

✔ Tips

- It's important to remember that an alias is not a copy of the item—it's a pointer. If you delete the original item, the alias will not open.

- You can use the Select New Original dialog (**Figure 99**) to reassign an original to an alias, as explained later in this chapter.

- By putting aliases of frequently used items together where you can quickly access them—such as on the desktop—you make the items more accessible without actually moving them.

- The Favorites and Recent Items features work with aliases. These features are discussed a little later in this chapter.

- You can name an alias anything you like, as long as you follow the file naming guidelines discussed in **Chapter 3**. An alias's name does not need to include the word *alias*.

- The icon for an alias looks very much like the icon for the original item but includes a tiny arrow in the bottom-left corner (**Figure 61**).

- You can move, copy, rename, open, and delete an alias just like any other file.

iTunes

iTunes alias

Figure 61
The icon for an alias looks like the original item's icon but includes a tiny arrow.

Figure 62
To create an alias, begin by selecting the item for which you want to make an alias.

Figure 63
Choose Make Alias from the File menu.

Figure 64
The alias appears with the original.

Figure 65
Select the alias's icon.

Figure 66
Choose Show Original from the File menu.

To create an alias

1. Select the item you want to make an alias for (**Figure 62**).

2. Choose File > Make Alias (**Figure 63**), or press ⌘⌘L.

   The alias appears right beneath the original item (**Figure 64**).

or

Hold down ⌘⌘Option and drag the item for which you want to make an alias to a new location. The alias appears in the destination location.

✔ Tip

- An alias's name is selected right after it is created (**Figure 64**). If desired, you can immediately type a new name to replace the default name.

To find an alias's original file

1. Select the alias's icon (**Figure 65**).

2. Choose File > Show Original (**Figure 66**), or press ⌘⌘R.

   If the folder in which the original resides is already open, its window becomes active with the original item selected.

or

If the folder in which the original resides is not open, Mac OS X opens a column view window with the original item selected (**Figure 67**).

Figure 67 The original item appears selected in its window.

WORKING WITH ALIASES

Favorites

Favorites enables you to add frequently used documents, applications, and other items to the Favorites submenu on the Go menu (**Figure 68**). This makes these items quick and easy to access.

✔ Tips

- Favorites also appear in the Open and Save Location dialogs, which are discussed in **Chapter 5**.

- The favorites feature works with aliases, which are discussed on the previous two pages.

- Your favorite item aliases are stored in the Favorites folder, in the Library folder, inside your home folder. You can learn more about your home folder in **Chapter 3**.

- The Mac OS X installer automatically creates a favorite item for your Documents folder (**Figure 68**), which is the default location for storing documents.

To add a favorite item

1. In the Finder, select the icon for the item that you want to add as a favorite item (**Figure 69**).

2. Choose File > Add to Favorites (**Figure 70**), or press ⌃ ⌘ T.

   The item is added to the Favorites submenu on the Go menu (**Figure 71**).

✔ Tip

- You can also add a currently selected folder to favorites by clicking the Add to Favorites button in the Open or expanded Save Location (**Figure 72**) dialogs. These dialogs are covered in **Chapter 5**.

Figure 68 Favorites are listed on the Favorites submenu on the Go menu.

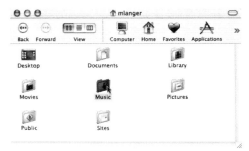

Figure 69 Select the item that you want to add as a favorite item.

Figure 70 Choose Add to Favorites from the File menu.

Figure 71 The item is added to the Favorites submenu on the Go menu.

Figure 72 You can click the Add to Favorites button in a Save Location dialog like this one to add the currently selected folder to your favorite items.

Figure 73 The Favorites folder contains icons for all your favorite items.

To use a favorite item

From the Favorites submenu on the Go menu (**Figures 68** and 71), choose the item you want to open.

To remove a favorite

1. Click the Favorites button in the toolbar of any Finder window.

   or

   Choose Go > Favorites (**Figures 68** and 71), or press ⌥⌘F.

   The Favorites folder window opens (**Figure 73**).

2. Drag the item that you want to remove out of the window.

3. Close the Favorites folder window.

   The item is removed from the Favorites submenu.

USING & REMOVING FAVORITES

Recent Items

Mac OS automatically tracks the things you open. It creates submenus of the most recently opened items in three categories—applications, documents, and folders—making it quick and easy to open them again.

✔ Tip

- You can specify how many recent applications and documents Mac OS X should track in the Recent Items submenu (**Figure 74**) by setting options in the General preferences pane. I cover System Preferences, including General preferences, in *Mac OS X Advanced: Visual QuickPro Guide*.

To open recent items

To open a recently used application or document, choose its name from the Recent Items submenu under the Apple menu (**Figure 74**).

or

To open a recently used folder, choose its name from the Recent Folders submenu under the Go menu (**Figure 75**).

✔ Tips

- Recent items works with aliases, which are discussed earlier in this chapter.

- Working with applications and documents is discussed in **Chapter 5**.

To clear the Recent Items submenu

Choose Apple > Recent Items > Clear Menu (**Figure 74**).

✔ Tip

- Clearing the Recent Items submenu does not delete any application or document files.

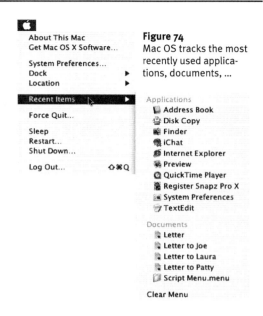

Figure 74
Mac OS tracks the most recently used applications, documents, ...

Figure 75
...and folders.

Figure 76
Choose Find from
the File menu.

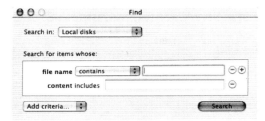

Figure 77 The Find window.

Everywhere
✓ Local disks
Home
Specific places

Figure 78 Use the Search in
pop-up menu to indicate where
you want to look for the file.

Figure 79 If you choose Specific places from the Search
in pop-up menu, the Find window expands to show all
mounted volumes.

Finding Files

The File menu's Find command (**Figure 76**)
enables you to search disks or specific disk
locations for files based on file name, content, or other criteria. You enter search
criteria in the Find window (**Figure 77**) and
click Search. The find feature displays a list
of items that match the criteria in a Search
Results window (**Figures 86** and **87**).

✔ Tips

- Mac OS X 10.2 moved the disk searching
  feature out of Sherlock and back into the
  Finder, where it was before Sherlock was
  developed. **Chapter 10** explains how to
  use Sherlock to search the Internet for a
  variety of information.

- The toolbar offers a quick way to find a
  file in the active window. Enter all or part
  of the file name in the Search box and
  press [Return]. The window displays only
  those files that match what you typed.

To find a file

1. Choose File > Find (**Figure 76**), or press
   [⌃][⌘][F] to display the Find window
   (**Figure 77**).

2. Choose the location you want to
   search from the Search in pop-up
   menu (**Figure 78**):

   ▲ **Everywhere** searches all mounted
     volumes.

   ▲ **Local disks** searches only volumes
     that are directly connected to your
     computer, including internal hard
     disks and inserted media such as
     CD-ROMs.

   ▲ **Home** searches your Home folder.

Continued on next page...

FINDING FILES

Continued from previous page.

▲ **Specific places** expands the Find window so you can toggle check marks for specific volumes you want to search (**Figure 79**).

3. To search by file name, choose an option from the pop-up menu in the file name line (**Figure 80**) and enter all or part of the file name in the edit box beside it (**Figure 81**).

    or

    To search by file content, enter text you expect to appear within the document in the content line (**Figure 82**).

    or

    To search by some other criteria, choose an option from the Add criteria pop-up menu (**Figure 83**). A line for that type of criteria appears in the window. (**Figure 84** shows the Find window with all criteria options added.) Choose an option from the pop-up menu on that line (if necessary) and enter search criteria beside it (if necessary).

4. To add additional criteria for the search, click the + button beside a line displaying that type of criteria. Then set options in that line (**Figure 85**). You can repeat this process for as many additional search criteria items as you like.

5. When you are finished setting search criteria, click Search. Mac OS X displays the Search Results window (**Figures 86** and **87**) with all files it found that match your search criteria.

Figure 80 Use the pop-up menu in the file name line to indicate how you want to match your search criteria...

Figure 81 ...and then enter the search criteria in the box beside it.

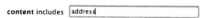

Figure 82 To search by content, simply enter the search criteria in the edit box on the content line.

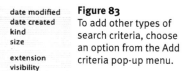

Figure 83 To add other types of search criteria, choose an option from the Add criteria pop-up menu.

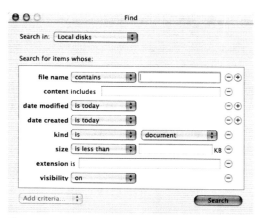

Figure 84 Here's what the Find window looks like with all kinds of criteria added. This is for illustrational purposes only—you'll never have to use all these options to find a file!

Figure 85 You can enter several lines of a specific type of search criteria.

FINDING FILES

Figure 86 Here are the results for the search criteria in Figure 81...

Figure 87 ...and here are the results for the criteria in Figure 82.

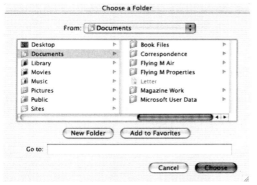

Figure 88 You can use the Choose a Folder dialog to specify folders to search.

✔ Tips

■ In step 2, if you choose Specific places from the Search in pop-up menu, you can click the Add button in the Find window (**Figure 79**) to display the Choose a Folder dialog (**Figure 88**). Use that dialog to locate and select specific folders to search. The Find feature remembers each folder you add until you remove it from the Find window by selecting it and clicking the Remove button. The Choose a Folder dialog looks and works very much like the Open dialog, which I cover in **Chapter 5**.

■ Search criteria are not case-sensitive. That means *Letter* is the same as *letter* or *leTTer*.

■ To remove search criteria you don't want to use, click the – button beside its line. The line disappears.

■ The find feature attempts to find files that match all search criteria. For example, the search criteria in **Figure 85** will find all files with names that contain the words *Letter* and *Joe*. The more criteria you enter, the narrower the search and the fewer items will be found.

■ Finding by content works with an index file that is automatically created and maintained by Mac OS X. You can keep this file small and improve your computer's indexing performance by specifying the languages you use in your files. I explain how to do this in my discussion of Finder Preferences at the beginning of this chapter.

■ The Relevance column in the Search Results window for finding files by content (**Figure 87**) indicates how often the search criteria were found in each file. The larger the Relevance bar, the more occurrences of the search criteria.

FINDING FILES

To learn where a found item resides on disk

Select the name of the item in the top half of the Search Results window. The path to the file appears in the bottom half of the window (**Figure 89**).

To work with found items

You can use commands on the File menu (**Figure 90**) to perform a number of tasks with selected items in the Search Results window (**Figures 86** and **87**):

◆ **Open** (⌘ ⌘ O) opens the selected item.

◆ **Open With** enables you to select an application to open the item with. This option, which I discuss in **Chapter 5**, only applies to document files.

◆ **Get Info** opens the Info window for the selected item. I tell you about the Info window on the next page.

◆ **Open Enclosing Folder** (⌘ ⌘ R) opens the folder in which the selected item resides.

◆ **Add to Favorites** (⌘ ⌘ T) adds the selected item as an alias to the Favorites folder. I tell you about Favorites earlier in this chapter.

◆ **Move to Trash** (⌘ ⌘ Delete) moves the selected item to the Trash.

✔ Tip

■ You can also use the Search Results window to move or copy an item. Drag the item from the top half of the window to a destination disk or folder. The item remains in the Search Results window but, if it is moved, its path changes.

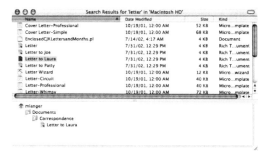

Figure 89 When you select an item in the top half of the Search Results window, its path appears in the bottom half of the window.

Figure 90
The File menu with a document selected in the top half of the Search Results window.

Figure 91
The Info window for a hard disk.

Figure 92
The Info window for a folder.

Figure 93
The Info window for an application.

Figure 94
The Info window for a document.

The Info Window

You can learn more about an item by opening its Info window (**Figures 91** through **94**). Depending on the type of icon (disk, folder, application, document, alias, etc.), the General information in the Info window will provide some or all of the following:

- ◆ **Icon** that appears in the Finder.

- ◆ **Name** of the item.

- ◆ **Kind** or type of item.

- ◆ **Size** of item or contents (folders and files only).

- ◆ **Where** item is on disk.

- ◆ **Created** date and time.

- ◆ **Modified** date and time.

- ◆ **Format** of item (disks only).

- ◆ **Capacity** of item (disks only).

- ◆ **Available** space on item (disks only).

- ◆ **Used** space on item (disks only).

- ◆ **Version** number or copyright date (files only).

- ◆ **Original** location on disk (aliases only).

- ◆ **Stationery Pad** check box to convert the file into a stationery format file, which is like a document template. (This option appears for documents only.)

- ◆ **Locked** check box to prevent the file from being deleted or overwritten (folders and files only).

✔ Tip

- ■ Other types of information available for a disk, folder, or file can be displayed by clicking triangles at the bottom of the info window (**Figures 91** through **94**).

THE INFO WINDOW

To open the Info window

1. Select the item for which you want to open the Info window (**Figure 95**).

2. Choose File > Get Info (**Figure 96**), or press ⌃⌘Ⅰ.

   The Info window for that item appears (**Figure 92**).

To enter comments in the Info window

1. Open the Info window for the item for which you want to enter comments.

2. Click the triangle beside Comments in the bottom of the window. The window expands to show the Comments box.

3. Type your comments into the Comments box (**Figure 97**). They are automatically saved.

✔ Tip

■ As discussed earlier in this chapter, you can set a window's list view to display comments entered in the Info window.

To lock an application or document

1. Open the Info window for the item you want to lock (**Figures 92** through **94**).

2. Turn on the Locked check box.

✔ Tip

■ Locked items cannot be deleted or over-written. They can, however, be moved.

Figure 95 Select the item for which you want to open the Info window.

Figure 96 Choose Get Info from the File menu.

Figure 97 You can enter information about the item in the Comments box.

Figure 98
You can click the Select New Original button in the Info window for an alias to assign a new original to the alias.

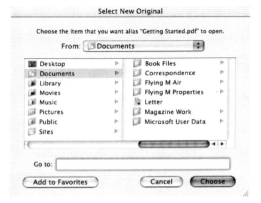

Figure 99 Use the Select New Original dialog to locate and choose a new original for an alias.

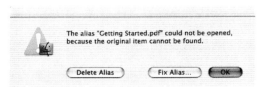

Figure 100 This dialog appears when you attempt to open an alias for which the original cannot be found.

To select a new original item for an alias

1. In the Info window for the alias (**Figure 98**), click the Select New Original button.

2. Use the Select New Original dialog that appears (**Figure 99**) to locate and select the item that you want to use as the original for the alias.

3. Click Choose. The item you selected is assigned to the alias.

✔ Tips

■ The Select New Original dialog is similar to an Open dialog, which is covered in **Chapter 5**.

■ If you try to open an alias for which the original cannot be found, a dialog like the one in **Figure 100** appears. Click Fix Alias to display the Select New Original dialog (**Figure 99**), and select a new original.

■ Aliases are discussed in detail earlier in this chapter.

To close the Info window

Click the Info window's close button.

or

1. Activate the Info window.

2. Choose File > Close Window, or press ⌃ ⌘ W.

✔ Tip

■ Closing the Info window saves all changes you made to its contents.

WORKING WITH THE INFO WINDOW

Undoing Finder Actions

The Mac OS X Finder includes limited support for the Undo command, which can reverse the most recently completed action. Say, for example, that you move a file from one folder to another folder. If you immediately change your mind, you can choose Edit > Undo Move (**Figure 101**) to put the file back where it was.

✔ Tips

■ Don't depend on the Undo command. Unfortunately, it isn't available for all actions (**Figure 102**).

■ The exact wording of the Undo command varies depending on the action and the item it was performed on. In **Figure 101**, for example, the command is Undo Move of "Letter to John" because the last action was to move a document icon named *Letter to John*.

■ The Undo command is also available (and generally more reliable) in most Mac OS applications. You'll usually find it at the top of the Edit menu.

To undo an action

Immediately after performing an action, choose Edit > Undo *action description* (**Figure 101**), or press ⌘⌘Z. The action is reversed.

To redo an action

Immediately after undoing an action, choose Edit > Redo *action description* (**Figure 103**). The action is redone—as if you never used the Undo command.

✔ Tip

■ Think of the Redo command as the Undo-Undo command since it undoes the Undo command.

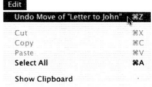

Figure 101
The Undo command enables you to undo the last action you performed.

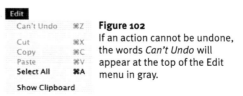

Figure 102
If an action cannot be undone, the words *Can't Undo* will appear at the top of the Edit menu in gray.

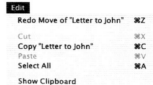

Figure 103
The Redo command undoes the Undo command.

Application Basics

Applications

Applications, which are also known as *programs*, are software packages you use to get work done. Here are some examples:

- ◆ **Word processors**, such as TextEdit and Microsoft Word, are used to write letters, reports, and other text-based documents.

- ◆ **Spreadsheets**, such as Microsoft Excel, have built-in calculation features that are useful for creating number-based documents such as worksheets and charts.

- ◆ **Databases**, such as FileMaker Pro, are used to organize information, such as the names and addresses of customers or the artists and titles in a record collection.

- ◆ **Graphics** and **presentation** programs, such as Adobe Photoshop and Microsoft PowerPoint, are used to create illustrations, animations, and presentations.

- ◆ **Communications** programs, such as Internet Connect and Microsoft Internet Explorer, are used to connect to other computers via modem or to the Internet.

- ◆ **Integrated** software, such as AppleWorks, combines "lite" versions of several types of software into one application.

- ◆ **Utility** software, such as Disk Utility and StuffIt Expander, performs tasks to manage computer files or keep your computer in good working order.

✔ Tips

- ■ Your Macintosh comes with some application software, some of which is discussed throughout this book.

- ■ Make sure the software you buy is Mac OS-compatible, and if possible, labeled "Built for Mac OS X." You may see Mac OS X applications referred to as *Carbon* or *Cocoa* applications. (Carbon and Cocoa are two methods for writing Mac OS X software.)

Mac OS X Applications vs. Classic Applications

Mac OS X supports two types of Mac OS applications:

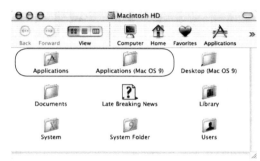

Figure 1 A typical Mac OS X setup includes two Applications folders.

◆ **Mac OS X applications** are those written specifically for Mac OS X. These programs take advantage of many of the new features of Mac OS X and use its new interface for menus, commands, and onscreen display. You can usually identify Mac OS X applications by the "Built for Mac OS X" label on them.

◆ **Classic applications** are those written for Mac OS 9.x and earlier but not rewritten for Mac OS X. These programs must be run in the Classic environment, which utilizes Mac OS 9.x.

You don't have to do anything special to run a Classic application. Mac OS X will automatically launch the Classic environment when it needs to.

✔ Tips

■ All of the applications that come with Mac OS X are Mac OS X applications.

■ If you upgraded to Mac OS X from a previous version of Mac OS, all of the applications that were on your computer before the upgrade are probably Classic applications.

■ Whenever possible, you should use Mac OS X applications. You'll find that applications run better and faster under Mac OS X than in the Classic environment.

■ Classic applications are covered in greater detail near the end of this chapter.

■ The hard disk window should include two applications folders, as shown in **Figure 1**: Applications and Applications (Mac OS 9).

Figure 2 A tiny triangle appears beneath each open application. Click an icon to make its application active.

Multitasking & the Dock

Mac OS uses a form of *multitasking*, which makes it possible for more than one application to be open at the same time. Only one application, however, can be *active*. You must make an application active to work with it. Other open applications continue running in the background.

Mac OS X features *preemptive multitasking*, a type of multitasking in which the operating system can interrupt a currently running task in order to run another task, as needed.

As discussed in **Chapter 2**, you can identify open applications by looking at the Dock; a tiny triangle appears beneath each application that is running (**Figure 2**).

You can also use the Dock to switch from one open application to another; simply click the application's icon in the Dock to make the application active.

✔ Tips

- Mac OS 8 and 9 use *cooperative multitasking*, a type of multitasking in which a running program can receive processing time only if other programs allow it. Each application must "cooperate" by giving up control of the processor in order to allow others to run.

- Mac OS X also features *protected memory*, a memory management system in which each program is prevented from modifying or corrupting the memory partition of another program. This means that if one application freezes up or bombs, your computer won't freeze up. You can continue using the other applications that are running.

- One application that is always open is Finder, which I cover in detail in **Chapters 2** through **4**.

- The active application is the one whose name appears at the top of the application menu—the menu to the right of the Apple menu—on the menu bar. The application menu is covered in more detail a little later in this chapter.

- Another way to activate an application is to click any of its windows. This brings the window to the foreground onscreen and makes the application active.

Using Applications & Creating Documents

You use an application by opening, or *launching*, it. It loads into the computer's memory. Its menu bar replaces the Finder's menu bar and offers commands that can be used only with that application. It may also display a document window and tools specific to that program.

Most applications create *documents*—files written in a format understood by the application. When you save documents, they remain on disk so you can open, edit, print, or just view them at a later date.

For example, you may use Microsoft Word to write a letter. When you save the letter, it becomes a Word document file that includes all the text and formatting you put into the letter, written in a format that Microsoft Word can understand.

Your computer keeps track of applications and documents. It automatically associates documents with the applications that created them. That's how your computer is able to open a document with the correct application when you open the document from the Finder.

✔ Tips

- You can launch an application by opening a document that it created.

- A document created by an application that is not installed on your computer is sometimes referred to as an *orphan* document since no *parent* application is available. An orphan document usually has a generic document icon (**Figure 3**).

Figure 3
An orphan document often has a generic document icon like this one.

Figure 4
Select the icon for the application that you want to open.

Figure 5
Choose Open from the File menu.

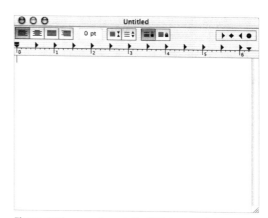

Figure 6 When you launch TextEdit by opening its application icon, it displays an empty document window.

Figure 7
Select the icon for the document you want to open.

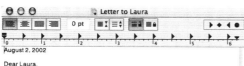

Figure 8 When you launch TextEdit by opening one of its documents, it displays the document.

To launch an application

Double-click the application's icon.

or

1. Select the application's icon (**Figure 4**).

2. Choose File > Open (**Figure 5**), or press ⌃⌘O.

or

If an icon for the application is in the toolbar or the Dock, click that icon once.

The application opens (**Figure 6**).

To open a document & launch the application that created it at the same time

Double-click the icon for the document that you want to open.

or

1. Select the icon for the document that you want to open (**Figure 7**).

2. Choose File > Open (**Figure 5**), or press ⌃⌘O.

or

If an icon for the document is in the toolbar or the Dock, click that icon once.

If the application that created the document is not already running, it launches. The document appears in an active window (**Figure 8**).

To open a document with drag & drop

1. Drag the icon for the document that you want to open onto the icon for the application with which you want to open it.

2. When the application icon becomes selected (**Figure 9**), release the mouse button. The application launches and displays the document (**Figure 8**).

✔ Tips

- Drag and drop is a good way to open a document with an application other than the one that created it.

- Not all applications can read all documents. Dragging a document icon onto the icon for an application that can't open it either won't launch the application or will display an error message.

- In step 1, the application icon can be in a Finder window, in the toolbar, or on the Dock.

To open a document with the Open With command

1. Select the icon for the document that you want to open (**Figure 7**).

2. Choose File > Open With to display the Open With submenu (**Figure 10**) and choose the application you want to use to open the file. The application you chose opens and displays the document.

✔ Tips

- The Open With feature is new in Mac OS X 10.2.

- The Open With submenu (**Figure 10**) will only list applications that are installed on your compuer and are capable of opening the selected document.

Figure 9 Drag the icon for the document you want to open onto the icon for the application you want to open it with.

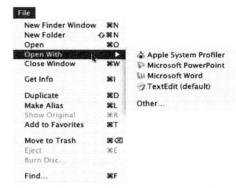

Figure 10 The Open With submenu lists installed applications that can open a selected document. The options that appear depend on what type of document is selected and what applications are installed on your computer.

Standard Application Menus

Apple's Human Interface Guidelines provide basic recommendations to software developers to ensure consistency from one application to another. Nowhere is this more obvious than in the standard menus that appear in most applications: the application, File, Edit, Window, and Help menus. You'll see these menus with the same kinds of commands over and over in most of the applications you use. This consistency makes it easier to learn Mac OS applications.

The next few pages provide a closer look at the standard menus you'll find in most applications.

✔ Tips

- The Finder, which is covered in **Chapters 2 through 4**, has standard menus similar to the ones discussed here.

- The Finder rules regarding the ellipsis character (…) and keyboard commands displayed on menus also apply to applications. **Chapter 2** explains these rules.

LEARNING ABOUT APPLICATIONS

The Application Menu

The application menu takes the name of the currently active application—for example, the TextEdit application menu (**Figure 11**) or the Internet Explorer application menu (**Figure 12**). It includes commands for working with the entire application.

To learn about an application

1. From the application menu, choose About *application name* (**Figures** 11 and 12).

2. A window with version and other information appears (**Figure 13**). Read the information it contains.

3. When you're finished reading about the application, click the window's close button.

To set application preferences

1. From the application menu, choose Preferences (**Figures** 11 and 12).

2. The application's Preferences window (**Figure 14**) or dialog appears. Set options as desired.

3. Click the window's close button.

   or

   Click the dialog's OK or Save button.

✔ Tip

■ Preference options vary greatly from one application to another. To learn more about an application's preferences, check its documentation or online help.

Figures 11 & 12
The TextEdit application menu (left), and the Internet Explorer application menu (right).

Figure 13 The About window for TextEdit provides its version number and other information.

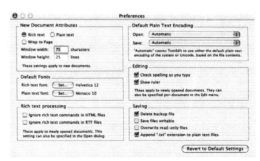

Figure 14 TextEdit's Preferences window offers a number of options you can set to customize the way TextEdit works.

To hide an application

From the application menu, choose Hide *application name* (**Figures 11** and **12**) or press ⌃⌘H. All of the application's windows, as well as its menu bar, are hidden from view.

✔ Tip

■ You cannot hide the active application if it is the only application that is open (the Finder) or if all the other open applications are already hidden.

To hide all applications except the active one

From the application menu, choose Hide Others (**Figures 11** and **12**).

To hide the active application while displaying another application

Hold down Option while displaying or switching to another application.

To display a hidden application

Click the application's icon (or any of its document icons) in the Dock (**Figure 2**).

To unhide all applications

From the application menu, choose Show All (**Figures 11** and **12**).

To quit an application

1. From the application menu, choose Quit *application name* (**Figures 11** and **12**), or press ⌘ ⌘ Q.

2. If unsaved documents are open, a dialog like the one in **Figure 15** appears for each unsaved document.

   ▲ Click Don't Save to quit without saving the document.

   ▲ Click Cancel or press Esc to return to the application without quitting.

   ▲ Click Save or press Return or Enter to save the document.

   The application closes all windows, saves preference files (if applicable), and quits.

✔ Tips

■ Closing all of an application's open windows is not the same as quitting. An application is still running until you quit it.

■ I tell you more about saving documents later in this chapter.

■ In Classic applications, the Quit command is on the File menu.

■ If an application is unresponsive and you cannot access its menus or commands, you can use the Force Quit command to make it stop running. I explain how near the end of this chapter.

Figure 15 This dialog appears when you close a TextEdit document that contains unsaved changes.

Figures 16, 17, & 18
The File menu in QuickTime Player (top left), TextEdit (bottom left), and Microsoft Internet Explorer (above).

Figure 19 Internet Explorer's New Window command opens a new Web browser window displaying the default Home page.

The File Menu

The File menu (**Figures 16**, **17**, and **18**) includes commands for working with files or documents. This section discusses the commands most often found under the File menu: New, Open, Close, and Save.

✔ Tip

- The Page Setup and Print commands are also found on the File menu. These commands are discussed in detail in **Chapter 8**.

To create a new document or window

Choose File > New (**Figure 17**).

or

Choose File > New Window (**Figure 18**).

or

Press ⌘N.

A new untitled document (**Figure 6**) or window (**Figure 19**) appears.

✔ Tip

- As shown in **Figures 16**, **17**, and **18**, the exact wording of the command for creating a new document or window varies depending on the application and what the command does. This command, however, is usually the first one on the File menu.

CREATING NEW DOCUMENTS & WINDOWS

To open a file

1. Choose File > Open (**Figures 16**, **17**, and **18**) or press ⌘⌥O to display the Open dialog (**Figure 20**).

2. Use any combination of the following techniques to locate the document you want to open:

   ▲ Use the From pop-up menu (**Figure 21**) to select a specific location.

   ▲ Click one of the items in either list to view its contents in the list on the right side of the window. (The list containing the item you clicked shifts to the left if necessary.)

   ▲ Use the scroll bar at the bottom of the two lists to shift lists. Shifting lists to the right enables you to see your path from the root directory (usually your hard disk).

   ▲ In the Go to field, enter the path from the currently selected folder to the folder you want to open. (This is an advanced technique that requires you to know the exact location of a folder or file.)

3. When the name of the file you want to open appears in the list on the right side of the window, use one of the following techniques to open it:

   ▲ Select it and then click Open or press Return or Enter.

   ▲ Double-click it.

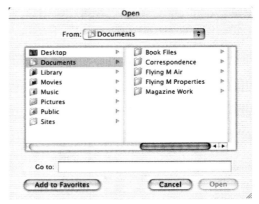

Figure 20 A standard Open dialog.

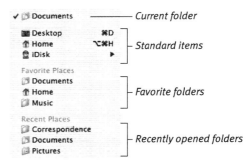

Figure 21 The From (and Where) pop-up menu includes several standard items, as well as your Favorite folders and up to five of the folders most recently accessed by the application.

OPENING FILES

Figure 22 TextEdit's Open Recent submenu makes it easy to reopen a recently opened document.

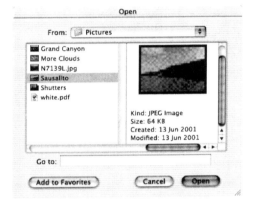

Figure 23 When you select a file in the Open dialog, the file's icon or a preview and other information for the file appears. This example shows Preview's Open dialog with a JPEG format file selected. The image in the right side of the dialog is the file's custom icon, which was created automatically by Photoshop when the image was saved.

✔ Tips

■ The exact wording of the Open command varies depending on the application and what you want to open. For example, the Open command on QuickTime Player's File menu (**Figure 16**) is Open Movie in New Player and the Open command on Internet Explorer's File menu (**Figure 18**) is Open File.

■ The Open Recent command, which is available on the File menu of some applications (**Figures 16** and **17**), displays a submenu of recently opened items (**Figure 22**). Choose the item you want to open it again.

■ The Open dialog (**Figure 20**) has many standard elements that appear in all Open dialogs.

■ In step 2, you can make a selected folder into a favorite item by clicking the Add to Favorites button.

■ In step 3, you can only select the files that the application can open; other files will either not appear in the list or will appear in gray. Some applications include a Show menu that enables you to display the types of files that appear in the Open dialog.

■ In step 3, selecting a file's name in the Open dialog displays its icon or a preview and other information for the file on the right side of the dialog (**Figure 23**).

■ Favorites are covered in **Chapter 4** and file paths are discussed in **Chapter 3**. iDisk is covered in detail in *Mac OS X Advanced: Visual QuickPro Guide*.

To close a window

1. Choose File > Close (**Figures 16**, **17**, and **18**), or press ⌃ ⌘ W.

   or

   Click the window's close button.

2. If the window contains a document with changes that have not been saved, a dialog sheet like the one in **Figure 15** appears.

   ▲ Click Don't Save to close the window without saving the document.

   ▲ Click Cancel or press (Esc) to keep the window open.

   ▲ Click Save or press (Return) or (Enter) to save the document.

✔ Tip

■ The exact appearance of the dialog sheet that appears when you close a document with unsaved changes varies depending on the application. All versions of the dialog should offer the same three options, although they may be worded differently. **Figure 15** shows the dialog that appears in TextEdit.

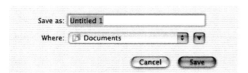

Figure 24 The Save dialog sheet can be collapsed to offer fewer options...

Figure 25 ...or expanded to offer more options.

Figure 26 Use the New Folder dialog to enter a name for a new folder.

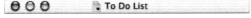

Figure 27 The name of the newly saved file appears in the window's title bar.

To save a document for the first time

1. Choose File > Save (**Figure 17**) or press ⌃⌘S to display the Save dialog (**Figure 24** or **25**).

2. Use the Where pop-up menu (**Figure 21**) to select a location in which to save the document.

   or

   If necessary, click the triangle beside the Where pop-up menu (**Figure 24**) to expand the dialog (**Figure 25**). Then use any combination of the following techniques to select a location in which to save the document:

   ▲ Click one of the items in either list to view its contents on the right side of the dialog. (The list containing the item you clicked shifts to the left if necessary.)

   ▲ Use the scroll bar at the bottom of the two lists to shift lists. Shifting lists to the right enables you to see your path from the root directory (usually your hard disk).

   ▲ Click the New Folder button to create a new folder inside the currently selected folder. Enter a name for the folder in the New Folder dialog that appears (**Figure 26**), and click Create.

3. When the name of the folder in which you want to save the document appears on the Where pop-up menu, enter a name for the document in the Save as edit box and click Save.

   The document is saved in the location you specified. The name of the file appears in the document window's title bar (**Figure 27**).

SAVING DOCUMENTS

✔ Tips

- Not all applications enable you to save documents. The standard version of QuickTime Player, for example, does not include a Save command on its File menu (**Figure 16**).

- The Save dialog (**Figure 24**) is also known as the Save Location dialog because it enables you to select a location in which to save a file.

- In step 1, you can also use the Save As command. The first time you save a document, the Save and Save As commands do the same thing: display the Save dialog.

- In step 2, you can make a selected folder into a favorite item by clicking the Add to Favorites button.

- Some applications automatically append a period and a three-character *extension* to a file's name when you save it. Extensions are used by Mac OS X and Windows applications to identify the file type.

- Favorites are covered in **Chapter 4** and file pathnames are discussed in **Chapter 3**.

Close button

Figure 28 A bullet in the close button of a document window indicates that the document has unsaved changes.

To save changes to a document

Choose File > Save (**Figure 17**), or press ⌘ ⌘ S.

The document is saved in the same location with the same name, thus overwriting the existing version of the document with the new version.

✔ Tip

■ Mac OS X includes two ways to indicate whether a window contains unsaved changes:

▲ A bullet character appears in the close button on the title bar of the window for a document with unsaved changes (**Figure 28**).

▲ A bullet character appears in the Window menu beside the name of the window for a document with unsaved changes (**Figure 32**). The Window menu is discussed a little later in this chapter.

SAVING CHANGES TO DOCUMENTS

To save a document with a new name or in a new location

1. Choose File > Save As (**Figures 17** and **18**) to display the Save dialog sheet (**Figure 24** or **25**).

2. Follow steps 2 and 3 in the section titled "To save a document for the first time" to select a location, enter a name, and save the document.

✔ Tips

■ Saving a document with a new name or in a new location creates a copy of the existing document. From that point forward, you work with the copy, not the original.

■ If you use the Save dialog to save a document with the same name as a document in the selected location, a confirmation dialog like the one in **Figure 29** appears. You have two options:

▲ Click Cancel or press ⌈Esc⌉ to return to the Save dialog and either change the document's name or the save location.

▲ Click Replace or press ⌈Return⌉ or ⌈Enter⌉ to replace the document on disk with the current document.

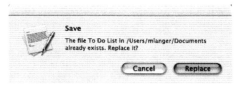

Figure 29 This dialog appears when you try to save a file with the same name as another file in a folder.

Edit	
Undo Typing	⌘Z
Redo	⇧⌘Z
Cut	⌘X
Copy	⌘C
Paste	⌘V
Delete	
Select All	⌘A
Find	▶
Spelling	▶
Speech	▶

Edit	
Undo Edit Person	⌘Z
Redo	⇧⌘Z
Cut	⌘X
Copy	⌘C
Paste	⌘V
Delete Person	
Remove From Group	
Select All	⌘A
Find	⌘F
Rename Group	
Edit Mailing List...	
Edit Card	⌘L

Figures 30 & 31
The Edit menus for
TextEdit (left) and Address Book (right).

The Edit Menu

The Edit menu (**Figures 30** and **31**) includes commands for modifying the contents of a document. Here's a quick list of the commands you're likely to find, along with their standard keyboard equivalents:

◆ **Undo** (⌘ Z) reverses the last editing action you made.

◆ **Redo** (Shift ⌘ X) reverses the last undo.

◆ **Cut** (⌘ X) removes a selection from the document and puts a copy of it in the Clipboard.

◆ **Copy** (⌘ C) puts a copy of a selection in the Clipboard.

◆ **Paste** (⌘ V) inserts the contents of the Clipboard into the document at the insertion point or replaces selected text in the document with the contents of the Clipboard.

◆ **Clear** or **Delete** removes a selection from the document. This is the same as pressing Delete when document contents are selected.

◆ **Select All** (⌘ A) selects all text or objects in the document.

✔ Tips

■ As you can see in **Figures 30** and **31**, not all Edit menu commands are available in all applications at all times.

■ Edit menu commands work with selected text or graphic objects in a document.

■ Most Edit menu commands are discussed in greater detail in **Chapter 7**, which covers TextEdit.

THE EDIT MENU

135

The Window Menu

The Window menu (**Figures** 32 and 33) includes commands for working with open document windows as well as a list of the open windows.

✔ Tips

■ The windows within applications have the same basic parts and controls as Finder windows, which are discussed in detail in **Chapter 2**.

■ A bullet character beside the name of a window in the Window menu indicates that the window contains a document with unsaved changes.

To close a window

1. Choose Window > Close Window (**Figures** 32 and 33).

2. If the window contains a document with changes that have not been saved, a Save Changes dialog sheet like the one in **Figure 15** appears.

   ▲ Click Don't Save to close the window without saving the document.

   ▲ Click Cancel or press Esc to keep the window open.

   ▲ Click Save or press Return or Enter to save the document.

To zoom a window

Choose Window > Zoom Window (**Figure 32**).

The window toggles between its full size and a custom size you create with the window's resize control.

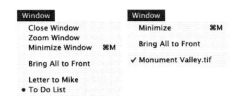

Figures 32 & 33 The Window menus for TextEdit (left) and Preview (right).

Figure 34 The icon for a minimized window appears in the Dock. If you look closely, you can see a tiny icon for the application in which it is open.

To minimize a window

Choose Window > Minimize Window (**Figure 32**) or Window > Minimize (**Figure 33**).

or

Press ⌃ ⌘ M.

The window shrinks down to the size of an icon and slips into the Dock (**Figure 34**).

To display a minimized window

With the application active, choose the window's name from the Window menu (**Figures 32** and **33**).

or

Click the window's icon in the Dock (**Figure 34**).

The window expands out of the Dock and appears onscreen.

To bring all of an application's windows to the front

Choose Window > Bring All to Front (**Figures 32** and **33**).

All of the application's open windows are displayed on top of open windows for other applications.

✔ Tip

- ■ Mac OS X allows an application's windows to be mingled in layers with other applications' windows.

To activate a window

Choose the window's name from the bottom of the Window menu (**Figures 32** and **33**).

MINIMIZING & DISPLAYING WINDOWS

The Help Menu

The Help menu (**Figures 35** and **36**) includes commands for viewing onscreen help information specific to the application. Choosing the primary Help command launches the Help Viewer application with help information and links (**Figures 37** and **38**).

✔ Tips

- Onscreen help is covered in detail in **Chapter 13**.

- Although the Help menu may only have one command for a simple application (**Figures 35** and **36**), it can have multiple commands to access different kinds of help for more complex applications.

Figures 35 & 36 The Help menu for Sherlock (left) and TextEdit (right).

Figure 37 Choosing Sherlock Help from Sherlock's Help menu displays this window,...

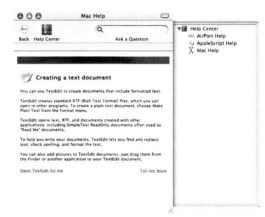

Figure 38 ...while choosing TextEdit Help from TextEdit's Help menu displays this window.

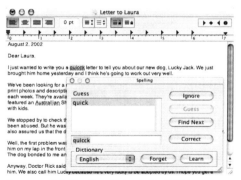

Figure 39 This Spelling dialog in TextEdit is an example of a modeless dialog—you can interact with the document while the dialog is displayed.

Figure 40 A standard Save Location dialog sheet is an example of a document modal dialog—you must address and dismiss it before you can continue working with the document it is attached to.

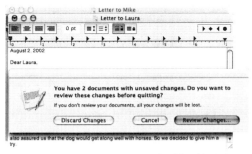

Figure 41 An application modal dialog like this Quit dialog requires your attention before you can continue working with the application.

Dialogs

Mac OS applications use *dialogs* to tell you things and get information from you. Think of them as the way your computer has a conversation—or dialog—with you.

Mac OS X has three main types of dialogs:

◆ *Modeless* dialogs enable you to work with the dialog while interacting with document windows. These dialogs usually have their own window controls to close and move them (**Figure 39**).

◆ *Document modal* dialogs usually appear as dialog *sheets* attached to a document window (**Figure 40**). You must address and dismiss these dialogs before you can continue working with the window, although you can switch to another window or application while the dialog is displayed.

◆ *Application modal* dialogs appear as movable dialogs (**Figure 41**). These dialogs must be addressed and dismissed before you can continue working with the application, although you can switch to another application while the dialog is displayed.

✔ Tips

■ You don't need to remember *modeless* vs. *modal* terminology to work with Mac OS X. Just understand how the dialogs differ and what the differences mean.

■ Some dialogs are very similar from one application to another. This chapter covers some of these standard dialogs , including Open (**Figure 20**), Save Location (**Figures 24**, **25**, and **40**), Save Changes (**Figure 15**), and Replace Confirmation (**Figure 29**). Two more standard dialogs—Page Setup and Print—are covered in **Chapter 8**.

To use dialog parts

- Click a *tab control* to view a *pane* full of related options (**Figure 42**).

- Use *scroll bars* to view the contents of *scrolling lists* (**Figure 43**). Click a list item once to select it or to enter it in a *combination box* (**Figure 43**).

- Enter text or numbers into *entry fields* (**Figure 44**), including those that are part of combination boxes (**Figure 43**).

- Click a *pop-up menu* (**Figures 43** and **44**) to display its options. Click a menu option to choose it.

- Click a *check box* (**Figure 45**) to toggle it on or off. (A check box is turned on when a check mark or X appears inside it.)

- Click a *radio button* (**Figure 45**) to choose its option. (A radio button is choosen when a bullet appears inside it.)

- Drag a *slider* control (**Figure 45**) to change a setting.

- Consult a preview area (**Figure 42**) to see the effects of your changes.

- Drag an image file into an *image well* (**Figure 44**).

- Click a *push button* (**Figures 42** and **44**) to activate it.

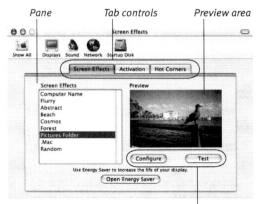

Figure 42 The Screen Effects pane of the System Preferences application.

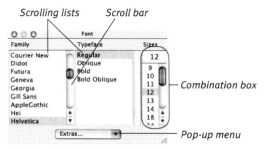

Figure 43 TextEdit's Font pane.

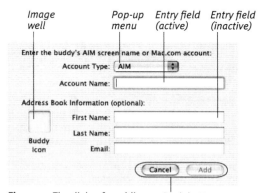

Figure 44 The dialog for adding buddy information to iChat.

USING DIALOGS

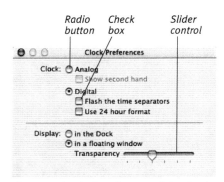

Radio button   *Check box*   *Slider control*

Figure 45 The Clock Preferences dialog for the Clock application.

✔ Tips

- An entry field with a dark border around it is the active field (**Figure 44**). Typing automatically enters text in this field. You can advance from one entry field to the next by pressing ⟨Tab⟩.

- If an entry field has a pair of arrows or triangles beside it you can click the triangles to increase or decrease a value already in the field.

- The default push button is the one that pulsates. You can always select a default button by pressing ⟨Enter⟩ and often by pressing ⟨Return⟩.

- You can usually select a Cancel button (**Figure 44**) by pressing ⟨Esc⟩.

- You can select as many check boxes (**Figure 45**) in a group as you like.

- One and only one radio button in a group can be selected (**Figure 45**). If you try to select a second radio button, the first button becomes deselected.

- If you click the Cancel button in a dialog (**Figure 44**), any options you set are lost.

- To select multiple items in a scrolling list, hold down ⟨⌘ ⌘⟩ while clicking each one. Be aware that not all dialogs support multiple selections in scrolling lists.

- There are other standard controls in Mac OS X dialogs. These are the ones you'll encounter most often.

USING DIALOGS

Using Classic Applications

When you open a Mac OS application that isn't Mac OS X-native, Mac OS X automatically launches the Classic environment, then opens the application within it. The application runs under Mac OS 9.x, which has slightly different interface elements.

This part of the chapter explains how you can manually start and stop the Classic environment, as well as how to use standard Open and Save As dialogs within Mac OS 9.x applications.

✔ Tips

- Mac OX 9.2 or later must be properly installed on your computer, as discussed in **Chapter 1**, for the Classic environment to work.

- The Classic environment in Mac OS X is discussed in greater detail in *Mac OS X Advanced: Visual QuickPro Guide*.

- Other aspects of the Classic environment, including Apple menu options, networking, and control panels, are covered in *Mac OS 9.1: Visual QuickStart Guide*.

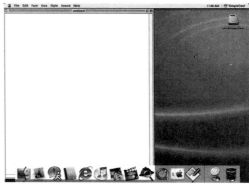

Figure 46 SimpleText running in the Classic environment.

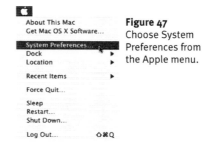

Figure 47 Choose System Preferences from the Apple menu.

Figure 48 The Classic icon in the System Preferences window.

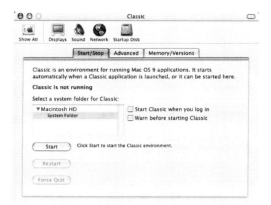

Figure 49 The Classic pane of System Preferences.

Figure 50 This window appears while the Classic environment starts up.

Figure 51 This dialog may appear the first time you start the Classic environment. If it does, click Update.

To start the Classic environment

Open any Mac OS application that is not Mac OS X-native. The Classic environment launches automatically, and the application opens within it (**Figure 46**).

or

1. Choose Apple > System Preferences (**Figure 47**), or click the System Preferences icon on the Dock.

2. In the System Preferences window that appears, click the Classic icon (**Figure 48**) to display the Classic pane (**Figure 49**).

3. If necessary, select the hard disk on which Mac OS 9.x is installed.

4. Click the Start button.

5. Wait while the Classic environment starts. A window with a progress bar that shows Mac OS 9.2 or later starting up (**Figure 50**) tracks its progress. When it's finished, the window disappears and the message "Classic is running" appears in the Classic pane (**Figure 52**).

✔ Tips

- The first time you start the Classic environment, a dialog like the one in **Figure 51** may appear. Click Update.

- If you often use Mac OS 9.x applications, you can configure your computer to automatically start the Classic environment when you start or log in to your computer. Just turn on the Start Classic when you log in check box in the Classic pane of System Preferences (**Figure 49**).

To stop the Classic environment

1. Choose Apple > System Preferences (**Figure** 47), or click the System Preferences icon in the Dock.

2. In the System Preferences window that appears, click the Classic icon (**Figure 48**) to display the Classic pane (**Figure 52**).

3. Click the Stop button.

4. Your computer switches to the Classic environment and attempts to Quit each open Mac OS 9.x application. Use any dialogs that appear to save changes to unsaved documents.

✔ Tip

■ You don't have to stop the Classic environment when you're finished working with Classic applications. Doing so, however, frees up computer resources and may make your computer run faster in Mac OS X.

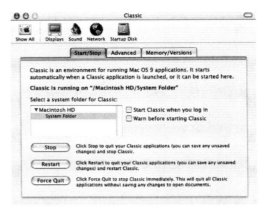

Figure 52 Once the Classic environment is running, you can use the Classic pane to stop it.

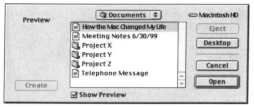

Figure 53
Choose Open from the application's—in this case SimpleText's—File menu.

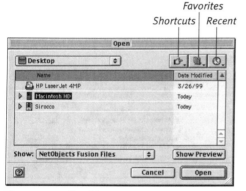

Figure 54 An Open dialog can look like this...

Favorites

Shortcuts   Recent

Figure 55 ...or like this.

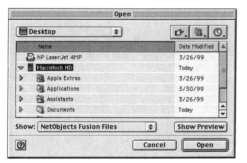

Figure 56 Use the pop-up menu above the scrolling list to choose a different folder in the hierarchy.

Figure 57 Click a triangle to display the items within its folder or disk.

To use a Mac OS 9.x Open dialog

1. Choose File > Open (**Figure 53**), or press ⌘⌘Ｏ.

   A dialog similar to the one in **Figure 54** or **55** appears.

2. Use any combination of these techniques to navigate to the file you want to open:

   ▲ To open an item in a scrolling list, click to select it and then click Open or double-click it.

   ▲ To back up out of the current folder to a previous folder in the file hierarchy, choose a folder from the pop-up menu above the scrolling list (**Figure 56**) or press ⌘⌘↑ to back up one folder level at a time.

   ▲ Click the triangle to the left of the name of a disk or folder that you want to open (**Figure 55**) to display its contents along with the contents of other disks or folders (**Figure 57**).

   ▲ Open several files at once by holding down ⇧Shift while clicking the names of the files you want to open. (This only works in applications that support it.)

   ▲ Choose an option from the Shortcuts button menu (**Figure 58**) to quickly access the desktop, mounted disks, or disks available over the network or Internet.

   ▲ Choose an item from the Favorites button menu (**Figure 59**) to open a Favorite item.

   ▲ Choose an item from the Recent button menu (**Figure 60**) to open an item you recently opened with that application.

Continued on next page...

USING THE OPEN DIALOG IN MAC OS 9.X

Continued from previous page.

---

3. Click to select the name of the file that you want to open, and then click Open (**Figure 61**) or press ⌐Return⌐ or ⌐Enter⌐.

or

Double-click the name of the file that you want to open.

✔ Tips

- To quickly view the items on the desktop, click the Desktop button (**Figure 54**) or press ⌘ ⌘ D. This enables you to open folders, files, and other disks on your desktop.

- Some Open dialogs offer a Show pop-up menu that lets you narrow down a file list by document or file type (**Figure 55**).

Figure 58
The Shortcuts button displays the desktop, network connections, and other mounted disks.

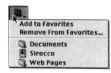

Figure 59
The Favorites button displays your Favorites.

Figure 60 The Recent button displays items recently opened with that application.

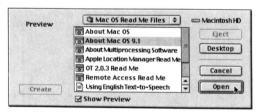

Figure 61 Select the file's name and click Open to open it within the application.

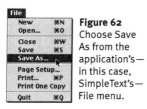

Figure 62
Choose Save As from the application's— in this case, SimpleText's— File menu.

Figure 63 A Save As dialog could look like this...

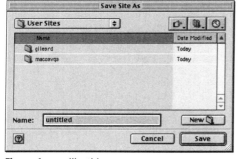

Figure 64 ...or like this.

✔ Tips

■ If you have never saved the document, you can also choose Save from the application's File menu or press ⌘ S to display the Save As dialog.

To use the Mac OS 9.x Save As dialog

1. Choose File > Save As (**Figure 62**). A dialog similar to the one in **Figure 63** or **64** appears.

2. Use any combination of these techniques to navigate to the folder in which you want to save the document:

   ▲ To open an item in a scrolling list, click to select it and then click Open or double-click the item.

   ▲ To back out of the current folder to a previous folder in the file hierarchy, choose a folder from the pop-up menu above the scrolling list (**Figure 56**) or press ⌘ ↑ to back up one folder level at a time.

   ▲ Choose an option from the Shortcuts button menu (**Figure 58**) to quickly access the desktop, mounted disks, or disks available over a network or the Internet.

   ▲ Choose an item from the Favorites button menu (**Figure 59**) to open a Favorite folder.

   ▲ Choose an item from the Recent button menu (**Figure 60**) to open a folder you recently opened with that application.

3. In the edit box beneath the scrolling list, enter the name that you want to give the document.

4. Click Save, or press [Return] or [Enter].

■ To quickly view the items on the desktop, click the Desktop button (**Figure 63**) or press ⌘ D. This enables you to open folders and other disks on your desktop.

USING THE SAVE AS DIALOG

Force Quitting Applications

Occasionally, an application may freeze, lock up, or otherwise become unresponsive. When this happens, you can no longer work with that application or its documents. Sometimes, you can't access any application at all!

Mac OS X includes the Force Quit command (**Figure 65**), which enables you to force an unresponsive application to quit. Then you can either restart it or continue working with other applications.

✱ Warning!

- When you force quit an application, any unsaved changes in that application's open documents may be lost. Use the Force Quit command only as a last resort, when the application's Quit command cannot be used.

✔ Tips

- Mac OS X's protected memory, which is discussed at the beginning of this chapter, makes it possible for applications to continue running properly on your computer when one application locks up.

- If more than one application experiences problems during a work session, you might find it helpful to restart your computer. This clears out RAM and forces your computer to reload all applications and documents into memory. You can learn more about troubleshooting Mac OS X in **Chapter 13**.

About This Mac
Get Mac OS X Software...
System Preferences...
Dock ▶
Location ▶
Recent Items ▶
Force Quit...
Sleep
Restart
Shut Down
Log Out... ⇧⌘Q

Figure 65
Choose Force Quit from the Apple menu.

Figure 66 Select the application you want to force to quit.

Figure 67 Use this dialog to confirm that you really do want to force quit the application.

To force quit an application

1. Choose Apple > Force Quit (**Figure 65**), or press ⌥ Option ⌘ ⌘ Esc.

2. In the Force Quit Applications window that appears (**Figure 66**), select the application you want to force to quit.

3. Click Force Quit.

4. A confirmation dialog like the one in **Figure 67** appears. Click Force Quit.

   The application immediately quits.

✔ Tip

■ If you selected Finder in step 2, the button to click in step 3 is labeled Relaunch.

FORCE QUITTING APPLICATIONS

Using Mac OS X Applications

Figure 1 The Mac OS X Applications folder.

Mac OS Applications

Mac OS X includes a variety of software applications that you can use to perform tasks on your computer.

This chapter covers the following Apple programs in the Applications folder (**Figure 1**):

◆ **Address Book**, which enables you to keep track of contact information for friends, family members, and business associates.

◆ **Calculator**, which enables you to perform quick calculations and graph formulas.

◆ **Chess**, which is a computerized version of the game of chess.

◆ **Clock**, which displays a live-action digital or analog clock.

◆ **DVD Player**, which enables you to play movies on DVD discs.

◆ **Image Capture**, which enables you to download image files from a digital camera and save them on disk.

◆ **Preview**, which enables you to view images and PDF files.

◆ **QuickTime Player**, which enables you to view QuickTime movies and streaming video.

◆ **Stickies**, which enables you to place colorful notes on your computer screen.

✔ Tips

■ Mac OS X includes a number of other applications that are discussed elsewhere in this book or in *Mac OS X Advanced: Visual QuickPro Guide*:

▲ TextEdit is covered in **Chapter 7**.

▲ Print Center is covered in **Chapter 8**.

▲ iChat, Internet Connect, Internet Explorer, and Mail are covered in **Chapter 9**.

▲ Sherlock is covered in **Chapter 10**.

▲ iMovie, iPhoto, and iTunes (as well as iDVD) are covered in **Chapter 11**.

▲ AppleScript is covered in **Chapter 12**.

▲ System Preferences and applications in the Utilities folder are covered in *Mac OS X Advanced: Visual QuickPro Guide*.

■ Mac OS X 10.2 also includes Acrobat Reader, which enables you to open and view PDF files created with Adobe Acrobat and other programs. You can learn more about Acrobat Reader on Adobe Systems' Web site, www.adobe.com/products/acrobat/readerstep.html.

■ The Mac OS X 10.2 installer places icons for some Mac OS X applications in the Dock (**Figure 2**).

Figure 2 The Dock includes icons for several Mac OS X applications.

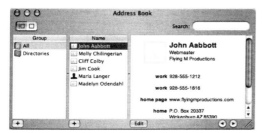

Figure 3 The main Address Book window, with several records already created.

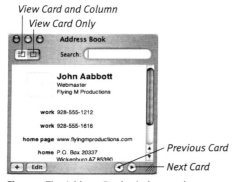

Figure 4 The Address Book window can be collapsed to display just one record's card.

Address Book

Address Book, which has been completely revised for Mac OS X 10.2, enables you to keep track of the names, addresses, phone numbers, e-mail addresses, and Web URLs of people you know. The information you store in Address Book's database can be used by Mail to send e-mail messages and iChat to send instant messages.

In this chapter, I provide enough information to get you started using Address Book for your contact management needs. You can explore the rest of Address Book's features on your own.

✔ Tips

- You must have an Internet connection to send e-mail or use iChat.

- Mail and iChat are covered in **Chapter 9**.

To launch Address Book

Double-click the Address Book icon in the Applications folder (**Figure 1**) to select it.

or

1. Click the Address Book icon in the Applications folder (**Figure 1**) to select it.

2. Choose File > Open, or press ⌘O.

or

Click the Address Book icon in the Dock (**Figure 2**).

Address Book's main window appears (**Figure 3**).

✔ Tip

- If the Address Book window looks more like what's shown in **Figure 4**, you can click the View Card and Column button in its upper-left corner to expand the view to show all three columns (**Figure 3**).

To add a new card

1. Click the Add New Person button (a plus sign) beneath the Name column in the main Address Book window (**Figure 3**).

   or

   Choose File > New Card (**Figure 5**), or press ⌘⌘N.

   A <No Name> record is created in the Name column and a blank address card appears beside it, with the *First* field active (**Figure 6**).

2. Enter information about the contact into appropriate fields. When a field is active, text appears within it to prompt you for information (**Figure 7**). Press Tab or click on a field to move from field to field.

3. To change the label that appears beside a field, click the tiny triangles beside it (**Figure 8**) to display a menu (**Figure 9**), then choose the label you prefer.

4. To add more fields, click the plus sign button beside a similar field (**Figure 8**). For example, to add another phone number field, click the plus sign beside a phone number. Then enter information and choose a field label as discussed in steps 2 and 3.

5. When you are finished entering information, click the Edit button to view the completed card (**Figure 10**).

✔ Tips

- You can enter information into any combination of fields; if you do not have information for a specific field, skip it and it will not appear in the completed card.

- In step 3, if you choose Custom from the pop-up menu, use the Adding new custom label dialog that appears (**Figure 11**) to enter a custom label and click OK.

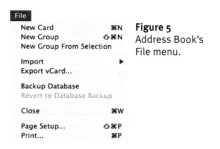

Figure 5
Address Book's File menu.

Figure 6 When you click the Add New Person button, Address Book creates an unnamed card record and selects the first field for entry.

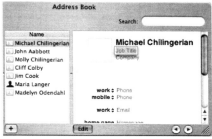

Figure 7 Each active field prompts you for entry information.

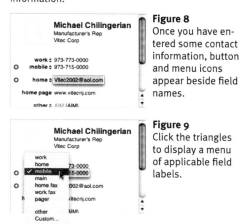

Figure 8
Once you have entered some contact information, button and menu icons appear beside field names.

Figure 9
Click the triangles to display a menu of applicable field labels.

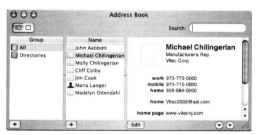

Figure 10 The completed contact record appears in the column on the right side of the window.

Figure 11 You can use this dialog to create a custom label for a record's card.

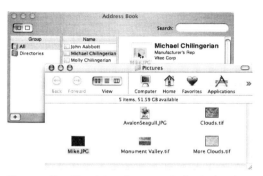

Figure 12 To add a picture for a record, simply drag its icon into the image well.

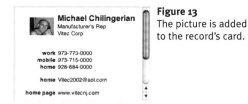

Figure 13 The picture is added to the record's card.

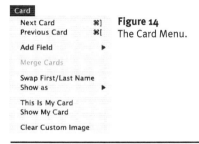

Figure 14 The Card Menu.

To edit a contact record

1. In the Name column of the Address Book window, select the contact you want to edit.

2. Click the Edit button.

3. Make changes as desired in the record's address card.

4. When you are finished making changes, click Edit again to save your changes and view the modified card.

To add a photo or logo to a contact record

1. In the Name column of the Address Book window, select the contact for which you want to add a picture or logo to display the contact card.

2. Drag the icon for the file containing the photo or logo you want to add from a Finder window to the image well in the address card window (**Figure 12**). When you release the mouse button, the image appears in the image well (**Figure 13**).

✔ Tip

- To remove a photo or logo from a contact record, select the contact and choose Card > Clear Custom Image (**Figure 14**).

To delete a contact record

1. In the Name column of the Address Book window, select the contact you want to delete.

2. Press (Delete).

3. In the confirmation dialog that appears, click Yes. The contact disappears.

To add information from a vCard

Drag the icon for the vCard from a Finder window to the Name column in the Address Book window (**Figure 15**).

or

Double-click the icon for a vCard file.

An Address Book contact card is created based on the vCard information (**Figure 16**).

✔ Tips

- *vCard* or *virtual address card* files are commonly used to share contact information electronically.

- vCard file names usually end with *.vcf*.

To save information as a vCard

Drag the name of a contact from the Name column of the Address Book window to a Finder window (**Figure 17**).

or

1. In the Name column of the Address Book window, select the name of the contact for which you want to save a vCard.

2. Choose File > Export vCard.

3. Use the Save dialog that appears (**Figure 18**) to enter a name and select a location for the vCard file. Then click Save.

The vCard file's icon appears where you dragged or saved it (**Figure 19**).

✔ Tips

- You can send your vCard via e-mail to anyone you like. This makes it easy for people to add your contact information to their contact database.

- The vCard format is recognized by most Mac OS and Windows contact management software.

Figure 15 Drag a vCard file's icon into the Address Book window's Name column.

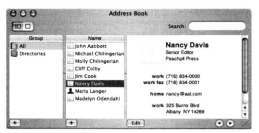

Figure 16 The vCard information is added to your Address Book as a contact card.

Figure 17 Drag the name of a contact from the Name column of the Address Book window to a Finder window.

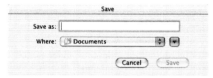

Figure 18 When you choose the Export vCard command, use the Save dialog that appears to save the selected address book record as a vCard.

Figure 19
A saved vCard file's icon looks like this.

Figure 20
When you click the Add New Group button, a new group appears in the Group column, with its default name selected.

Figure 21
Enter a new name for the group and press Return to save it.

Figure 22
To add a contact to a group, simply drag its name to the group name.

Figure 23
To see which contacts are in a group, select the name of the group.

To organize contact cards into groups

1. Click the Add New Group button (a plus sign) under the Group column of the Address Book window (**Figure 3**).

   or

   Choose File > New Group (**Figure 5**) or press Shift ⌃ ⌘ N.

2. A new entry appears in the Group column. Its name, *Group Name*, is selected (**Figure 20**). Enter a new name for the Group and press Return to save it (**Figure 21**).

3. Repeat steps 1 and 2 to add as many groups as you need to organize your contacts.

4. Select All in the Group column.

5. Drag a contact name from the Name column onto the name of the group you want to associate it with in the Group column. When a box appears around the group name (**Figure 22**), release the mouse button to add the contact to that group.

6. Repeat step 5 to organize contact cards as desired.

✔ Tips

- To see which contact cards are in a group, click the name of the group in the Group column. The Name column changes to display only those contacts in the selected group (**Figure 23**).

- A contact can be included in more than one group.

- The Directories entry in the Group field enables you to use an LDAP server to search for an e-mail address. This is an advanced feature that is beyond the scope of this book.

ORGANIZING CONTACTS INTO GROUPS

To remove a contact from a group

1. In the Group column, select the group you want to remove the contact from (**Figure 23**).
2. In the Name column, select the contact you want to remove.
3. Press [Delete].
4. In the confirmation dialog that appears (**Figure 24**), click Yes. The contact is removed from that group but remains in the Address Book database.

✖ Warning

- If you delete a contact from the All group, you will remove the contact from the Address Book database.

To remove a group

1. In the Group column, select the group you want to remove (**Figure 23**).
2. Press [Delete].
3. In the confirmation dialog that appears (**Figure 25**), click Yes. The group is removed but all contacts within it remain in the Address Book database.

✔ Tip

- You cannot remove the All group.

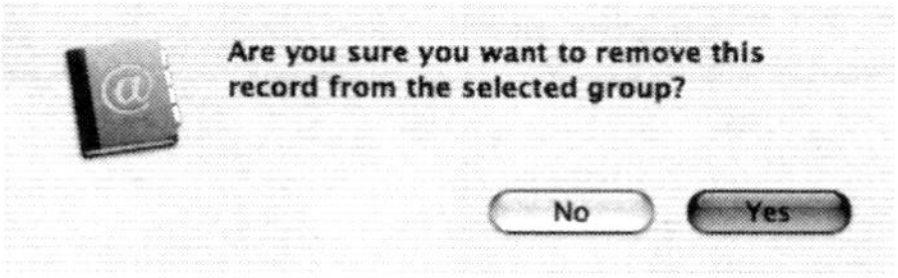

Figure 24 This dialog confirms that you want to delete a record from a group,...

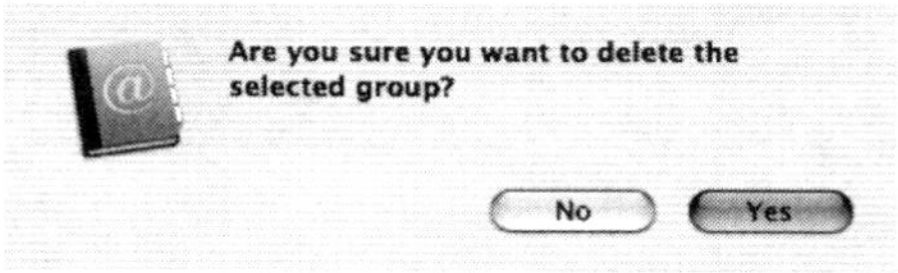

Figure 25 ...and this dialog confirms that you want to delete a group.

Figure 26 Enter all or part of a contact name in the Search box to find that contact.

To search for a contact card

1. In the Group column, select the name of the group in which you expect to find the contact.

2. Enter all or part of the contact name in the Search box at the top of the Address Book window (**Figure 26**).

   The names of contacts that match what you typed appear in the Name column (**Figure 26**).

✔ Tips

- In step 1, if you're not sure which group a contact is in, select All.

- Search results begin appearing in the Name column as soon as you begin entering search characters in the Search box. The more you enter, the fewer results are displayed.

- If no contact cards match your search criteria, the Name column will be empty.

Calculator

Calculator displays a simple calculator that can perform addition, subtraction, multiplication, and division, as well as complex mathematical calculations and conversions.

✔ Tip

- The Calculator has been around since the early days of the Macintosh. With Mac OS X 10.2, Apple gave it the first major upgrade I can remember—and I've been using Macs since 1989!

To launch Calculator

Double-click the Calculator icon in the Applications folder (**Figure 1**).

or

1. Click the Calculator icon in the Applications folder (**Figure 1**) to select it.

2. Choose File > Open, or press ⌃ ⌘ O.

The Calculator window appears (**Figure 27**).

To perform basic calculations

Use your mouse to click buttons for numbers and operators.

or

Press keyboard keys corresponding to numbers and operators.

The numbers you enter and the results of your calculations appear at the top of the Calculator window.

✔ Tip

- You can use the Cut, Copy, and Paste commands to copy the results of calculations into documents. **Chapter 7** covers the Cut, Copy, and Paste commands.

Figure 27
The Calculator looks and works like a $10 pocket calculator.

USING THE CALCULATOR

Figure 28 Clicking the Paper Tape button displays a drawer that tracks all of your entries.

Figure 29 The File menu includes commands for saving and printing the paper tape.

Figure 30 Clicking the Advanced button expands the Calculator to display mathematical functions.

To keep track of your entries

Click the Paper Tape button in the Calculator window.

A drawer slides out of the right side of the window. It displays everything you enter into Calculator (**Figure 28**).

✔ Tips

■ To hide the paper tape drawer, click the Paper Tape button again.

■ To start with a fresh tape, click the Clear Tape button.

■ You can use commands under the File menu (**Figure 29**) to save or print the paper tape.

To perform advanced calculations

1. Click the Advanced button in the Calculator window. The window expands to show a variety of complex mathematical functions (**Figure 30**).

2. Click buttons for the functions, values, and operators to perform your calculations.

✔ Tips

■ To hide advanced functions, click the Basic button.

To perform conversions

1. Enter the value you want to convert.

2. Choose the conversion you want from the Convert menu (**Figure** 31).

3. In the dialog that appears, set options for the conversion you want to perform. **Figure** 32 shows an example that converts speed from miles per hour to kilometers per hour.

4. Click OK. The original value you entered is converted and appears at the top of the Calculator window.

✔ Tips

- The Convert menu's Recent Conversions submenu makes it easy to repeat conversions you have done recently.

- If you have an Internet connection, you can choose Convert > Update Currency Exchange Rates and then use the Convert menu to perform currency conversions.

Figure 31 The Convert menu lists a variety of common conversions.

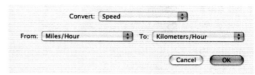

Figure 32 Set conversion options in a dialog like this.

Figure 33 The Chess window displays a three-dimensional chess board.

Figure 34 This Alert appears if you try to start a new game while another game is active.

Chess

Chess is a computerized version of the classic strategy game of chess. Your pieces are white and you go first; the computer's pieces are black.

To launch Chess

Double-click the Chess icon in the Applications folder (**Figure 1**).

or

1. Click the Chess icon in the Applications folder (**Figure 1**) to select it.

2. Choose File > Open, or press ⌃ ⌘ O.

The Chess window appears (**Figure 33**).

To move a chess piece

Drag the piece onto any valid square on the playing board.

✔ Tips

■ The computer moves automatically after each of your moves.

■ If you attempt to make an invalid move, an alert sounds and the piece returns to where it was.

■ If Speakable Items is enabled, you can use spoken commands to move chess pieces. Speakable Items is covered in *Mac OS X Advanced: Visual QuickPro Guide*.

To start a new game

1. Choose Game > New.

2. If you are already in the middle of a game, an alert dialog (**Figure 34**) appears:

    ▲ **No** starts a new game without saving the current one.

    ▲ **Cancel** dismisses the dialog and returns you to the current game.

    ▲ **Save** displays a Save Location dialog that you can use to save the game.

CHESS

Clock

Clock displays an analog or digital clock, either in the Dock or in a floating window on screen.

To launch Clock

Double-click the Clock icon in the Applications folder (**Figure 1**).

or

1. Click the Clock icon in the Applications folder (**Figure 1**) to select it.

2. Choose File > Open, or press ⌃⌘O.

The Clock either appears in the Dock (**Figure 35**) or as a floating window (**Figure 36**).

To set Clock preferences

1. Choose Clock > Preferences to display the Clock Preferences window (**Figure 37**).

2. Set Clock options by selecting a radio button and toggling check boxes as desired:

   ▲ **Analog** displays an analog clock (**Figures 35** and **36**). Use the check box to determine whether you want the second hand to display.

   ▲ **Digital** displays a digital clock (**Figure 38**). Use check boxes to determine whether it should flash time separators to mark seconds or use 24-hour format.

3. Set Display options as desired by selecting a radio button:

   ▲ **In the Dock** displays the clock in the Dock (**Figure 35**).

   ▲ **In a floating window** displays the clock in a floating window on screen (**Figures 36** and **38**). If you select this option, you can use the slider to set the transparency of the window.

Figure 35 The Clock in the Dock (not to be confused with the Cat in the Hat).

Figure 36
A floating analog clock window.

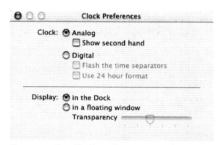

Figure 37 The Clock Preferences window.

Figure 38
A floating digital clock window.

✔ Tip

■ The clock that appears in the menu bar can be customized with the Date & Time pane of System Preferences. System Preferences are covered in detail in *Mac OS X Advanced: Visual QuickPro Guide*.

Figure 39 DVD Player either starts with a blank Viewer window and Controller palette...

Figure 40 ...or begins playing the DVD-Video. (This DVD is an example from Martin Sitter's book, *DVD Studio Pro 1.5: Visual QuickPro Guide.*)

Figure 41 This dialog may appear the first time you insert a DVD-Video.

DVD Player

DVD Player enables you to play DVD-Video on your Macintosh.

✔ Tip

■ To use DVD Player, your Macintosh must have a DVD-ROM drive or SuperDrive. For that reason, the Mac OS X installer only installs DVD Player on computers that have one of these drives. If you can't find DVD Player in your Applications folder, chances are that your computer can't play DVD-Video anyway.

To launch DVD Player

Insert a DVD-Video into your computer. DVD Player should launch and do one of two things:

◆ Display a black Viewer window with a floating Controller palette (**Figure 39**).

◆ Immediately begin DVD play (**Figure 40**).

If DVD Player does not launch at all, then:

Double-click the DVD Player icon in the Applications folder (**Figure 1**).

or

1. Click the DVD Player icon in the Applications folder (**Figure 1**) to select it.

2. Choose File > Open or press ⌃ ⌘ O.

✔ Tip

■ If a Drive Region Code dialog like the one in **Figure 41** appears the first time you play a DVD-Video, click the Set Drive Region button to set DVD Player's region to match that of the disc you inserted. Then click OK to dismiss the confirmation dialog that appears.

To display the Controller

Move the mouse while the DVD is playing.

or

Choose Window > Show Viewer (the menu appears, if necessary, when you point to it), or press Control C.

The Controller palette appears (**Figure 42a** or **42b**).

✔ Tips

■ You can change the appearance of the Controller from horizontal (**Figure 42a**) to vertical (**Figure 42b**) by choosing an option from the Controller Type submenu under the Controls menu (**Figure 43**).

■ To display additional DVD controls on the Controller palette, click the three tiny dots on the right (**Figure 42a**) or bottom (**Figure 42b**) of the Controller. **Figure 44** shows a horizontal Controller expanded to show these controls.

To control DVD play

Click buttons on the Controller palette (**Figure 42a, 42b**, or **44**).

or

Choose a command from the Controls menu (**Figure 43**).

✔ Tip

■ The Pause button on the Controller (**Figures 42a** and **42b**) and the Pause command on the Controls menu (**Figure 43**) change into a Play button and a Play command when a DVD is not playing.

To resize the Viewer window

Choose an option from the Video window (**Figure 45**) or press the corresponding shortcut key.

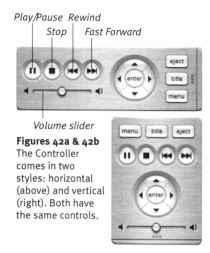

Play/Pause Rewind
Stop Fast Forward

Volume slider

Figures 42a & 42b
The Controller comes in two styles: horizontal (above) and vertical (right). Both have the same controls.

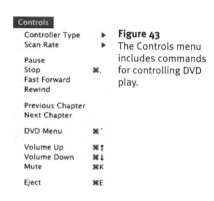

Figure 43
The Controls menu includes commands for controlling DVD play.

Figure 44 A horizontal Controller, expanded to show additional control buttons. Point to a button to learn its name.

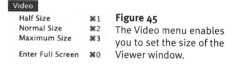

Figure 45
The Video menu enables you to set the size of the Viewer window.

Image Capture

Image Capture is an application that performs two functions:

◆ Download image files from a digital camera to your computer's hard disk.

◆ Operate your scanner to scan and save images.

In this part of the chapter, I explain how to download images from a digital camera with Image Capture.

✔ Tips

■ Some digital cameras and scanners require that driver software be installed on Mac OS X before the camera or scanner can be used. Consult the documentation that came with your scanner or camera or check the device manufacturer's Web site for Mac OS X compatibility and driver information.

■ Not all digital cameras or scanners are compatible with Image Capture. Generally speaking, if Image Capture does not "see" your camera or scanner when it is connected and turned on, the camera or scanner is probably not compatible with Image Capture and Image Capture cannot be used.

■ You can also download images from a digital camera using iPhoto, which offers additional features for managing photos saved to disk. I tell you about iPhoto in **Chapter 11**.

To launch Image Capture

1. Attach your digital camera to your computer's USB or Firewire port, using the applicable cable.

2. Turn the digital camera on and, if necessary, set it to review mode. The Image Capture window should appear (**Figure 46**). If it does not, then:

   Double-click the Image Capture icon in the Applications folder (**Figure 1**).

   or

1. Click the Image Capture icon in the Applications folder (**Figure 1**) to select it.

2. Choose File > Open, or press ⌥ ⌘ O.

✔ Tips

- If iPhoto is installed on your computer, it may launch instead of Image Capture. If so, you must manually launch Image Capture as instructed here to use it.

- You can specify which application should launch when you attach a digital camera or scanner. Choose Image Capture > Preferences to display the Image Capture Preferences window (**Figure 47**). Then use the pop-up menus for Camera Preferences and Scanner Preferences to choose the applications you prefer and click the window's close button to dismiss it.

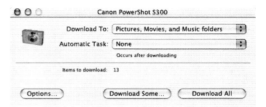

Figure 46 Image Capture's main window is named for the camera you have attached and turned on.

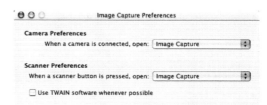

Figure 47 You can set options in the Image Capture Preferences window to choose applications for working with your digital camera and scanner.

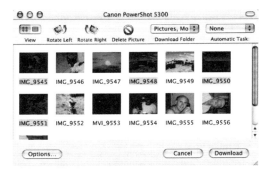

Figure 48 Use this window to select the images you want to download.

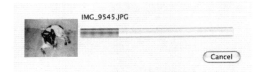

Figure 49 A progress window appears as the pictures are downloaded. (This is my new dog, Lucky Jack.)

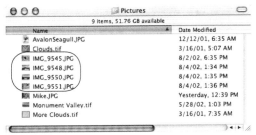

Figure 50 Image Capture switches to the Finder and opens the folders where it downloaded the images and/or movies. In this example, it has downloaded four images from my Canon Digital Elph to the Pictures folder.

To download images from a digital camera

To download all images on the camera, click the Download All button in the main Image Capture window (**Figure 46**).

or

1. To download some of the images on the camera, click the Download Some button in the main Image Capture window (**Figure 46**).

2. A window full of thumbnail images appears (**Figure 48**). Select the images you want to download. To select more than one image, hold down ⌃ ⌘ while clicking each image.

3. Click the Download button.

A dialog sheet appears, showing the progress of the download (**Figure 49**). When it disappears, the download is complete and Image Capture displays the window(s) for the folder(s) in which it downloaded the pictures (**Figure 50**).

✔ Tip

■ You can also use the thumbnail window (**Figure 48**) to delete images on the camera. Select the images you want to delete and click the Delete Picture button (the red circle with a line through it). Then click Delete in the confirmation dialog sheet that appears.

DOWNLOADING IMAGES

169

Preview

Preview, which was revised for Mac OS X 10.2, is a program that enables you to open and view two kinds of files:

◆ **Image files** (**Figure 51**), including files in JPEG, TIFF, PICT, and GIF formats.

◆ **PDF** or **Portable Document Format files** (**Figure 52**) created with Mac OS X's Print command, Adobe Acrobat software, or other software capable of creating PDFs.

✔ Tips

■ I explain how to create PDF files with the Print command in **Chapter 8**.

■ You can also open PDF files with Adobe Systems' Acrobat Reader software, which is installed with Mac OS X 10.2. (Look for it in your Applications folder, **Figure 1**.) You can learn more about Acrobat Reader—and download a copy of the software, if you need it—on the Adobe Web site, www.adobe.com/products/ acrobat/readstep.html. Adobe Acrobat Reader is free.

Figure 51 Here's an image file opened with Preview...

Figure 52 ...and here's a PDF file opened with Preview.

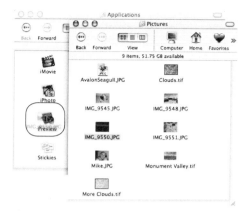

Figure 53 One way to open a file with Preview is to drag the file's icon onto the Preview icon.

info.pdf   photo.jpg

Figure 54
You can also double-click a Preview document's file icon.

Figure 55
Here's the View menu with a multi-page PDF file open. Not all commands are available when an image file is open.

Figure 56 You can display thumbnails for a multi-page document.

To open a file with Preview

Drag the document file's icon onto the Preview icon in the Applications folder (**Figure 53**).

or

Double-click the icon for a Preview document (**Figure 54**).

Preview launches and displays the file in its window (**Figures 51** and **52**).

✔ Tips

- You can also use Preview's Open command to open any compatible file on disk. I explain how to use an application's Open command in **Chapter 5**.

- You can use options on a Preview window's toolbar (**Figures 51** and **52**) or Preview's View menu (**Figure 55**) to zoom in or out, rotate the window's contents, or view a specific page.

- If a document has multiple pages, you can click the Thumbnails button in the window's toolbar to display or hide a drawer with thumbnail images of each page (**Figure 56**). Click a thumbnail to move quickly to that page.

QuickTime Player

QuickTime is a video and audio technology developed by Apple Computer, Inc. It is widely used for digital movies as well as streaming audio and video available via the Internet. QuickTime Player is an application you can use to view QuickTime movies and streaming Internet content.

✔ Tips

- There are two versions of QuickTime Player: the standard version, which is included with Mac OS X, and the Pro version, which enables you to edit and save QuickTime files. You can learn about QuickTime Pro on Apple's QuickTime Web site, www.apple.com/quicktime/, and in *QuickTime 6: Visual QuickStart Guide*.

- Internet access is covered in **Chapter 9**.

To launch QuickTime Player

Click the QuickTime Player icon in the Dock (**Figure 2**).

or

Open the QuickTime Player icon in the Applications folder (**Figure 1**).

A QuickTime Player window appears (**Figure 57**).

✔ Tips

- When you launch QuickTime Player, a dialog like the one in **Figure 58** may appear. Click Later to dismiss it.

- The first time you launch QuickTime Player, a dialog like the one in **Figure 59** may appear. Click OK to dismiss the dialog, then follow the instructions on the next page to set QuickTime Connection Speed preferences.

Figure 57 A QuickTime Player window.

Figure 58 When you launch QuickTime Player, Apple tries to sell you QuickTime Pro.

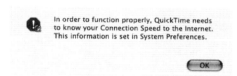

Figure 59 This dialog appears the first time you launch QuickTime Player.

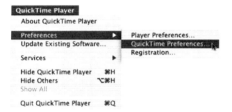

Figure 60 You can manually open the Quick-Time preferences pane by choosing QuickTime Preferences from the Preferences submenu under the QuickTime Player menu.

Figure 61 The Connection tab of the QuickTime preferences pane.

Figure 62 Connection Speed options.

To set connection speed options

1. If a dialog like the one in **Figure 59** appears when you launch QuickTime, click OK.

   or

   Choose QuickTime Player > Preferences > QuickTime Preferences (**Figure 60**).

2. Mac OS X opens System Preferences and displays the QuickTime Preferences pane. If necessary, click the Connection tab to display its options (**Figure 61**).

3. Choose a speed from the Connection Speed pop-up menu (**Figure 62**).

4. Choose System Preferences > Quit System Preferences, or press ⌘Q.

✔ Tips

- The dialog in **Figure 59** automatically appears just the first time you launch QuickTime Player.

- Once set, you do not need to change the QuickTime connection speed options unless you change your Internet connection speed—for example, switch from dialup to DSL.

- System Preferences, including QuickTime preferences, are covered in detail in *Mac OS X Advanced: Visual QuickPro Guide*.

To open a QuickTime movie file

Double-click the QuickTime movie file icon (**Figure 63**).

If QuickTime Player is not already running, it launches. The movie's first frame appears in a window (**Figure 64**).

✔ Tip

■ You can also open a QuickTime movie file by using the Open Movie in New Player command on QuickTime Player's File menu (**Figure 65**). The Open dialog is covered in **Chapter 5**.

To control movie play

You can click buttons and use controls in the QuickTime Player window (**Figure 64**) to control movie play:

◆ **Go To Start** displays the first movie frame.

◆ **Fast Rewind** plays the movie backward quickly, with sound.

◆ **Play** starts playing the movie. When the movie is playing, the Play button turns to a **Pause** button, which pauses movie play.

◆ **Fast Forward** plays the movie forward quickly, with sound.

◆ **Go To End** displays the last movie frame.

◆ **Time line** tracks movie progress. By dragging the slider, you can scroll through the movie without sound.

◆ **Volume** changes movie volume; drag the slider left or right.

To specify movie size

Select a size option from the Movie menu (**Figure 66**). The size of the movie's window changes accordingly.

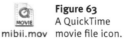

Figure 63
A QuickTime
mibii.mov movie file icon.

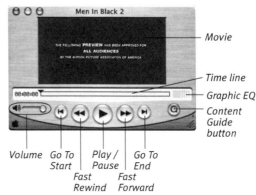

Movie

Time line

Graphic EQ

Content Guide button

Volume | Go To Start | Play / Pause | Go To End

Fast Rewind | Fast Forward

Figure 64 The first frame of the movie appears in a QuickTime Player window.

Figure 65 QuickTime Player's File menu. There are more menu commands in QuickTime Pro.

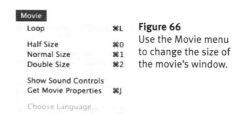

Figure 66
Use the Movie menu to change the size of the movie's window.

Figure 67 Use this dialog to enter the Internet address for the movie you want to watch.

Figure 68 QuickTime's Content Guide, with the What's On button selected.

Figure 69 Clicking the More What's On link displays this Web page.

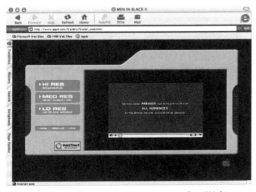

Figure 70 QuickTime content can appear in a Web browser window, like this.

To open QuickTime content on the Internet

1. If necessary, connect to the Internet.

Then:

2. Choose File > Open URL in New Player (**Figure 65**).

3. Enter the URL for the movie you want to watch in the Open URL dialog that appears (**Figure 67**), and click OK. Your computer downloads the movie you specified and displays it in a QuickTime Player window.

or

2. Click the Content Guide button in a QuickTime window to display the Quick-Time Content Guide (**Figure 68**).

3. Click one of the Content Guide buttons.

4. A graphic for the featured content appears in the right side of the window (**Figure 68**). Click the More link below it.

5. QuickTime launches your Web browser and opens the Web page for the content category you selected in step 3 (**Figure 69**).Use the Web browser to locate and display content that interests you. Quick-Time movies appear within the browser window (**Figure 70**) or within a Quick-Time Player window.

✔ Tips

- QuickTime content available on the Web includes *streaming* audio or video *channels*. This requires a constant connection to the Internet while content is downloaded to your computer. Streaming content continues downloading until you close its window.

- I tell you more about the Internet and using Web browser software in **Chapter 9**.

Stickies

Stickies is an application that displays computerized "sticky notes" that you can use to place reminders on your screen.

To launch Stickies

Double-click the Stickies icon in the Applications folder (**Figure 1**).

or

1. Click the Stickies icon in the Applications folder (**Figure 1**) to select it.

2. Choose File > Open, or press ⌃⌘O.

The default Stickies windows appear (**Figure 71**).

✔ Tips

■ Read the text in the default Stickies windows (**Figure 71**) to learn more about Stickies and how the Mac OS X version differs from previous versions.

■ Sticky notes remain on the desktop until you quit Stickies.

■ When you quit Stickies, all notes are automatically saved to disk and will reappear the next time you launch Stickies.

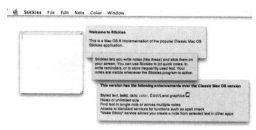

Figure 71 The default windows that appear when you first launch Stickies tell you a little about the program.

Figure 72
Stickies' File
menu.

To create a sticky note
To create a sticky note

1. Choose File > New Note (**Figure 72**) or press ⌃⌘N to display a blank new note (**Figure 73**).

2. Type the text that you want to include in the note (**Figure 74**).

✔ Tip

■ You can use options under the Color and Note menus (**Figures 75** and **76**) to change the appearance of notes or note text. Common text formatting options are covered in **Chapter 7**.

To print sticky notes

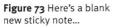

Figure 73 Here's a blank new sticky note...

Figure 74 ...and here's the same note with a reminder typed in.

1. To print just one sticky note, click it to activate it and then choose File > Print Active Note (**Figure 72**) or press ⌃⌘P.

   or

   To print all sticky notes, choose File > Print All Notes (**Figure 72**).

2. Use the Print dialog that appears to set options for printing and click the Print button (**Figure 77**).

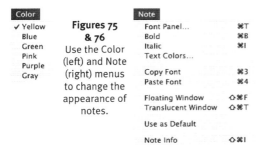

Figures 75 & 76 Use the Color (left) and Note (right) menus to change the appearance of notes.

✔ Tip

■ **Chapter 8** covers the Print dialog and printing.

Figure 77 The Print dialog.

To close a sticky note

1. Click the close box for the sticky note you want to close.

   or

   Activate the sticky note you want to close and choose File > Close (**Figure 72**) or press ⌃ ⌘ W.

2. A Close dialog like the one in **Figure 78** may appear.

   ▲ Don't Save closes the note without saving its contents.

   ▲ Cancel leaves the note open.

   ▲ Save displays the Export dialog (**Figure 79**), which you can use to save the note as plain or formatted text in a file on disk. Enter a name and select a disk location for the note's contents, then choose a file format and click Save.

✔ Tip

■ Once a sticky note has been saved to disk, it can be opened and edited with TextEdit or any other program capable of opening text files.

Figure 78 The Close dialog asks if you want to save note contents.

Figure 79 Use the Export dialog to save a note as plain or formatted text in a file on disk.

Using TextEdit

Figure 1
The TextEdit application icon.

TextEdit

Figure 2
A TextEdit document's icon.

Letter.rtf

TextEdit

TextEdit (**Figure 1**), which was updated for Mac OS X 10.2, is a basic text editing application that comes with Mac OS. As its name implies, TextEdit lets you create, open, edit, and print text documents (**Figure 2**), including the "Read Me" files that come with many applications.

This chapter explains how to use TextEdit to create, edit, format, open, and save documents.

✔ Tips

- Although TextEdit offers many of the basic features found in a word processing application, it falls far short of the feature list of word processors such as Microsoft Word and the word processing components of integrated software such as AppleWorks.

- If you're new to computers, don't skip this chapter. It not only explains how to use TextEdit, but it provides instructions for basic text editing skills—like text entry and the Copy, Cut, and Paste commands —as well as text formatting, that you'll use in all Mac OS-compatible applications.

Launching & Quitting TextEdit

Like any other application, you must launch TextEdit before you can use it. This loads it into your computer's memory so your computer can work with it.

To launch TextEdit

Double-click the TextEdit application icon in the Applications folder window (**Figure 3**).

or

1. Select the TextEdit application icon in the Applications folder window (**Figure 3**).

2. Choose File > Open, or press ⌃ ⌘ O.

   TextEdit launches. An untitled document window appears (**Figure 4**).

✔ Tip

■ As illustrated in **Figure 4**, the TextEdit document window has the same standard window parts found in Finder windows. I tell you how to use Finder windows in **Chapter 2**; TextEdit and other application windows work the same way.

Figure 3 You can find TextEdit in the Applications folder.

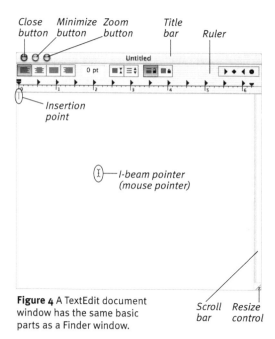

Figure 4 A TextEdit document window has the same basic parts as a Finder window.

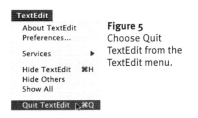

Figure 5
Choose Quit
TextEdit from the
TextEdit menu.

Figure 6 A dialog sheet like this appears when you quit TextEdit with an unsaved document open.

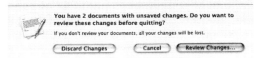

Figure 7 A dialog like this appears when you quit TextEdit with multiple unsaved documents open.

To quit TextEdit

1. Choose TextEdit > Quit TextEdit (**Figure 5**), or press ⌃ ⌘ Q.

2. If a single unsaved document is open, a dialog sheet like the one in **Figure 6** appears, attached to the document window.

   ▲ Click Don't Save to quit without saving the document.

   ▲ Click Cancel or press [Esc] to return to the application without quitting.

   ▲ Click Save or press [Return] or [Enter] to save the document.

   or

   If multiple unsaved documents are open, a dialog like the one in **Figure 7** appears:

   ▲ Click Discard Changes to quit TextEdit without saving any of the documents.

   ▲ Click Cancel or press [Esc] to return to the application without quitting.

   ▲ Click Review Changes or press [Return] or [Enter] to view each unsaved document with a dialog like the one in **Figure 6** to decide whether you want to save it.

   TextEdit closes all windows and quits.

✔ Tip

■ You learn more about saving TextEdit documents later in this chapter.

Entering & Editing Text

You enter text into a TextEdit document by typing it in. Don't worry about making mistakes; you can fix them as you type or when you're finished. This section tells you how.

✔ Tip

■ The text entry and editing techniques covered in this section work exactly the same in most word processors, as well as many other Mac OS applications.

To enter text

Type the text you want to enter. It appears at the blinking insertion point (**Figure 8**).

✔ Tips

■ It is not necessary to press ⎛Return⎞ at the end of a line. When the text you type reaches the end of the line, it automatically begins a new line. This is called *word wrap* and is a feature of all word processors. By default, in TextEdit, word wrap is determined by the width of the document window.

■ The insertion point moves as you type.

■ To correct an error as you type, press ⎛Delete⎞. This key deletes the character to the left of the insertion point.

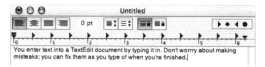

Figure 8 The text you type appears at the blinking insertion point.

ENTERING TEXT

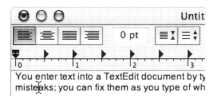

Figure 9 Position the mouse pointer...

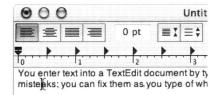

Figure 10 ...and click to move the insertion point.

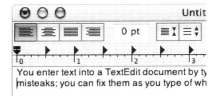

Figure 11 Position the insertion point...

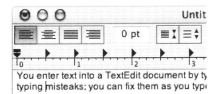

Figure 12 ...and type the text that you want to appear.

To move the insertion point

Press ⬅, ➡, ⬆, or ⬇ to move the insertion point left, right, up, or down one character or line at a time.

or

1. Position the mouse pointer, which looks like an I-beam pointer, where you want the insertion point to appear (**Figure 9**).

2. Click the mouse button once. The insertion point appears at the mouse pointer (**Figure 10**).

✔ Tips

■ Since the text you type appears at the insertion point, it's a good idea to know where the insertion point is *before* you start typing.

■ When moving the insertion point with the mouse, you must click to complete the move. If you simply point with the I-beam pointer, the insertion point will stay right where it is (**Figure 9**).

To insert text

1. Position the insertion point where you want the text to appear (**Figure 11**).

2. Type the text that you want to insert. The text is inserted at the insertion point (**Figure 12**).

✔ Tip

■ Word wrap changes automatically to accommodate inserted text.

MOVING THE INSERTION POINT, INSERTING TEXT

To select text by dragging

Drag the I-beam pointer over the text you want to select (**Figure 13**).

To select text with Shift-click

1. Position the insertion point at the beginning of the text you want to select (**Figure 14**).

2. Hold down (Shift) and click at the end of the text you want to select. All text between the insertion point's original position and where you clicked becomes selected (**Figure 15**).

✔ Tip

■ This is a good way to select large blocks of text. After positioning the insertion point as instructed in step 1, use the scroll bars to scroll to the end of the text you want to select. Then Shift-click as instructed in step 2 to make the selection.

To select a single word

Double-click the word (**Figure 16**).

✔ Tip

■ In some applications, such as Microsoft Word, double-clicking a word also selects the space after the word.

To select all document contents

Choose Edit > Select All (**Figure 17**), or press (⌃ ⌘ A).

✔ Tip

■ There are other selection techniques in TextEdit and other applications. The techniques on this page work in every application.

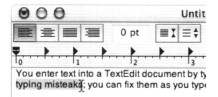

Figure 13 Drag the I-beam pointer over the text that you want to select.

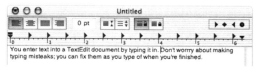

Figure 14 Position the insertion point at the beginning of the text you want to select.

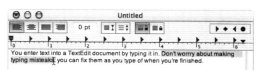

Figure 15 Hold down (Shift) and click at the end of the text you want to select.

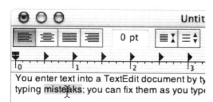

Figure 16 Double-click the word that you want to select.

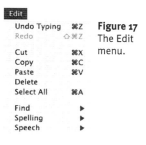

Figure 17 The Edit menu.

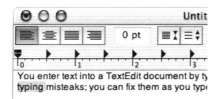

Figure 18 Select the text that you want to delete.

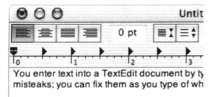

Figure 19 When you press Delete, the selected text disappears.

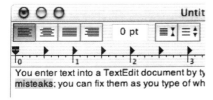

Figure 20 Select the text that you want to replace.

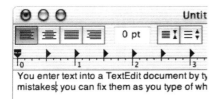

Figure 21 The text you type replaces the selected text.

To delete text

1. Select the text that you want to delete (**Figure 18**).

2. Press Delete or Del. The selected text disappears (**Figure 19**).

✔ Tip

- You can delete a character to the left of the insertion point by pressing Delete. You can delete a character to the right of the insertion point by pressing Del.

To replace text

1. Select the text that you want to replace (**Figure 20**).

2. Type the new text. The selected text is replaced by what you type (**Figure 21**).

DELETING & REPLACING TEXT

Basic Text Formatting

TextEdit also offers formatting features that you can use to change the appearance of text.

✔ Tip

- This chapter covers the most commonly used formatting options in TextEdit. Explore the other options on your own.

To apply font formatting

1. Select the text to which you want to apply a different font or font size (**Figure 22**).

2. Choose Format > Font > Show Fonts (**Figure 23**), or press ⌘⌘T to display the Fonts panel (**Figure 24**).

3. To change the font, select a font family from the Family list. If the family contains more than one typeface, you can also make a selection from the Typeface list.

4. To change the character size, either enter a new size in the Sizes text entry field or select one of the sizes in the Sizes list.

5. Preview your changes in the document window behind the Fonts panel (**Figure 25**). Make additional changes as desired.

6. Repeat steps 1 and 3 through 5 for any other text you want to apply formatting to.

7. When you are finished using the Fonts panel, close it by clicking its close button.

✔ Tips

- Generally speaking, a *font* is a style of typeface.

- The Font panel's Family list displays all fonts that are properly installed in your System. This list may differ from the one illustrated in **Figure 24**.

- The larger the text size, the less text appears onscreen or on a printed page.

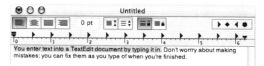

Figure 22 Select the text you want to format.

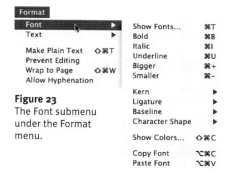

Figure 23
The Font submenu under the Format menu.

Figure 24 The Fonts panel.

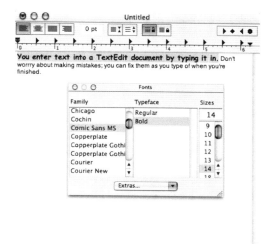

Figure 25 The changes you make in the Font panel are immediately applied to the selected text.

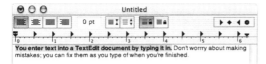

Figure 26 The style you chose is applied.

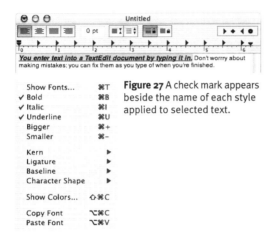

Figure 27 A check mark appears beside the name of each style applied to selected text.

To apply a different font style

1. Select the text you want to apply a different style to (**Figure 22**).

2. Choose a style command from the Font submenu under the Format menu (**Figure 23**) or press its keyboard equivalent. The style options are:

   ▲ **Bold**, or ⌃ ⌘ B, makes text characters appear thicker or darker.

   ▲ **Italic**, or ⌃ ⌘ I, makes text appear slanted.

   ▲ **Underline**, or ⌃ ⌘ U, puts a single underline under text.

   The style you chose is applied to the selected text (**Figure 26**).

✔ Tips

- You can apply more than one style to text (**Figure 27**). Simply select each style you want to apply.

- A check mark appears on the Font submenu beside each style applied to a selection (**Figure 27**).

- To remove an applied style, choose it from the Font submenu again.

- Some styles are automatically applied when you select a specific typeface for a font family in the Fonts panel (**Figure 25**). Similarly, if you select a typeface in the Fonts panel, certain style options become unavailable for characters with that typeface applied. For example, if you apply Comic Sans MS Bold font, as shown in **Figure 25**, the Italic option is not available on the Font submenu for that text.

APPLYING FONT STYLES

To change paragraph alignment

1. Select the paragraph(s) for which you want to change alignment (**Figure 28**).

2. Choose an alignment option from the Text submenu under the Format menu (**Figure 29**), or press its keyboard equivalent, or click an alignment button on the ruler (**Figure 30**). The alignment options are:

   ▲ **Align Left**, or ⌘{, aligns text characters against the left side of the window.

   ▲ **Center** centers text characters between the left and right side of the window (**Figure 31**).

   ▲ **Justify** adjusts the spacing between words so all lines of the paragraph except the last fill the space between the left and right sides of the window.

   ▲ **Align Right**, or ⌘}, aligns text characters against the right side of the window.

   The alignment option you chose is applied to the selected paragraph(s) (**Figure 31**).

✓ Tip

■ Alignment options affect all lines in a paragraph.

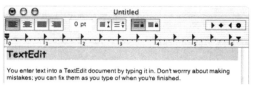

Figure 28 Select the paragraph you want to change the alignment of.

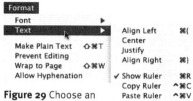

Figure 29 Choose an option from the Text submenu under the Format menu.

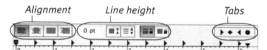

Figure 30 You can use buttons on the ruler to set alignment, line height, and tabs. Point to a ruler button to learn its name and function.

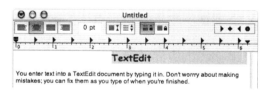

Figure 31 The alignment option you chose is applied.

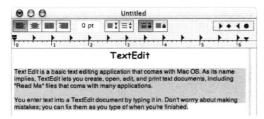

Figure 32 Select the paragraph(s) for which you want to change line height.

Figure 33 In this example, line height is set to 18, which is 6 points more than the 12-point font size.

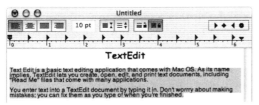

Figure 34 In this example, line height is set to 10, which is 2 points less than the 12-point font size. Because the Fixed Line Height button is selected, the lines are forced to a 10-point spacing, thus squishing them together.

To set line height

1. Select the paragraph(s) for which you want to change line height (**Figure 32**).

2. Enter a value in the Line Height box on the ruler (**Figure 30**) to specify an exact line height.

   or

   Click the Decrease Line Height or Increase Line Height button on the ruler (**Figure 30**) to decrease or increase the amount of space between lines.

   The settings take effect immediately (**Figure 33**).

✔ Tips

- Two other line height buttons on the ruler enable you to fine-tune line height settings:

  ▲ **Flexible Line Height** makes it possible for line height to change based on the size of the largest font character in the line.

  ▲ **Fixed Line Height** forces line height to adhere to your settings, no matter how large font characters in the line are (**Figure 34**).

- Changes in line height cannot be seen unless the value is greater than the largest font character or the Fixed Line Height option is selected.

- To reset line height, enter 0 (zero) in the Line Height box on the Ruler (**Figure 30**).

SETTING LINE HEIGHT

To set tab stops

Add and remove tab stops from the bottom half of the ruler as follows:

◆ To remove a tab stop, drag it from the ruler into the document window (**Figure 35**). When you release the mouse button, the tab is removed.

◆ To add a tab stop, drag one of the tab icons on the ruler—left, center, right, or decimal—into position on the ruler (**Figure 36**). When you release the mouse button, the tab is placed.

✔ Tips

■ A tab stop is the position the insertion point moves to when you press Tab.

■ Tab settings affect entire paragraphs. When you press Return to begin a new paragraph, the tab stops you set for the current paragraph are carried forward.

To use tab stops

1. Add and remove tab stops as instructed above.

2. Position the insertion point at the beginning of the paragraph for which tab stops are set (**Figure 37**).

3. If desired, enter text at the beginning of the line (**Figure 38**).

4. Press Tab.

5. Enter text at the tab stop (**Figure 39**).

6. Repeat steps 4 and 5 until you have entered text as desired at all tab stops. **Figure 40** shows an example.

7. Press Return.

8. Repeat steps 2 through 7 for each paragraph you want to use the tab stops for. **Figure 41** shows a completed table using tab stops.

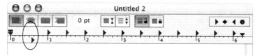

Figure 35 Drag the tab off the ruler. (The mouse pointer disappears as you do this, so it isn't easy to illustrate!)

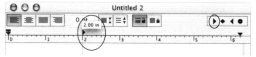

Figure 36 Drag one of the tab icons from the top half of the ruler into position on the ruler. Although the mouse pointer disappears as you drag, a tiny box with the tab location in it appears as you drag.

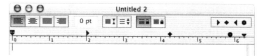

Figure 37 Start by setting tabs and positioning the insertion point at the beginning of the line.

Figure 38 If desired, enter text at the beginning of the line.

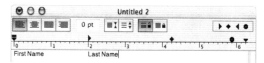

Figure 39 Press Tab and enter text at the first tab stop.

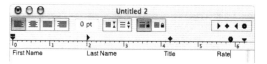

Figure 40 The first line of a table created with tabs.

Figure 41 A completed table. Note how the text lines up with each type of tab stop.

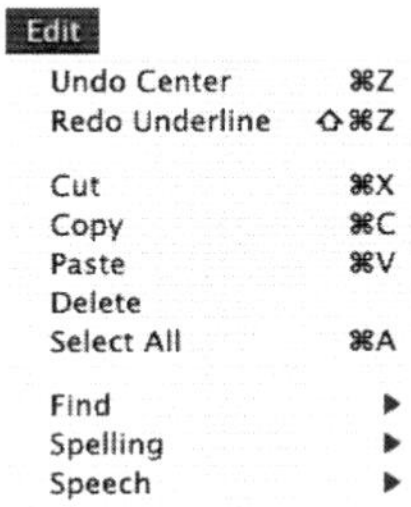

Edit	
Undo Center	⌘Z
Redo Underline	⇧⌘Z
Cut	⌘X
Copy	⌘C
Paste	⌘V
Delete	
Select All	⌘A
Find	▸
Spelling	▸
Speech	▸

Figure 42
The Edit menu with Undo and Redo commands displayed. If one of these commands were not available, it would be gray.

Undoing & Redoing Actions

The Undo command enables you to reverse your last action, thus offering an easy way to fix errors immediately after you make them. The Redo command, which is available only when your last action was to use the Undo command, reverses the undo action.

✔ Tips

- The Undo and Redo commands are available in most applications and can be found at the top of the Edit menu.

- Unlike most applications, TextEdit supports multiple levels of undo (and redo). That means you can undo (or redo) several actions, in the reverse order that they were performed (or undone).

- The exact wording of the Undo (and Redo) command depends on what was last done (or undone). For example, if the last thing you did was center text in a paragraph, the Undo command will be Undo Center (**Figure 42**).

To undo the last action

Choose Edit > Undo (**Figure 42**), or press ⌘Z. The last thing you did is undone.

✔ Tip

- To undo multiple actions, choose Edit > Undo repeatedly.

To redo an action

After using the Undo command, choose Edit > Redo (**Figure 42**), or press Shift ⌘Z. The last thing you undid is redone.

✔ Tip

- To redo multiple actions, choose Edit > Redo repeatedly.

Copy, Cut, & Paste

The Copy, Cut, and Paste commands enable you to duplicate or move document contents. Text that is copied or cut is placed on the Clipboard, where it can be viewed if desired and pasted into a document.

✔ Tip

- Almost all Mac OS-compatible applications include the Copy, Cut, and Paste commands on the Edit menu. These commands work very much the same in all applications.

To copy text

1. Select the text that you want to copy (**Figure 43**).

2. Choose Edit > Copy (**Figure 44**), or press ⌘ C.

   The text is copied to the Clipboard so it can be pasted elsewhere. The original remains in the document.

To cut text

1. Select the text that you want to cut (**Figure 43**).

2. Choose Edit > Cut (**Figure 44**), or press ⌘ X.

   The text is copied to the Clipboard so it can be pasted elsewhere. The original is removed from the document.

To paste Clipboard contents

1. Position the insertion point where you want the Clipboard contents to appear (**Figure 45**).

2. Choose Edit > Paste (**Figure 44**), or press ⌘ V.

   The Clipboard's contents are pasted into the document (**Figure 46**).

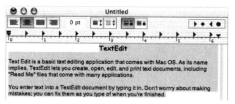

Figure 43 Select the text you want to copy or cut.

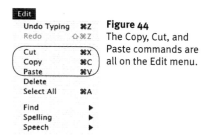

Figure 44 The Copy, Cut, and Paste commands are all on the Edit menu.

Figure 45 Position the insertion point where you want the contents of the Clipboard to appear.

Figure 46 The contents of the Clipboard are pasted into the document.

✔ Tip

- The Clipboard contains only the last item that was copied or cut. Using the Paste command, therefore, pastes in the most recently cut or copied selection.

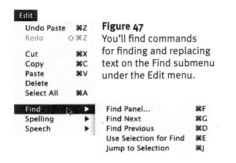

Figure 47
You'll find commands for finding and replacing text on the Find submenu under the Edit menu.

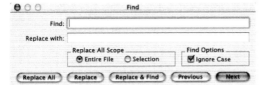

Figure 48 The Find panel.

Find & Replace

TextEdit's find and replace features enable you to quickly locate or replace occurrences of text strings in your document.

✔ Tip

■ Most word processing and page layout applications include find and replace features. Although these features are somewhat limited in TextEdit, full-featured applications such as Microsoft Word and Adobe InDesign enable you to search for text, formatting, and other document elements as well as plain text.

To find text

1. Choose Edit > Find > Find Panel (**Figure 47**), or press ⌃⌘F. The Find panel appears (**Figure 48**).

2. Enter the text that you want to find in the Find field.

3. To perform a case-sensitive search, turn off the Ignore Case check box in the Find Options area. With this check box turned off, *word* will not match *Word*.

4. Click Next, or press Return or Enter. If the text you entered in the Find field is found, it is highlighted in the document.

✔ Tip

■ To find subsequent or previous occurrences of the Find field entry, choose Edit > Find > Find Next or Edit > Find > Find Previous (**Figure 47**) or press ⌃⌘G or ⌃⌘D.

FINDING TEXT

To replace text

1. Choose Edit > Find > Find Panel (**Figure 47**), or press ⌃⌘F. The Find panel appears (**Figure 48**).

2. Enter the text that you want to replace in the Find field.

3. Enter the replacement text in the Replace with field (**Figure 49**).

4. If necessary, select one of the options in the Replace All Scope area:

   ▲ **Entire File** searches the entire file.

   ▲ **Selection** searches only selected text.

5. To perform a case-sensitive search, turn off the Ignore Case check box in the Find Options area. With this check box turned off, *word* will not match *Word*.

6. Click the buttons at the bottom of the Find pane to find and replace text:

   ▲ **Replace All** replaces all occurrences of the Find word with the Replace word.

   ▲ **Replace** replaces the currently selected occurrence of the Find word with the Replace word.

   ▲ **Replace & Find** replaces the currently selected occurrence of the Find word with the Replace word and then selects the next occurrence of the Find word.

   ▲ **Previous** selects the previous occurrence of the Find word.

   ▲ **Next** selects the next occurrence of the Find word.

7. When you're finished replacing text, click the Find panel's close button to dismiss it.

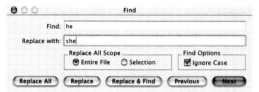

Figure 49 You can set up the Find panel to find and replace text.

✖ Warning!

■ Use the Replace All button with care! It will not give you an opportunity to preview and approve any of the replacements it makes.

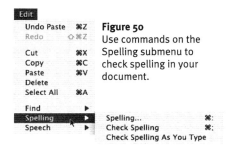

Figure 50
Use commands on the Spelling submenu to check spelling in your document.

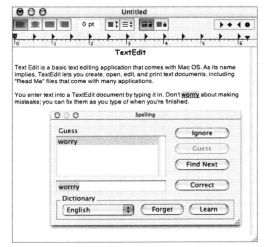

Figure 51 Use the Spelling panel to resolve possible misspelled words.

Checking Spelling

TextEdit includes a spelling checker that you can use to manually or automatically check spelling in your document.

To manually check spelling

1. Choose Edit > Spelling > Spelling (**Figure 50**) or press Shift ⌃ ⌘ ; to display the spelling panel and start the spelling check.

   TextEdit selects and underlines the first possible misspelled word it finds. The word appears in a field in the Spelling panel and any suggested corrections appear in the Guess list (**Figure 51**).

2. You have several options:
   ▲ To replace the word with a guess, select the replacement word and click Correct.
   ▲ To enter a new spelling for the word, enter it in the field where the incorrect spelling appears and click Correct.
   ▲ To ignore the word, click Ignore.
   ▲ To skip the word and continue checking, click Find Next.
   ▲ To add the word to TextEdit's dictionary, click Learn. TextEdit will never stop at that word again in any document.

3. Repeat step 2 for each word that TextEdit identifies as a possible misspelling.

4. When you're finished checking spelling, click the Spelling panel's close button to dismiss it.

✔ Tip

■ You can use the Forget button in the Spelling dialog (**Figure 51**) to remove a word that you previously added to the dictionary. Select the Word in the Guess list, then click the Forget button. The word is removed.

MANUALLY CHECKING SPELLING

To check spelling as you type

1. Choose Edit > Spelling > Check Spelling As You Type (**Figure 50**).

   As you enter text into the document, TextEdit checks the spelling of each word. It places a dashed red underline under each word that isn't in its dictionary. (**Figure 52**).

2. Manually correct a misspelled word using standard text editing techniques covered near the beginning of this chapter.

   or

   Hold down [Control] and click on a misspelled word. Then choose a correct spelling from the contextual menu that appears (**Figure 53**). The misspelled word is replaced with the word you chose.

✔ Tips

- In Mac OS X 10.2, the Check Spelling As You Type option in TextEdit may automatically be enabled. To disable it, choose Edit > Spelling > Check Spelling As You Type.

- If you display a contextual menu as instructed in step 2 (**Figure 53**), you can also use the Ignore Spelling or Learn Spelling commands to ignore the underlined word or add it to the dictionary.

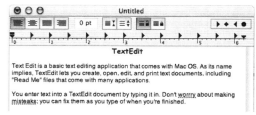

Figure 52 With automatic spelling check enabled, Text-Edit underlines possible misspelled words as you type.

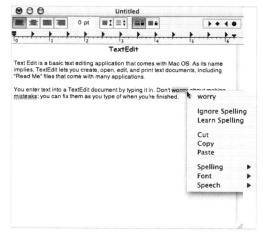

Figure 53 You can display a contextual menu that lists corrections and other options for an unknown word.

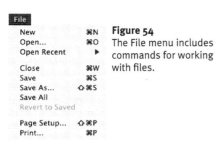

Figure 54
The File menu includes commands for working with files.

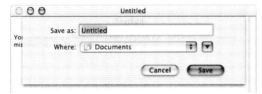

Figure 55 Use the Save As dialog to enter a name and select a location for saving a file.

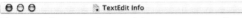

Figure 56 The name of a saved document appears in its title bar.

Saving & Opening Files

When you're finished working with a Text-Edit document, you may want to save it. You can then open it another time to review, edit, or print it.

To save a document for the first time

1. Choose File > Save (**Figure 54**), or press ⌃ ⌘ S.

   or

   Choose File > Save As (**Figure 54**), or press Shift ⌃ ⌘ S.

2. Use the Save As dialog sheet that appears (**Figure 55**) to enter a name and select a location for the file.

3. Click Save, or press Return or Enter.

   The document is saved with the name you entered in the location you specified. The name of the document appears on the document's title bar (**Figure 56**).

✔ Tips

■ I explain how to use the Save As dialog in **Chapter 5**.

■ There's only one difference between the Save and Save As commands:

  ▲ The Save command opens the Save As dialog only if the document has never been saved.

  ▲ The Save As command always opens the Save As dialog.

■ By default, TextEdit creates Rich Text Format (RTF) files and appends the *.rtf* extension to the files it saves. This extension does not appear unless the Always show file extensions option is enabled in Finder Preferences. I discuss Finder preferences in **Chapter 4**.

■ To save a TextEdit document as a plain text document (with a *.txt* extension), choose Format > Make Plain Text. Then follow steps 1 through 3 above. Keep in mind, however, that if you save a document as a plain text document, any formatting applied to document text will be lost.

To save changes to an existing document

Choose File > Save (**Figure 54**), or press
⌃ ⌘ S.

The document is saved. No dialog appears.

Figure 57 A bullet in the document window's close button...

✔ Tips

- TextEdit identifies a document with changes that have not been saved by displaying a bullet in the document window's close button (**Figure 57**) and to the left of the document's name in the Window menu (**Figure 58**).

- It's a good idea to save changes to a document frequently as you work with it. This helps prevent loss of data in the event of a system crash or power outage.

Window
Close Window
Zoom Window
Minimize Window   ⌘M
Bring All to Front
Mac OS Apps
• TextEdit Info

Figure 58
...or beside its name in the Window menu indicates that the document has unsaved changes.

To save an existing document with a new name or in a new location

1. Choose File > Save As (**Figure 54**).

2. Use the Save As dialog that appears (**Figure 55**) to enter a different name or select a different location (or both) for the file.

3. Click Save, or press Return or Enter.

   A copy of the document is saved with the name you entered in the location you specified. The new document name appears in the document's title bar. The original document remains untouched.

✔ Tip

- You can use the Save As command to create a new document based on an existing document—without overwriting the original document with your changes.

SAVING DOCUMENTS

Figure 59 Use the Open dialog to locate and open a file.

To open a document

1. Choose File > Open (**Figure 54**), or press ⌃ ⌘O.

2. Use the Open dialog that appears (**Figure 59**) to locate and select the document that you want to open.

3. Click Open, or press Return or Enter.

✔ Tip

■ I explain how to use the Open dialog in **Chapter 5**.

To close a document

1. Choose File > Close (**Figure 54**), or press ⌃ ⌘W.

2. If the document contains unsaved changes, a Close dialog like the one in **Figure 6** appears.

   ▲ Click Don't Save to close the document without saving it.

   ▲ Click Cancel or press Esc to return to the document without closing it.

   ▲ Click Save or press Return or Enter to save the document.

   The document closes.

Printing

Printing

On a Mac OS system, printing is handled by the operating system rather than the individual applications. You choose the Print command in the application that created the document you want to print. Mac OS steps in, displaying the Print dialog and telling the application how to send information to the printer. There are two main benefits to this:

◆ If you can print documents created with one application, you can probably print documents created with any application on your computer.

◆ The Page Setup and Print dialogs, which are generated by Mac OS, look very much the same in every application.

This chapter covers most aspects of printing on a computer running Mac OS X.

To print (an overview)

1. If necessary, add your printer to the Printer List.

2. Open the document that you want to print.

3. If desired, set options in the Page Setup dialog, and click OK.

4. Set options in the Print dialog, and click Print.

Printer Drivers

A *printer driver* is software that Mac OS uses to communicate with a specific kind of printer. It contains information about the printer and instructions for using it. You can't open and read a printer driver, but your computer can.

There are basically two kinds of printers:

◆ A **PostScript** printer uses PostScript technology developed by Adobe Systems. Inside the printer is a *PostScript interpreter*, which can process PostScript language commands to print high-quality text and graphics. Examples of PostScript printers include most Apple LaserWriter printers and Hewlett-Packard LaserJet printers.

◆ A **non-PostScript** printer relies on the computer to send it all of the instructions it needs for printing text and graphics. It cannot process PostScript commands. Examples of non-PostScript printers include Apple ImageWriters and Style-Writers, Hewlett-Packard DeskJet printers, and most Epson Stylus printers. Non-PostScript printers are generally more common for home and small business use, primarily because they are less expensive than PostScript printers. Their print quality is quite acceptable for most purposes.

A standard installation of Mac OS X installs many commonly used printer drivers. When you buy a printer, it should come with a CD that includes its printer driver software; if your computer does not recognize your printer, you'll need to install this software to use it.

✔ Tips

■ If you do not have a printer driver for your printer, you may not be able to print.

■ To install a printer driver, follow the instructions that came with its installer or installation disc.

■ If you need to install printer driver software for your printer, make sure it is Mac OS X compatible. If your printer did not come with Mac OS X compatible printer software, you may be able to get it from the printer manufacturer's Web site.

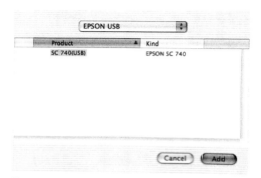

Figure 1 Print Center can be found in the Utilities folder inside the Applications folder.

Figure 2 The Printer List window with two printers.

Printers

Show Printer List

Make Default   ⌘D
Add Printer...
Delete Printer
Configure Printer
Show Info   ⌘I

Show Jobs   ⌘O
Stop Jobs

Figure 3
The Printers menu includes commands for working with the Printer List and printers.

Print Center

Print Center (**Figure 1**) is an application that enables you to manage printers and print jobs. It has two main components:

◆ **Printer List** window (**Figure 2**) lists all of the printers your computer "sees." Use this window to select and configure printers.

◆ **Printer Queue** window (**Figure 43** and **44**) lists all the print jobs sent to a specific printer. Use this window to check the status of and cancel print jobs, as discussed later in this chapter.

✔ Tip

■ Print Center replaces the Chooser and Desktop Printer Utility software that were used for the same functions in Mac OS 9.x and earlier. Desktop printers are not available in Mac OS X.

To open Print Center

1. Click the Applications icon in the toolbar of any Finder window to open the Applications folder.

2. Open the Utilities folder.

3. Open the Print Center application (**Figure 1**).

The Printer List window (**Figure 2**) should appear automatically. If it does not, follow the instructions below to display it.

✔ Tip

■ You can also open Print Center by choosing Edit Printer List from the Printer pop-up menu (**Figure 18**) in the Print dialog.

To display the Printer List window

Choose Printers > Show Printer List (**Figure 3**).

The Printer List window appears (**Figure 2**).

To add a printer

1. Choose Printers > Add Printer (**Figure 3**).

   or

   Click the Add Printer button in the Printer List window (**Figure 2**).

2. A dialog sheet appears. Choose an option from the top pop-up menu (**Figure 4**) to indicate the type of printer connection. The dialog sheet changes to offer appropriate options; **Figures 5** through **8** show examples.

3. If you chose AppleTalk, Directory Services, or Epson AppleTalk, choose a network option from the second pop-up menu. Then wait while Print Center looks for printers and displays a list of what it finds (**Figure 5**). Select the printer you want to add, and click Add.

   or

   If you chose IP Printing, enter an IP (Internet Protocol) address or domain name and set other options in the dialog (**Figure 6**). Then click Add.

   or

   If you chose USB, Epson Firewire, Epson USB, or Lexmark Inkjet Networking, Print Center displays a list of printers connected to the computer (**Figure 7**). Select the printer you want to add, and click Add.

   The printer appears in the Printer List window (**Figure 2**).

Figure 4
Use this pop-up menu to choose the type of printer connection.

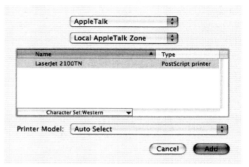

Figure 5 Options for adding an AppleTalk printer,...

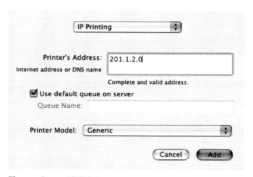

Figure 6 ...an IP Printer, ...

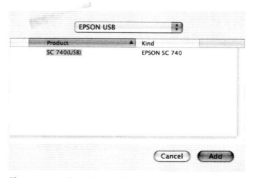

Figure 7 ...and an Epson USB printer.

ADDING PRINTERS

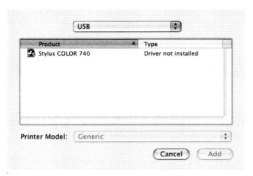

Figure 8 If your computer finds a printer but not the corresponding printer driver, it displays a question mark over the printer icon. In this example, I can still use the printer by choosing the Epson USB option, as shown in **Figure 7,** but if this wasn't an Epson printer, I'd have to install the driver to use it.

✔ Tips

■ You only have to add a printer if it does not already appear in the Printer List window (**Figure 2**). This needs to be done only once; Mac OS will remember all printers that you add.

■ In step 3, if you chose AppleTalk, Directory Services, or Epson AppleTalk and you're not sure what to select from the second pop-up menu, ask your network administrator.

■ If you're not sure how to set options for an LPR Printer using IP (**Figure 6**), ask your network administrator.

■ If your printer is properly connected but it does not appear in step 3 (**Figures 5** and **7**), or if a question mark appears over its icon (**Figure 8**), you may have to install printer driver software for it. Printer drivers are discussed earlier in this chapter.

To delete a printer

1. In the Printer List window (**Figure 2**), select the printer you want to delete.

2. Choose Printers > Delete Printer (**Figure 3**).

   or

   Click the Delete button in the Printer List window (**Figure 2**).

   The printer is removed from the list.

To set the default printer

1. In the Printer list window (**Figure 2**), select the printer you want to set as the default.

2. Choose Printers > Make Default (**Figure 3**), or press ⌃ ⌘ D.

   The name of the printer you selected becomes bold, indicating that it is the default printer.

✔ Tip

- The default printer is the one that is automatically chosen when you open the Print dialog.

Figure 9 Select the printer you want to configure.

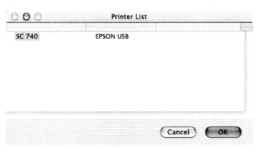

Figure 10 If a list of printers appears, select the one you want to configure, and click OK.

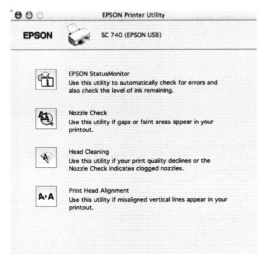

Figure 11 Here are the configuration options for an Epson Stylus 740i printer. Your configuration options may differ.

To configure a printer

1. Select the printer you want to configure in the Printer List window (**Figure 9**).

2. Click the Configure button.

   Print Center launches the configuration software for your printer. In my case, it launches Epson Printer Utility.

3. If a list of printers appears (**Figure 10**), select the printer you want to configure, and click OK.

4. Follow the instructions that appear in the configuration window to configure or maintain your printer. **Figure 11** shows an example of the options available for an Epson Stylus 740i printer in the Epson Printer Utility window.

5. When you are finished configuring the printer, close the configuration window.

✔ Tips

■ In step 2, if the Configure button in the Printer List window is gray or faded, the printer cannot be configured through Print Center.

■ It's not possible to show all configuration options for all printers. The instructions and illustrations here should be enough to get you started with your printer. Consult the manual that came with your printer for more information.

CONFIGURING PRINTERS

The Page Setup Dialog

The Page Setup dialog lets you set page attributes prior to printing, including the printer the document should be formatted for, paper size, orientation, and scale.

To set Page Attributes

1. Choose File > Page Setup (**Figures 12a**, **12b**, and **12c**) to display the Page Setup dialog sheet (**Figure 13**).

2. If necessary, choose Page Attributes from the Settings pop-up menu (**Figure 14**).

3. If necessary, select the correct printer from the Format for pop-up menu (**Figure 15**).

4. Select a paper size from the Paper Size pop-up menu (**Figure 16**).

5. Select an Orientation option by clicking it.

6. Enter a scaling percentage in the Scale field.

7. Click OK to save your settings and dismiss the Page Setup dialog.

✔ Tips

- The Format for pop-up menu should list all of the printers that appear in the Print Center's Printer List window (**Figure 2**).

- Options in each of the above steps vary depending on the printer selected from the Format for pop-up menu. Additional options may be available for your printer; check the documentation that came with the printer for details.

Figures 12a, 12b, & 12c
The Page Setup and Print commands appear on most File menus, including Text-Edit (top left), Preview (top right), and Internet Explorer (bottom left).

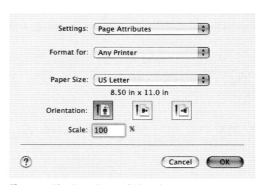

Figure 13 The Page Setup dialog sheet.

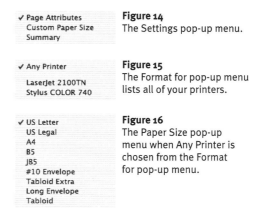

Figure 14
The Settings pop-up menu.

Figure 15
The Format for pop-up menu lists all of your printers.

Figure 16
The Paper Size pop-up menu when Any Printer is chosen from the Format for pop-up menu.

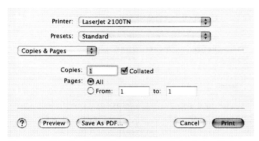

Figure 17 The Copies & Pages pane of the Print dialog.

✓ LaserJet 2100TN
Stylus COLOR 740

Edit Printer List...

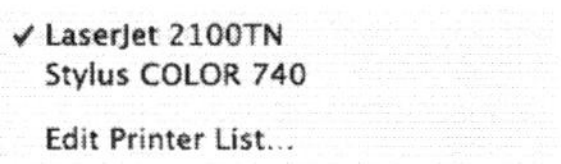

Figure 18
The Printer
pop-up menu.

The Print Dialog

The Print dialog enables you to set printing options and send the print job to the printer. Like the Page Setup dialog, the Print dialog is a standard dialog, but two things can cause its appearance and options to vary:

◆ Print options vary depending on the selected printer.

◆ Additional options may be offered by specific applications.

This section explains how to set the options available for most printers and applications.

✔ Tips

■ If your Print dialog includes options that are not covered here, consult the printer's documentation.

■ For information about using Print options specific to an application, consult the application's documentation.

To open the Print dialog

Choose File > Print (**Figures 12a**, **12b**, and **12c**), or press ⌃ ⌘ P.

The Copies & Pages pane of the Print dialog appears (**Figure 17**).

To select a printer

In the Print dialog (**Figure 17**) choose a printer from the Printer pop-up menu (**Figure 18**).

✔ Tips

■ The Printer pop-up menu (**Figure 18**) includes all printers that appear in Print Center's Printer List window (**Figure 2**).

■ Choosing Edit Printer List from the Printer pop-up menu (**Figure 18**) opens Print Center and displays its Printer List window so you can add a printer. Adding printers is covered earlier in this chapter.

THE PRINT DIALOG

To set Copies & Pages options

1. In the Print dialog, choose Copies & Pages from the third pop-up menu (**Figure 19a** or **19b**) to display Copies & Pages options (**Figure 17**).

2. In the Copies field, enter the number of copies of the document to print.

3. To collate multiple copies, turn on the Collated check box.

4. In the Pages area, select either the All radio button to print all pages or enter values in the From and To fields to print specific pages.

To set Layout options

1. In the Print dialog, choose Layout from the third pop-up menu (**Figure 19a** or **19b**) to display Layout options (**Figure 20**).

2. To set the number of pages that should appear on each sheet of paper, choose an option from the Pages per Sheet pop-up menu (**Figure 21**). The preview area of the dialog changes accordingly (**Figure 22**).

3. To indicate the order in which multiple pages should print on each sheet of paper, select a Layout Direction option. The preview area of the dialog changes accordingly (**Figure 22**).

4. To place a border around each page, choose an option from the Border pop-up menu (**Figure 23**).

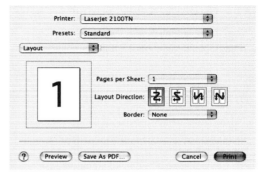

```
✓ Copies & Pages        ✓ Copies & Pages
  Layout                   Layout
  Output Options           Output Options
  Error Handling           Print Settings
  Paper Feed               Color Management
  Image Quality            Summary
  Printer Features
  Summary
```

Figures 19a & 19b The pop-up menu beneath the Presets pop-up menu offers different options depending on the printer that is selected. The menu on the left is for a Hewlett-Packard LaserJet printer connected via network and the menu on the right is for an Epson Stylus Color printer connected directly to the computer via USB. This menu may also include an option that enables you to set printing options that are specific to the application from which you are printing—for example, a Microsoft Word option would enable you to set Word-specific options.

Figure 20 The Layout pane of the Print dialog.

```
✓ 1
  2
  4
  6
  9
  16
```

Figure 21
The Pages per Sheet pop-up menu.

Figure 22
The Preview area indicates the number of pages to be printed per sheet, as well as the page order.

```
1  2  3
4  5  6
```

```
✓ None

  Single hairline
  Single thin line

  Double hairline
  Double thin line
```

Figure 23
The Border pop-up menu.

SETTING COPIES, PAGES, & LAYOUT OPTIONS

Figure 24 The Output Options pane of the Print dialog.

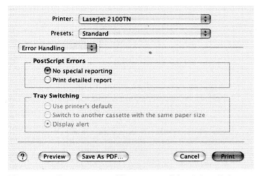

Figure 25 The Error Handling pane of the Print dialog.

To set Output options

1. In the Print dialog, choose Output Options from the third pop-up menu (**Figure 19a** or **19b**) to display the Output Options pane (**Figure 24**).

2. To save the document as a file (instead of printing it), turn on the Save as File check box, then choose an option from the Format pop-up menu:

   ▲ **PDF** creates a portable document format (PDF) file that can be read with Preview on Mac OS X or Adobe Acrobat Reader on any computer.

   ▲ **PostScript** writes PostScript language code to a file that can then be downloaded to and interpreted by a PostScript printer or imagesetter.

✔ Tip

■ When you turn on the Save as File check box, the Print button in the Print dialog turns into a Save button.

To set Error Handling options

1. In the Print dialog, choose Error Handling from the third pop-up menu (**Figure 19a**) to display Error Handling options (**Figure 25**).

2. To specify how the printer should report PostScript errors, select one of the PostScript Errors radio buttons.

3. To specify how the printer should handle an out-of-paper situation for a multiple-tray printer, select one of the Tray Switching radio buttons.

✔ Tips

■ These options are only available for PostScript printers.

■ Tray switching options are only available for printers with multiple paper trays.

To set Paper Feed options

1. In the Print dialog, choose Paper Feed from the third pop-up menu (**Figure 19a**) to display Paper Feed options (**Figure 26**).

2. To specify how paper trays should be used for paper feed, select one of the radio buttons.

3. To specify which paper tray(s) should be used for paper feed, choose options from the pop-up menu(s) (**Figure 27**).

✔ Tip

■ The options offered in the Paper Feed pane of the Print dialog (**Figure 26**) vary depending on your printer. The options here are for an HP LaserJet 2100TN printer.

To set Image Quality options

1. In the Print dialog, choose Image Quality from the third pop-up menu (**Figure 19a**) to display Image Quality options (**Figure 28**).

2. Use the pop-up menus to set image quality options.

✔ Tips

■ The options offered in the Image Quality pane of the Print dialog (**Figure 28**) vary depending on your printer. The options here are for an HP LaserJet 2100TN printer.

■ To get more information about image quality options offered by your printer, consult the manual that came with your printer.

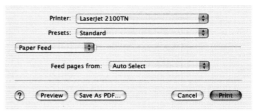

Figure 26 The Paper Feed pane of the Print dialog.

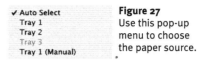

Figure 27
Use this pop-up menu to choose the paper source.

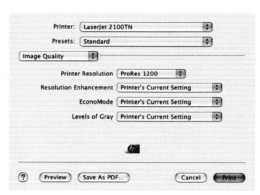

Figure 28 The Image Quality pane of the Print dialog for an HP LaserJet 2100TN printer.

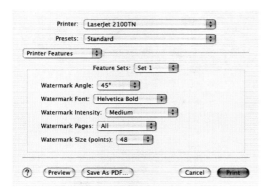

Figure 29 The Set 1 Printer Features pane of the Print dialog for a LaserJet 2100TN.

Figure 30 The Print Settings pane of the Print dialog for an Epson Stylus Color printer.

✓ Plain Paper
  360 dpi Ink Jet Paper
  Photo Quality Ink Jet Paper
  Photo Paper
  Photo Quality Glossy Film
  Ink Jet Transparencies

Figure 31
The Media Type pop-up menu for an Epson Stylus Color printer.

To set Printer Features options

1. In the Print dialog, choose Printer Features from the third pop-up menu (**Figure 19a**) to display Printer Features options (**Figure 29**).

2. Select an option from the Feature Sets pop-up menu to display the group of options you want to set.

3. Set options as desired in the pane.

4. Repeat steps 2 and 3 to set all options to your specifications.

✔ Tips

- These options are not available for all printers.

- When available, these options vary greatly from printer to printer. The options shown here are for an HP LaserJet 2100TN printer, which has a variety of watermark and resolution features.

To set Print Settings options

1. In the Print dialog, choose Print Settings from the third pop-up menu (**Figure 19b**) to display the Print Settings pane (**Figure 30**).

2. Select the type of paper you will print on from the Media Type pop-up menu (**Figure 31**).

3. For a color printer, select an Ink option.

4. Set Mode options as desired. These options vary from printer to printer; check the documentation that came with your printer for details.

To set Color Management options

1. In the Print dialog, choose Color Management from the third pop-up menu (**Figure 19b**) to display Color Management options (**Figure 32**).

2. To indicate the color management method, select one of the radio buttons near the top of the pane.

3. If you selected Color Controls, set options in the dialog as desired.

✔ Tips

■ Color management methods and options are far beyond the scope of this book.

■ ColorSync is discussed in *Mac OS X Advanced: Visual QuickPro Guide*.

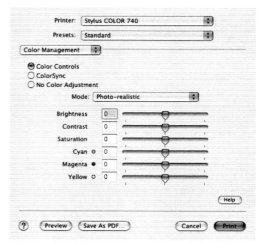

Figure 32 The Color Management pane of the Print dialog with Color Controls selected.

Figure 33 Choose Save As from the Presets pop-up menu.

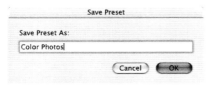

Figure 34 The Save Preset dialog.

Figure 35 The preset is added to the menu and chosen as the current preset.

Figure 36 The Preset pop-up menu with several presets added.

To save settings as a preset

1. In the Print dialog (**Figure 17**), choose Save As from the Presets pop-up menu (**Figure 33**).

2. Enter a name for the settings in the Save Preset dialog that appears (**Figure 34**).

3. Click OK.

   The name you entered is added to the Presets pop-up menu and choosen (**Figure 35**).

✔ Tip

■ It's a good idea to save settings if you often have to change the Print dialog's settings. This can save time when you need to print.

To save changes to preset settings

In the Print dialog (**Figure 17**), choose Save from the Presets pop-up menu (**Figure 35**). Your changes to the preset settings are saved.

To use preset settings

In the Print dialog (**Figure 17**), choose the name of the preset settings you want to use from the Presets pop-up menu (**Figure 36**).

All Print dialog settings are set according to the saved settings.

To delete a preset setting

1. In the Print dialog (**Figures 17**), choose the name of the preset settings you want to delete from the Presets pop-up menu (**Figure 36**).

2. Choose Delete from the Presets pop-up menu (**Figure 35**).

   The preset setting is deleted.

To preview a document

1. In the Print dialog (**Figure 17**), click the Preview button. The Print dialog disappears and Mac OS opens Preview. A moment later, the document appears in a Preview window (**Figure 37**).

2. When you're finished previewing the document, you have three options:

   ▲ Choose File > Print (**Figure 12b**) or press ⌃⌘P to display the Print dialog and print the document from Preview.

   ▲ Choose File > Save As (**Figure 12b**) to display a Save Location dialog (**Figure 38**) and save the document as a PDF file from within Preview.

   ▲ Choose Preview > Quit Preview (**Figure 39**) or press ⌃⌘Q to quit Preview and return to the original document.

✔ Tips

- Preview is covered in **Chapter 6**. The Save Location dialog is covered in **Chapter 5**.

- Some applications, such as Internet Explorer, include a Print Preview command on their File menu (**Figure 12c**).

Figure 37 The Preview button displays the document in a Preview window. You can use controls in the window's toolbar or commands in the View menu to scroll through document contents.

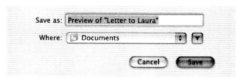

Figure 38 Use a standard Save Location dialog to save the document as a PDF file.

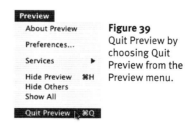

Figure 39 Quit Preview by choosing Quit Preview from the Preview menu.

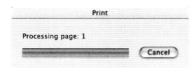

Figure 40 A progress window like this appears as a print job is spooled to the print queue.

Figure 41 When you turn on the Save as File check box, the Print button turns into a Save button.

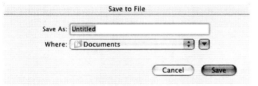

Figure 42 Use this dialog to enter a name, select a location, and Save a document as a file.

To print

In the Print dialog (**Figure 17**), click Print.

The print job is sent to the print queue, where it waits for its turn to be printed. A progress window like the one in **Figure 40** appears as it is sent or *spooled*.

✔ Tips

- You can normally cancel a print job as it is being spooled to the print queue or printer by pressing ⌘.. Any pages spooled *before* you press ⌘., however, may be printed anyway.

- Canceling a print job that has already been spooled to a print queue is discussed later in this chapter.

To save a document as a PDF file

1. In the Output Options pane of the Print dialog (**Figure 24**), turn on the Save as File check box and choose PDF from the Format pop-up menu (**Figure 41**).

2. Set other options in other panes of the Print dialog as desired.

3. Click Save (**Figure 41**).

4. A Save to File dialog like the one in **Figure 42** appears. Use it to enter a name and choose a disk location for the PDF file.

✔ Tips

- In Mac OS X 10.2, you can skip steps 1 through 3 by clicking the Save as PDF button in the Print dialog (**Figure 17**). Then use the Save to File dialog that appears to name and save the file as discussed in step 4.

- Using the Save dialog is covered in **Chapter 5**.

Print Queues

As mentioned earlier in this chapter, Print Center can also be used to manage print queues. A *print queue* is a list of documents or *print jobs* waiting to be printed. When you click the Print button to send a document to a printer, you're really sending it to the printer's queue, where it waits its turn to be printed.

Print Center's queue windows enable you to check the progress of print jobs that are printing; to stop printing; and to hold, resume, or cancel a specific print job.

To open a printer's queue window

1. Open Print Center.

2. In the Printer List window (**Figure 2**), double-click the name of the printer for which you want to open the queue.

   or

   In the Printer List window (**Figure 2**) select the name of the printer for which you want to open the queue, and choose Printers > Show Jobs (**Figure 3**) or press ⌘O.

   The printer's queue window appears (**Figure 43** or **44**).

✔ Tips

- Instructions for opening Print Center are provided earlier in this chapter.

- When a document is in the print queue, the Print Center icon appears in the Dock (**Figure 45**). Click the icon to open the Print Center.

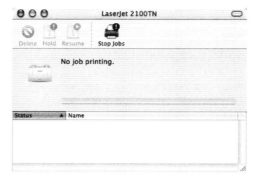

Figure 43 A printer's queue window, with no documents in the queue...

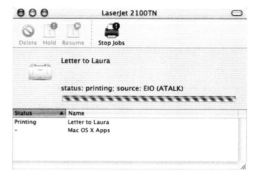

Figure 44 ...and the same printer's queue window with two documents in the queue, one of which is printing.

Figure 45 When print jobs are in a printer's queue, the Print Center icon appears in the Dock.

Figures 46a & 46b The Printers menu with a print queue window open. The last command will either stop (left) or start (right) the print jobs, depending on whether the queue is stopped.

Figure 47 The queue status appears in the queue window.

Figure 48 When you select a print job that is not on hold, the Delete and Hold buttons become active.

Figures 49a & 49b The Jobs menu with a print job that is waiting or printing selected (left) and the Jobs menu with a print job that is on hold selected.

Figure 50 The word "Hold" appears in the status column for any job on hold.

To stop print jobs

Click the Stop Jobs button in the Print Queue window (**Figures 43** and **44**).

or

Choose Printers > Stop Jobs (**Figure 46a**).

Any printing stops and the words "Jobs Stopped" appear in the print queue window (**Figure 47**).

To restart print jobs

Click the Start Jobs button in the Print Queue window (**Figure 47**).

or

Choose Printers > Start Jobs (**Figure 46b**).

The next print job starts printing.

To hold a specific print job

1. In the printer's queue window (**Figure 44**), select the print job you want to hold.

2. Click the Hold button (**Figure 48**).

   or

   Choose Jobs > Hold Job (**Figure 49a**).

   The word "Hold" appears in the Status column beside the job name in the queue window (**Figure 50**). If the job was printing, printing stops and another job in the queue begins to print.

To resume a specific print job

1. In the printer's queue window (**Figure 50**), select the print job you want to resume.

2. Click the Resume button (**Figure 51**).

   or

   Choose Jobs > Resume Job (**Figure 49b**).

   The word "Hold" disappears from the Status column beside the job name in the queue window. If no other jobs are printing, the job begins to print.

To cancel a specific print job

1. In the printer's queue window (**Figure 44**), select the print job you want to cancel.

2. Click the Delete button (**Figure 48 or 51**).

   or

   Choose Jobs > Delete Job (**Figure 49a** or **49b**).

   The job is removed from the print queue. If it was printing, printing stops.

Figure 51 When you select a print job that is on hold, the Resume button becomes active.

Figure 52 This dialog appeared when the printer wasn't turned on.

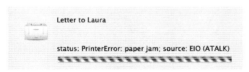

Figure 53 This message appeared in the printer queue window when the printer got a paper jam.

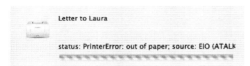

Figure 54 This dialog appeared in the printer queue window when the printer ran out of paper.

Figure 55 This dialog appeared when I confused my computer by purposely causing multiple printing errors, just so I could take these screen shots. (Ah, the things I do for readers.)

Figure 56 If you put a print job on hold while you fixed a printing problem, select it and click Resume to resume printing.

Troubleshooting Printing Problems

When a printing problem occurs, Mac OS can often give you hints to help you figure out why. Here are some examples:

◆ A dialog like the one in **Figure 52** appears when your computer can't find the selected printer. Check to make sure the printer is properly connected and turned on.

◆ A message like the one in **Figure 53** appears when your printer has a paper jam. Clear the jam.

◆ A dialog like the one in **Figure 54** appears when your printer is out of paper. Add paper!

◆ A dialog like the one in **Figure 55** appears when your computer knows there's a printing problem but can't figure out what it is.

To continue printing after a printing problem

If you get an error dialog like the one in **Figure 52**:

1. Click the Stop Jobs button to put the job on hold.

2. Fix the problem (if you can).

3. Select the document in the queue window (**Figure 56**).

4. Click the Resume button.

or

If you get an error message in the printer queue window, like the ones in **Figures 53** and **54**, fix the problem.

Continued on next page...

TROUBLESHOOTING PRINTING PROBLEMS

Continued from previous page.

or

If you get an error dialog like the one in **Figure 55**:

1. Click OK to dismiss the dialog.

2. Fix the problem (if you can).

If the problem is fixed, the document should print.

✔ Tip

- If you have printing problems that Mac OS can't help you identify, check the troubleshooting section of the documentation that came with your printer.

Connecting to the Internet

Connecting to the Internet

The *Internet* is a vast, worldwide network of computers that offers information, communication, online shopping, and entertainment for the whole family.

There are two ways to connect to the Internet:

◆ In a *direct* or *network connection*, your computer has a live network connection to the Internet all the time. This is relatively common for workplace computers on companywide networks. For home use, *cable modems* and *DSL*, which work like direct connections, are gaining popularity.

◆ In a *modem* or *dial-up connection*, your computer uses its modem to dial in to a server at an *Internet Service Provider* (*ISP*), which gives it access to the Internet. Access speed is limited by the speed of your modem.

This chapter explains how to configure your system for an Internet connection, connect to the Internet, and use the Internet applications and utilities included with Mac OS X.

✔ Tips

■ An ISP is a business that provides access to the Internet for a fee.

■ The *World Wide Web* is part of the Internet. The Web and the *Web browser* software you use to access it are covered later in this chapter.

TCP/IP, PPP, & Internet Connect

Your computer accesses the Internet via a TCP/IP connection. *TCP/IP* is a standard Internet *protocol*, or set of rules, for exchanging information.

A TCP/IP connection works like a pipeline. Once established, Internet applications—such as your Web browser and e-mail program—reach through the TCP/IP pipeline to get the information they need. When the information has been sent or received, it stops flowing through the pipeline. But the pipeline is not disconnected.

If you have a direct or network connection to the Internet, the Internet is accessible all the time. But if you connect via modem, you need to use Internet Connect software. This software, which comes with Mac OS, uses PPP to connect to TCP/IP networks via modem. *PPP* is a standard protocol for connecting to networks.

When you connect via modem using Internet Connect, you set up a temporary TCP/IP pipeline. Internet applications are smart enough to automatically use Internet Connect to connect to the Internet when necessary. When you're finished accessing Internet services you should tell Internet Connect to disconnect.

✔ Tip

- Internet Connect replaces the Remote Access software found in Mac OS 9.x and earlier.

Manually Setting Internet Configuration Options

If you set up your Internet connection as part of the setup process discussed in **Chapter 1**, your computer should be ready to connect to the Internet and you can skip ahead to the sections that discuss Internet connection software. But if you didn't set up your connection or your Internet connection information has changed since setup, you'll have to do some manual configuration.

Mac OS X includes two System Preferences panels that you can use to manually set up an Internet configuration:

◆ **Network** enables you to set the server IP address and domain name information, as well as proxy and PPP dialup information.

◆ **Internet** enables you to set a wide variety of configuration options, including options for .Mac, iDisk, Email, and Web.

The following two sections explain the configuration options in these System Preference panels in case you ever need or want to modify your settings.

✔ Tip

■ If your Internet configuration is working fine, don't change it! Internet connections follow one of the golden rules of computing: *If it ain't broke, don't fix it.*

Network Preferences

The Network pane of System Preferences enables you to configure your modem or network connection:

◆ For **modem or network connections**, you can set options to configure your TCP/IP address and proxy information.

◆ For **modem connections only**, you can set options for your PPP connection to the Internet and your modem.

◆ For **network connections only**, you can set options for your PPPoE connection to a cable or DSL server and AppleTalk connection to an internal network.

✔ Tips

■ A discussion of AppleTalk network connections is beyond the scope of this book. You can learn more about networking in *Mac OS X Advanced: Visual QuickPro Guide*.

■ *PPPoE*, which stands for *Point to Point Protocol over Ethernet*, is a connection method used by some cable and DSL ISPs.

■ Before you set Network preferences, make sure you have all the information you need to properly configure the options. You can get all of the information you need from your ISP or network administrator.

To open Network preferences

1. Choose Apple > System Preferences (**Figure 1**), or click the System Preferences icon on the Dock.

2. In the System Preferences window that appears (**Figure 2**), click the Network icon to display the Network pane (**Figure 3**).

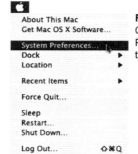

Figure 1
Choose System Preferences from the Apple menu.

Figure 2 The System Preferences window.

Figure 3 The Network pane of System Preferences with the TCP/IP tab selected for a modem connection.

Figure 4 The Configure pop-up menu in the TCP/IP tab of the Network preferences pane.

Figure 5 If your ISP has provided you with a static IP address, the TCP/IP tab should include all address information.

Figure 6 The PPP tab should include all of the information your computer needs to dial in and log on to the ISP's server. (Yes, my dog has an e-mail address.)

To set up a modem connection

1. In the Network pane of System Preferences (**Figure 3**), choose Modem or Internal Modem from the Show pop-up menu above the tabs.

2. If necessary, click the TCP/IP tab to display its options (**Figure 3**).

3. If your ISP's instructions say that IP address and domain name information will be assigned automatically (i.e., you have a *dynamic* IP address), choose Using PPP from the Configure pop-up menu (**Figure 4**). Then enter the domain information in the fields. **Figure 3** shows an example. (This is the most commonly used option for dial-up connections to ISPs.)

   or

   If your ISP provided a *static* IP address and domain name server information for your connection, choose Manually from the Configure pop-up menu (**Figure 4**) and enter the information provided in each of the fields that appear. **Figure 5** shows an example.

   or

   If you plan to use an AOL connection for accessing the Internet, choose AOL Dialup from the Configure pop-up menu (**Figure 4**). You can then skip the remaining steps.

4. Click the PPP tab to display its options.

5. Enter the dialup information provided by your ISP. **Figure 6** shows an example.

6. Click the Modem tab to display its options (**Figure 7**).

7. Choose your modem type from the Modem pop-up menu.

Continued on next page...

SETTING UP A MODEM CONNECTION

Continued from previous page.

8. To minimize errors and speed up data transfer, turn on the "Enable error correction and compression in modem" check box.

9. To instruct your computer to wait until it "hears" a dial tone before it dials, turn on the "Wait for dial tone before dialing" check box. This, however, can prevent the computer from dialing if you have an unusual dial tone.

10. Select a dialing radio button:

   ▲ **Tone** enables you to dial with touch-tone dialing.

   ▲ **Pulse** enables you to dial with pulse dialing. Select this option only if touchtone dialing is not available on your telephone line.

11. Select a Sound radio button:

   ▲ **On** plays dialing and connection sounds through the modem or computer speaker.

   ▲ **Off** dials and connects silently.

12. If you have call waiting and want to be alerted for incoming calls, turn on the check box labeled "Notify me of incoming calls while connected to the Internet." You can then toggle settings two options:

   ▲ **Play alert sound when receiving a call** plays an audible alert when an incoming call is detected while you're connected to the Internet.

   ▲ **Remind me *n* seconds before disconnecting me** displays a reminder dialog the number of seconds you specify before disconnecting you from the Internet to answer the incoming call.

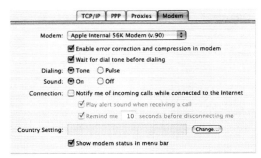

Figure 7 The Modem tab enables you to set options for your modem.

Modem status icon

Figures 8 & 9
You can display a modem status icon in the menu bar (top). Clicking the icon displays a menu of commands for accessing the Internet.

13. To change the Country Setting for your location, click the Change button beside Country Setting. This displays the Date & Time preferences pane so you can set country options.

14. To include a modem status icon and menu in the menu bar (**Figures 8** and **9**), turn on the "Show modem status in menu bar" check box.

15. Click the Apply Now button in the bottom of the Network preferences pane (**Figure 3**) to save your changes to Network preferences.

✔ Tips

■ Do not use the settings illustrated here. Use the settings provided by your ISP.

■ In step 5, if you turn on the Save password check box, you won't have to enter your password when you connect to the Internet. Be aware, however, that anyone who accesses your computer will be able to connect to the Internet with your account.

■ The Modem menu in step 7 includes dozens of modems, so yours should be listed. If it isn't, choose another model from the same manufacturer or one of the Hayes models.

■ The "Enable error correction and compression in modem" option in step 8 is not available for all modems.

■ In step 11, you may want to keep modem sounds on until you're sure you can connect. This enables you to hear telephone company error recordings that can help you troubleshoot connection problems. You can always turn sound off later.

■ If you do not have call waiting or don't want to be bothered by incoming calls if you do, keep the Notify me check box turned off in step 12.

SETTING UP A MODEM CONNECTION

To set up a network connection

1. In the Network pane of System Preferences, choose the network option from the Show pop-up menu. This option will probably be labeled "Built-in Ethernet," but it could have another name.

2. If necessary, click the TCP/IP tab to display its options.

3. Choose one of the options from the Configure pop-up menu (**Figure 10**). The option you select determines the appearance of the rest of the tab—**Figures 11** through 14 show examples.

4. Enter the appropriate IP addresses and domain names in the fields.

5. If you have a DSL connection via PPPoE, click the PPPoE tab to display its options. Turn on the Connect using PPPoE check box and enter the connection information provided by your ISP. **Figure 15** shows an example.

6. Click the Apply Now button at the bottom of the Network preferences pane (**Figure 11**) to save your changes to Network preferences.

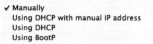

Figure 10 The Configure menu in the TCP/IP pane for a network connection offers four options.

Figure 11 Examples of various configurations for a network TCP/IP connection: manual,...

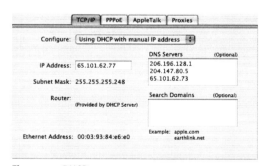

Figure 12 ...DHCP, ...

Figure 13 ...DHCP with a fixed IP address,...

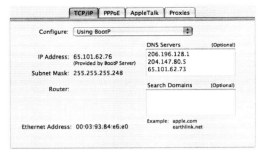

Figure 14 ...and using BootP.

Figure 15 You can use the PPPoE tab to set up a PPPoE connection to a DSL server.

✔ Tips

- Do not use the settings illustrated here. Use the settings provided by your ISP or network administrator.

- DHCP is a type of network addressing system.

- If you're not sure which option to choose in step 3, ask your network administrator.

- In step 5, if you turn on the Save password check box, you won't have to enter your password when you connect to the Internet. Be aware, however, that anyone who accesses your computer with your login will also be able to connect to the Internet with your account.

To set proxy options

1. In the Network pane of System Preferences, click the Proxies tab to display its options (**Figure 16**).

2. Turn on the check box beside each proxy option you need to set up. Then enter appropriate information for each one.

3. Click Apply Now to save your changes to Network preferences.

✖ Warning!

■ Do not change settings in the Proxies tab of Network preferences unless instructed by your ISP or network administrator. Setting invalid values may prevent you from connecting to the Internet.

✔ Tips

■ Proxies are most often required for network connections; they are seldom required for dialup connections.

■ Proxies tab options are the same for modems as for network connections.

■ Proxies enable your Internet connection to work with security setups such as firewalls, that protect network computers from hackers. For more information about proxy settings on your network, consult your network administrator.

Figure 16 The Proxies tab of the Network preferences pane.

Internet Preferences

The Internet pane of System Preferences includes tabs you can use to set options for accessing Internet features:

- ◆ **.Mac** enables you to enter your .Mac member name and password so you can access .Mac features on Apple's Web site.

- ◆ **iDisk** enables you to check the status of your iDisk disk space and set options for your iDisk Public folder.

- ◆ **Email** enables you to set your default e-mail reader application, e-mail address, and e-mail server information.

- ◆ **Web** enables you to set your default Web browser, home page, and file download location.

✔ Tip

- ■ .Mac and iDisk are discussed briefly in **Appendix B** and in greater detail in *Mac OS X Advanced: Visual QuickPro Guide*.

To open Internet preferences

1. Choose Apple > System Preferences (**Figure 1**), or click the System Preferences icon on the Dock.

2. In the System Preferences window that appears (**Figure 2**), click the Internet icon to display its options (**Figures 17** and **18**).

INTERNET PREFERENCES

To set Email options

1. In the Internet pane of System Preferences, click the Email tab to display its options (**Figure 17**).

2. To specify your e-mail application, choose an option from the Default Email Reader pop-up menu. The default selection is Mail, which is discussed in this chapter, but you can choose any e-mail program that is listed or choose Select to use an Open dialog to locate and select the program you want to use.

3. Fill in the fields with address and connection information for your e-mail address. This information should have been provided by your ISP or network administrator.

✔ Tip

- If you turn on the Use .Mac Email account check box, all other options are filled in automatically based on your .Mac login information and you can skip step 3. .Mac is discussed briefly in **Appendix B**.

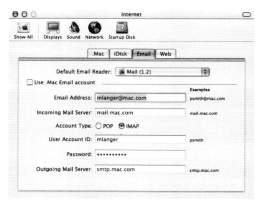

Figure 17 The Internet pane of System Preferences for Email...

Figure 18 ...and Web.

Figure 19 Use a dialog like this to select the location in which you want to save downloaded files.

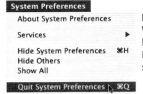

Figure 20
When you quit System Preferences, all of your Internet preferences settings are saved.

To set Web options

1. In the Internet pane of System Preferences, click the Web tab to display its options (**Figure 18**).

2. To specify your Web browser application, choose an option from the Default Web Browser pop-up menu. The default option is Internet Explorer, which is discussed in this chapter, but you can choose any Web browser that is listed or choose Select to use an Open dialog to locate and select the program you want to use.

3. To set your default Home page—the page that automatically appears when you first launch your Web browser—enter a URL in the Home Page box.

4. To change the default location to which files are downloaded by the Web browser, click the Select button. Then use the dialog that appears (**Figure 19**) to locate and select a folder in which to save files. When you click the Select button, the location appears in the Web tab of the Internet preferences pane (**Figure 18**).

✔ Tip

■ *URL* is defined and discussed later in this chapter.

To save Internet preferences

Choose System Preferences > Quit System Preferences (**Figure 20**), or press ⌘ ⌘ Q.

The System Preferences application quits, and all of your settings are saved.

Connecting to an ISP

You can establish a PPP connection to your ISP by using Internet Connect to dial in.

✔ Tip

■ If you have a network connection to the Internet, you are always connected.

To connect to an ISP

1. Open the Internet Connect icon in the Applications folder (**Figure 21**).

2. Check the settings in the main Internet Connect window that appears (**Figure 22**).

3. Click the Connect button. Internet Connect dials your modem. It displays the connection status in its Status area (**Figure 23**).

   When Internet Connect has successfully connected, the Connect button turns into a Disconnect button and the Status area fills with connection information (**Figure 24**).

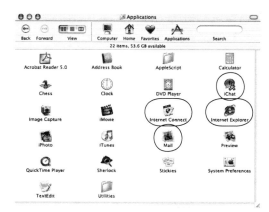

Figure 21 The Applications folder includes a number of applications for accessing the Internet.

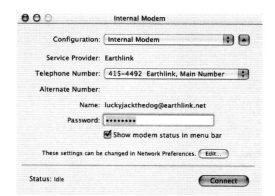

Figure 22 Internet Connect's main window.

Figure 23 The Status area displays connection status information while you are connecting...

Figure 24 ...and after you have connected.

CONNECTING TO AN ISP

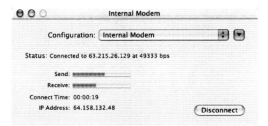

Figure 25 You can collapse Internet Connect's window to show only connection status.

✔ Tips

■ If the main Internet Connect window does not display your configuration settings as shown in **Figure 22**, click the triangle beside the Configuration pop-up menu. This will expand the window to show all settings (**Figure 22**).

■ The settings that appear in the Internet Connect window (**Figure 22**) should reflect settings you made in the PPP tab of the Network preferences pane (**Figure 6**). If you need to make changes, click the Edit button and follow the instructions provided earlier in this chapter.

■ You can click the triangle beside the Configuration pop-up menu to collapse the window and display only the status area (**Figure 25**).

■ Internet Connect does not have to be open while you are connected to the Internet.

To disconnect from an ISP

1. Open or switch to Internet Connect (**Figures 22** and **25**).

2. Click the Disconnect button (**Figures 24** and **25**). The connection is terminated.

DISCONNECTING FROM AN ISP

Internet Applications

Mac OS X includes three applications for accessing the Internet:

Figure 26 You can open Mail, iChat, and Internet Explorer by clicking their icons in the Dock.

◆ **Mail** is an Apple program that enables you to send and receive e-mail messages.

◆ **iChat** is an Apple program that enables you to exchange instant messages with .Mac and AOL users.

◆ **Internet Explorer** is a Microsoft program that enables you to browse Web sites and download files from FTP sites.

This section provides brief instructions for using these three programs—just enough to get you started. You can explore the other features of these programs on your own.

✔ Tips

■ Mail and Internet Explorer are set as the default e-mail and Web browser programs. If you prefer to use other applications, be sure to change the appropriate settings in the Internet preferences pane, as discussed earlier in this chapter.

■ Mac OS 9.x, which is bundled with Mac OS X to handle Classic applications, includes Outlook Express, an e-mail application and Netscape Communicator, a Web browser.

To open an Internet application

Use one of the following techniques:

◆ Open the icon for the application in the Applications folder (**Figure 21**).

◆ Click the icon for the application in the Dock (**Figure 26**).

Figure 27 The Mail main window with the Mailbox drawer and an incoming message displayed.

Mail

Mail (**Figure 27**) is an e-mail application from Apple Computer, Inc. It enables you to send and receive e-mail messages using your Internet e-mail account.

Here's how it works. Imagine having a mailbox at the post office. As mail comes in, the postmaster sorts it into the boxes—including yours. To get your mail, you need to go to the post office to pick it up. While you're there, you're likely to drop off any letters you need to send.

E-mail works the same way. Your e-mail is delivered to your e-mail server—like the post office where your mailbox is. The server software (like the postmaster) sorts the mail into mailboxes. When your e-mail client software (Mail, in this case) connects to the server via the Inernet, it picks up your incoming mail and sends any outgoing messages it has to send.

If you set up your Internet connection and provided e-mail information when you first configured Mac OS X, that information is automatically stored in Mail so it's ready to use. Just open mail and it automatically makes that virtual trip to the post office to get and send messages.

In this part of the chapter, I explain how to set up an e-mail account with Mail, just in case you need to add an account. I also explain how to compose, send, read, and retrieve e-mail messages.

✔ Tip

■ The first time you open Mail, a dialog appears, asking if you want to import e-mail addresses from another e-mail program. If you do, click Yes and follow the instructions that appear onscreen to perform the import.

MAIL

To set up an e-mail account

1. Choose Mail > Preferences.

2. In the Mail Preferences window that appears, click the Accounts button to display its options (**Figure 28**).

3. Click the Add Account button.

4. In the Account Information pane of the dialog that appears (**Figure 29**), enter the account and server information for the e-mail account.

5. Click OK to save your settings and dismiss the dialog. The account appears in the Mail Preferences window (**Figure 30**).

6. Click the Mail Preferences window's close button to dismiss it.

✔ Tips

■ You only have to set up an e-mail account once. Mail will remember all of your settings.

■ Your ISP or network administrator can provide all of the important information you need to set up an e-mail account, including the account name, password, and mail servers.

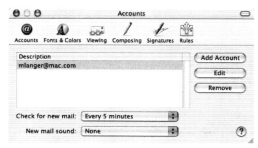

Figure 28 The Accounts pane of the Mail Preferences window.

Figure 29 The Account Information pane enables you to enter basic information for your e-mail account.

Figure 30 The account you added appears in the list.

Figure 31 Clicking the Compose button opens a New Message window like this one.

Figure 32 Here's a short message ready to be sent. The dashed underlines indicate potential spelling errors caught by Mail's built-in spelling checker; these lines aren't sent with the messages.

Figure 33 You can use Mail to send an e-mail message to someone in your Address Book by simply entering the person's name in the To field. Mail fills in the e-mail address automatically.

To create & send a message

1. Click the Compose button at the top of the Mail main window (**Figure 27**). The New Message window appears (**Figure 31**).

2. Enter the e-mail address of the message recipient in the To field, and press [Tab] twice.

3. Enter a subject for the message in the Subject field, and press [Tab].

4. Type your message into the large box at the bottom of the window. When you are finished, the window might look like the one in **Figure 32**.

5. Click the Send button near the top of the window. The message window closes and Mail sends the message.

✔ Tips

■ If you are writing to a person who has an entry in Address Book, you can simply enter the person's name into the To field in step 2. As you type, Mail attempts to match what you enter to what's in Address Book. When it finds a match, it fills in the rest for you, as shown in **Figure 33**. Address Book is covered in **Chapter 6**.

■ If you have a modem connection to the Internet, you must connect before you can send a message.

To retrieve e-mail messages

1. Click the Get Mail button at the top of the main window (**Figure 27**).

2. Mail connects to the Internet (if necessary), then connects to your e-mail server and downloads messages waiting for you. Incoming messages appear in a list when you select the In icon in the Mailbox drawer (**Figures 27** and **34**).

✔ Tips

- A blue bullet character appears beside each unread e-mail message (**Figure 34**).

- You can toggle the display of the Mailbox drawer by clicking the Mailboxes button in the main Mail window (**Figure 34**).

- You can configure Mail to have multiple mailboxes, one for each account. (This is how previous versions of Mail worked by default.) Use commands under the Mailbox menu to customize mailboxes.

Figure 34 When you select a message in the top half of the window, its content appears in the bottom half.

Figure 35 Double-click a message to open it in its own window.

Figure 36 When you click the Reply button, a pre-addressed message window appears.

To read a message

1. Click the message that you want to read. It appears in the bottom half of the main Mail window (**Figure 34**).

2. Read the message.

✔ Tips

- You can also double-click a message to display it in its own message window (**Figure 35**).

- To reply to the message, click Reply. A preaddressed message window with the entire message quoted appears (**Figure 36**). Type your reply, and click Send.

- To forward the message to another e-mail address, click Forward. A message window containing a copy of the message appears. Enter the e-mail address for the recipient in the To field, and click Send.

- To add a message's sender to the Address book, select the message (**Figure 34**) and choose Message > Add Sender To Address Book or press ⌃⌘Y. Mail automatically adds the person's name and e-mail address to the Address Book. You can open address book and add additional information for the record as desired. Address Book is covered **Chapter 6**.

iChat

iChat, which is brand new in Mac OS X 10.2, enables you to exchange instant messages and conduct live group chats with .Mac and AOL users via AOL Instant Messaging (AIM) technology.

Here's how it works. The first time you open iChat, you configure it with the .Mac account names and AOL screen names of your buddies who use iChat or AIM. Then, while you're connected to the Internet with iChat running, iChat does two things:

◆ It tells iChat and AIM users that you're available to receive instant messages and participate in chats.

◆ It tells you when your buddies are connected via iChat or AIM and available to receive instant messages and participate in chats.

When a buddy is available, sending him an instant message is as easy as clicking a button and typing what you want to say. If more than one buddy is available, you can open a chat window and invite them to participate together.

In this part of the chapter, I explain how to set up an iChat buddy list, invite a buddy to a chat, and participate in a group chat.

✔ Tips

■ To use iChat, you must have a .Mac or AOL account.

■ iChat enables you to chat with .Mac and AOL account holders using iChat or AIM only. As this book went to press, iChat did not support any other instant messaging technology.

ICHAT

Figure 37 When you first start iChat, you're prompted to enter information about your .Mac or AOL account.

Figure 38 A dialog like this asks whether you want to enable Rendezvous messaging.

Figures 39 & 40 Your Buddy list window starts out small while it's connecting to AIM (above), then expands once you're connected (right).

Figure 41 A Rendezvous window also appears if Rendezvous messaging is enabled.

To set up iChat

1. Open iChat as discussed earlier in this chapter.

2. In the Welcome to iChat dialog that appears (**Figure 37**), enter your name, account type, account name, and password in the appropriate boxes. Then click OK.

3. The Rendezvous dialog shown in **Figure 38** appears next. You have two options:

   ▲ **No** leaves Rendezvous messaging turned off. Choose this option if you are not connected to a network or you do not plan to use iChat with other people on your network.

   ▲ **Yes** turns on Rendezvous messaging. This enables you to use iChat with local network users.

4. A Buddy List window with a "Connecting" message appears next (**Figure 39**). Wait while iChat connects to AIM. The Buddy List expands to show all of your buddies (**Figure 40**).

✔ Tips

■ Rendezvous is a new type of networking that's part of Mac OS X. You can learn more about networking in *Mac OS X Advanced: Visual QuickPro Guide*.

■ If you have enabled Rendezvous messaging, two windows appear—a Buddy List window (**Figure 40**) and a Rendezvous window (**Figure 41**). The instructions in this chapter do not cover using iChat with Rendezvous.

■ If you set a picture for yourself in Address Book, that picture automatically appears for you in iChat (**Figures 39** through **41**). I explain how to use Address Book in **Chapter 6**.

To add a buddy

1. Click the Add a new buddy button at the bottom of the Buddy List window (**Figure 42**).

   or

   Choose Buddies > Add a Buddy, or press ⇧⌘A.

2. A dialog sheet like the one in **Figure 43** appears. You have two choices:

   ▲ To add a person in your Address Book to your Buddy List, select a name in the dialog and click Select Buddy.

   ▲ To add a person not in your Address Book to your Buddy List, click the New Person button. Then fill out the form that appears by entering information about the person you want to add (**Figure 44**). Click Add.

✔ Tips

■ You can add as many .Mac and AOL accounts as you like to your buddy list. **Figure 45** shows an example of a buddy list with several buddies added.

■ If your Buddy List remains empty after adding buddies, you may have the list configured to show only available buddies. Choose View > Show Offline Buddies to display all buddies in the list, regardless of availability.

To remove a buddy

1. Select the name of the buddy you want to remove.

2. Press Delete.

3. Click OK in the confirmation dialog that appears.

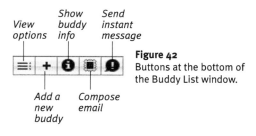

View options — Show buddy info — Send instant message

Add a new buddy — Compose email

Figure 42
Buttons at the bottom of the Buddy List window.

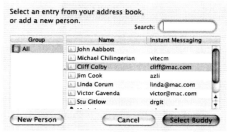

Figure 43 To add a person from your address book to your Buddy List, select his or her record and click Select Buddy.

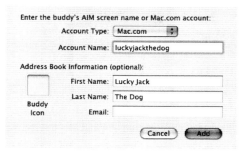

Figure 44 To add a new person (or my dog, in this example) to your Buddy List, fill in this form. (Of course, if my dog could chat, I wouldn't be writing computer books for a living.)

Figure 45
A Buddy List with buddies. Buddies who are available appear in black type with a bullet beside their names. Buddies who are offline appear in gray type.

Figure 46
Select a buddy who is available for chatting. If the buddy has a custom icon, it appears when he becomes available. From that point forward, it is saved in iChat.

To send an instant message

1. In the Buddy List, select the name of a buddy who is available for chatting (**Figure 46**).

2. Click the Send instant message button at the bottom of the Buddy List window (**Figure 42**). A window like the one in **Figure 47** appears.

3. Enter your message in the box at the bottom of the window. As you type, a "cloud" appears beside your icon to indicate that you're writing something (**Figure 48**).

4. Press Return. The comment appears in the top half of the window beside your icon (**Figure 49**).

5. Wait for your buddy to answer. His comments appear in the top half of the window beside his icon (**Figure 50**). If your buddy starts typing again, a "cloud" appears beside his icon (**Figure 51**).

6. Repeat steps 3 through 5 to continue your instant message conversation in the window. **Figure 52** shows a typical conversation between two Mac OS X geeks, one of whom is writing a book.

Figure 47
As you prepare to type, a "cloud" appears beside your icon.

Figure 48
Type your message in the box.

Figure 49 When you press Return, your message appears in the top half of the window.

Figure 50 When your buddy responds, his message appears beside his icon.

Figure 51
A "cloud" appears beside your buddy's icon as he types.

Figure 52
The start of a long and geekish conversation.

To initiate a group chat

1. Choose File > New Chat, or press ⌃⌘N. An Instant Message window with a Participants list appears (**Figure 53**).

2. Drag the name of a buddy you'd like to participate in the chat from the Buddy List to the Participants list (**Figure 54**). When you release the mouse button, the buddy's name appears in the list (**Figure 55**).

3. Repeat step 2 for each buddy you'd like to participate in the chat.

4. Enter your message in the box at the bottom of the window (**Figure 56**) and press ⟨Return⟩. It appears in the top half of the window and *(Deciding...)* appears beneath each participant name in the Participant list (**Figure 57**).

5. Wait while the buddies you invited to the chat decide whether they want to join. If they do join in, their comments appear in the message window (**Figures 58** and **59**).

6. Enter another message in the box at the bottom of the window and press ⟨Return⟩. The message is added to the message window (**Figure 60**).

7. Repeat steps 5 and 6 to continue the conversation.

Figure 53 To initiate a group chat, start with an Instant Message window like this.

Figure 54 Drag a buddy name into the Participants list.

Figure 55 The buddy you dragged appears in the Participants list.

Figure 56 Enter your message in the box at the bottom of the Instant Message window.

Figure 57 Your message appears in the message window while the participants decide whether they want to chat.

INITIATING GROUP CHATS, LEAVING CHATS

Figure 58 As this illustration shows, the first participant to join in is Linda. Victor is still deciding.

Figure 59 Victor joins in.

Figure 60 And the chat is underway.

Figure 61 A chat invitation appears in a little window like this.

Figure 62 Click the window to expand it.

To accept a chat invitation

1. When another iChat user invites you to chat, his message appears in a window on your desktop (**Figure 61**). Click the window to display a box at the bottom of the window for entering your messages (**Figure 62**).

2. Enter your message in the box at the bottom of the window (**Figure 63**) and press Return. The message appears in the main window, which expands, if necessary to list all chat participants (**Figure 64**).

3. Continue chatting as discussed on the previous two pages.

Figure 63 Enter your message in the bottom of the window.

Figure 64 When you press Return to join the chat, the window expands further. If the chat has more than two participants, the Participants list also appears.

To turn down a chat invitation

1. Click the chat invitation window (**Figure 61**) to expand it (**Figure 62**).

2. Click the Close button to close the window without entering any comments.

To block someone from trying to send you instant messages

1. Click the chat invitation window (**Figure 61**) to expand it (**Figure 62**).

2. Click the Block button.

✔ Tip

■ The block feature is a good way to keep an annoying user from bugging you. After all, even though the user might not be on your buddy list, you could be on his!

To leave a chat

Close the message window.

or

Choose iChat > Quit iChat.

✔ Tip

■ When a user leaves a chat, a message informing you that he has left appears in the message window (**Figure 65**).

Figure 65 iChat tells you when a chat participant leaves the chat.

Mouse pointer when pointing to a clickable link

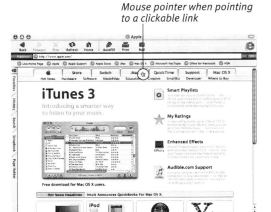

Figure 66 When you launch Internet Explorer, it displays the default home page.

Figure 67 Clicking the link in **Figure 66** displays this page.

Internet Explorer

Internet Explorer is a popular Web browser application from Microsoft. It enables you to view, or *browse*, pages on the World Wide Web.

A Web *page* is a window full of formatted text and graphics (**Figures 66** and **67**). You move from page to page by clicking text or graphic links or by opening *URLs* (*uniform resource locators*) for specific Web pages. These two methods of navigating the World Wide Web can open a whole world of useful or interesting information.

✔ Tips

- The version of Internet Explorer included with Mac OS X is Mac OS X compatible. It has been customized to start with a specific home page and offers buttons with links to Apple and Microsoft pages.

- You can easily identify a link by pointing to it; the mouse pointer turns into a pointing finger and the link destination appears in the status bar at the bottom of the window (**Figure 66**).

- The first time you start Internet Explorer, a dialog asks whether you want to set Explorer as your default browser. If you plan on always using Explorer, click Yes. Otherwise, turn on the Don't show this message again check box and click No.

To follow a link

1. Position the mouse pointer on a text or graphic link. The mouse pointer turns into a pointing finger (**Figure 66**).

2. Click. After a moment, the page or other location for the link you clicked will appear (**Figure 67**).

To view a specific URL

Enter the URL in the Address field near the top of the Internet Explorer window (**Figure 68**), and press Return or Enter.

To return to the home page

Click the Home button at the top of the Internet Explorer window (**Figure 68**).

✔ Tip

- You can change the default home page by specifying a different page's URL in the Web tab of the Internet preferences pane (**Figure 18**). The page you specify will load each time you launch Internet Explorer. The Internet pane is discussed earlier in this chapter.

To save a page as a favorite

1. Display the Web page that you want to save as a favorite.

2. Choose Favorites > Add Page to Favorites (**Figure 69**), or press ⌃ ⌘ D.

   The name of the page is added to the Favorites menu (**Figure 70**).

✔ Tips

- Once a page has been added to the Favorites menu, you can display it by selecting its name from the menu.

- Favorites are also referred to as *bookmarks*.

Figure 68 Enter the URL in the Address field at the top of the Internet Explorer window, and press Enter.

Figure 69 The Add Page to Favorites command adds the currently displayed page to the Favorites menu,...

Figure 70 ...as shown here.

Using Sherlock

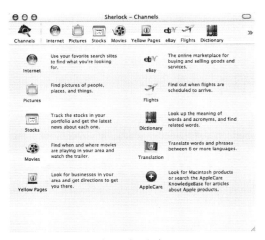

Figure 1 Sherlock's Channels window.

Figure 2 You can launch Sherlock by opening its icon in the Applications folder...

Figure 3 ...or by clicking the Sherlock icon in the Dock.

Sherlock

Sherlock (**Figure 1**), which has been completely reworked for Mac OS X 10.2, is Apple's Internet search utility. It enables you to search for information found on Web sites all over the world, including stock quotes and news, business listings, movie show times in your area, flight information, and more.

This chapter explains how to use Sherlock's search features to search the Internet.

✔ Tips

- Previous versions of Sherlock included disk searching capabilities. These features have been moved from Sherlock to the Finder's Find command, which I discuss in **Chapter 4**.

- To use Sherlock, your computer must have access to the Internet. **Chapter 9** covers accessing the Internet.

To launch Sherlock

Use one of these techniques:

- ◆ Open the Sherlock icon in the Applications folder (**Figure 2**).

- ◆ Click the Sherlock icon in the Dock (**Figure 3**).

Sherlock opens and displays its Channels window (**Figure 1**).

Channels

Sherlock's interface (**Figure 1**) includes a feature called *channels*, which enables you to organize search sites based on the types of information they can find for you. Sherlock comes preconfigured with ten channels:

◆ **Internet** enables you to search the Internet for general information.

◆ **Pictures** enables you to search for pictures of people, places, and things.

◆ **Stocks** enables you to track prices and get news about stocks in your portfolio.

◆ **Movies** enables you to get information about movie locations and show times, as well as watch movie trailers.

◆ **Yellow Pages** enables you to search for businesses and get driving directions.

◆ **eBay** enables you to participate in online auctions on eBay.

◆ **Flights** enables you to get information about flight arrivals.

◆ **Dictionary** enables you to look up words and acronyms to get their meanings and synonyms.

◆ **Translation** enables you to translate words and phrases between several languages.

◆ **AppleCare** enables you to search for Macintosh products and technical information.

To open a channel

Click the icon for the channel in Sherlock's Channels window (**Figure 1**) or in the toolbar at the top of any Sherlock window.

or

Choose the name of the channel from the Channel menu (**Figure 4**).

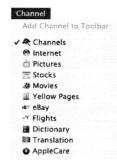

Figure 4
You can open a channel by choosing its name from the Channel menu.

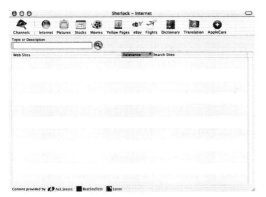

Figure 5 Use Sherlock's Internet channel to search the Internet for general information.

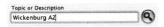

Figure 6 Enter a search word or phrase in the box.

Figure 7 Sherlock displays matches, in order of relevance, in its window.

The Internet Channel

You can use Sherlock to search the Internet for Web sites with information about topics that interest you. Unlike most other Internet search engines, Sherlock can search multiple directories (or *search sites*) at once. Best of all, you don't need to know special search syntax. Just enter a search word or phrase in plain English, select the search sites you want to use, and put Sherlock to work. It displays matches in order of relevance, so the most likely matches appear first.

✔ Tip

- Sherlock utilizes the search sites that are listed at the bottom of the Internet window (**Figure 5**). These sites may change.

To search for Web content

1. Open the Internet channel (**Figure 5**).

2. Enter a search word or phrase in the Topic or Description box near the top of the window (**Figure 6**).

3. Click the magnifying glass button to begin the search.

4. After a moment, the matches begin to appear. You can begin working with matches immediately or wait until Sherlock has finished searching (**Figure 7**).

✔ Tips

- When entering words in step 2, enter at least two or three words you expect to find in documents about the topic you are searching for. This helps narrow down the search, resulting in more useful matches.

- To perform a new search, follow steps 2 and 3. A new results list replaces the original list.

To work with found sites

1. Scroll through the list of items found (**Figure 7**) to locate an item that interests you.

2. To open an item's Web page, double-click it. Your Web browser launches and displays the page in its window (**Figure 8**).

✔ Tips

- You can sort the items found list in the Sherlock window (**Figure 7**) by clicking one of its column headings. To reverse the sort order, just click the same column heading again.

- To open a separate Sherlock window to perform a new search (without disturbing the items found list), choose File > New (**Figure 9**), or press ⌘ ⌘ N.

Figure 8 Double-clicking the name of a Web page displays the page in your Web browser window. Here's my favorite Web site for my favorite western town.

Figure 9 Sherlock's File menu.

Figure 10 Sherlock's Pictures channel.

Figure 11 A search using the word *helicopters* results in pictures of all kinds of helicopters.

The Pictures Channel

Sherlock's Pictures channel enables you to search for pictures of people, places, and things. You can use these pictures for a variety of things, from writing school reports to building Web pages to creating advertising campaigns.

✔ Tip

- Most of the photos that Sherlock finds are stock photography images that are protected by U.S. copyright law. These images must be licensed or purchased before they can be used.

To search for pictures

1. Open the Pictures channel (**Figure 10**).

2. Enter a search word or phrase in the Picture Topic or Description box near the top of the window.

3. Click the magnifying glass button to begin the search.

4. After a moment, the matches begin to appear as thumbnail images. You can begin working with matches immediately or wait until Sherlock has finished searching (**Figure 11**).

✔ Tip

- To perform a new search, follow steps 2 and 3. A new results list replaces the original list.

SEARCHING FOR PICTURES

To work with found photos

1. Scroll through the thumbnail images found (**Figure** 11) to locate a photo that interests you.

2. Click the photo to select it. The URL for the photo's location on the Web appears in the bottom of the Sherlock window (**Figure 12**).

3. To open a photo Web page, double-click it. Your Web browser launches and displays the page in its window (**Figure 13**). The page will include licensing information if it applies.

✔ Tip

■ To open a separate Sherlock window to perform a new search (without disturbing the items found list), choose File > New (**Figure 9**), or press ⌘ ⌘ N.

Figure 12 When you select a photo's thumbnail, the URL for its location on the Web appears in the bottom of the Sherlock window.

Figure 13 Double-clicking a thumbnail image displays a Web page with more information about the photo, including licensing information.

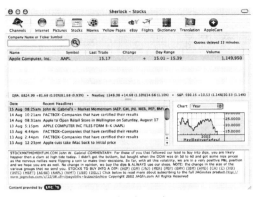

Figure 14 Sherlock's Stocks channel.

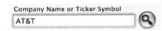

Figure 15 You can enter a ticker symbol (if you know it) or a company name, like this.

Figure 16 If you enter a company name, Sherlock displays a list of companies to choose from.

Figure 17 The company you added appears in the window.

The Stocks Channel

Sherlock's Stocks channel enables you to get stock quotes, news headlines and stories, and charts for stocks. You enter the company name or ticker symbol and put Sherlock to work. It retrieves the information and displays it in the Stocks window.

✔ Tip

■ Although the stock quotes are delayed 15 minutes, they are constantly updated as long as the Stocks window is open.

To look up stock information for a company

1. Open the Stocks channel. Sherlock connects to the Internet and retrieves information about the last companies you looked up, which it displays in its window (**Figure 14**).

2. Enter the name or ticker symbol for a company in the Company Name or Ticker Symbol box near the top of the window (**Figure 15**).

3. Click the magnifying glass button to begin the search.

4. If you entered a company name, Sherlock displays a dialog sheet like the one in **Figure 16**. Scroll through the list, select the company you want, and click Add.

   The company name and information appears in the window (**Figure 17**).

✔ Tips

■ In step 1, the first time you open the Stocks channel, it displays information for Apple Computer, Inc.

■ In step 4, you can select multiple companies by holding down ⌘ as you click each one.

To view news stories

Click a headline in the Stocks window. The story appears in the bottom of the window (**Figures** 14 and 17).

or

Double-click a headline in the Stocks window. Sherlock launches your default Web browser and opens the Web page with the story you double-clicked (**Figure 18**).

To view a different chart

Choose an option from the Chart pop-up menu (**Figure 19**). The chart changes accordingly.

To remove a company from the list

1. Select the company you want to remove from the list.

2. Press (Delete). The company disappears.

✔ Tip

■ The fewer companies in the list, the quicker Sherlock can display and update information. This also speeds up the Stocks channel's loading time.

Figure 18 The news story that appears in the bottom of **Figure 14**, when viewed in a Web browser window.

Figure 19 The Chart menu offers three charting options.

VIEWING NEWS STORIES & CHARTS

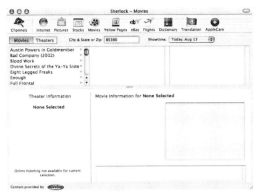

Figure 20 The Movies channel with the Movies option selected.

Figure 21 When you select a movie, a list of nearby theaters appears, along with movie info.

Figure 22 When you select a theater, a list of show-times and theater location information appears. (Yes, the closest theater showing this current movie is nearly 44 miles away. That's part of the charm of living in Wickenburg, on the edge of nowhere.)

The Movies Channel

Sherlock's Movies channel (**Figures 20** and **23**) offers a great way to get local movie listings and show times, without picking up the phone. For some theaters, you can even buy your movie tickets online.

To search for movie show times

1. Open the Movies channel.

2. Enter your zip code in the City & State or Zip box.

3. If necessary, click the Movies button on the far left side of the window. After a moment, a list of current movies appears in the leftmost list (**Figure 20**).

4. Select the name of a movie that you'd like to see. A list of theaters showing the movie appears in the middle list and information about the movie, including a QuickTime movie trailer, appears in the bottom right of the window (**Figure 21**).

5. Select the name of the theater where you'd like to see the movie. A list of showtimes appears in the rightmost list and the theater location appears in the bottom left of the window (**Figure 22**).

6. Repeat steps 4 and 5 to find other show-times for movies.

✔ Tips

- In step 4, you can play the movie trailer by clicking the play button when the movie is finished downloading from the Internet. I explain how to play QuickTime movies in **Chapter 6**.

- In step 5, if a Buy Tickets button appears with the theater location (**Figure 22**), you can click the button to display a secure Web page where you can purchase tickets online.

To search theater schedules

1. Open the Movies channel.

2. Enter your zip code in the City & State or Zip box.

3. If necessary, click the Theaters button on the far left side of the window. After a moment, a list of nearby theaters appears in the leftmost list (**Figure 23**).

4. Select the name of a theater you'd like to see the schedule for. A list of movies playing at that theater appears in the middle list and additional information about the theater appears in the bottom left of the window (**Figure 24**).

5. Select the name of the movie you'd like to see. A list of showtimes appears in the rightmost list and information about the movie, including a QuickTime movie trailer, appears in the bottom right of the window (**Figure 25**).

6. Repeat steps 4 and 5 to find other theater schedules.

✔ Tips

- In step 5, you can play the movie trailer by clicking the play button when the movie is finished downloading from the Internet. I explain how to play QuickTime movies in **Chapter 6**.

- In step 4, if a Buy Tickets button appears with the theater location, you can click the button to display a secure Web page where you can purchase tickets online.

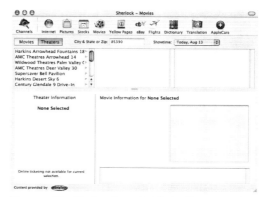

Figure 23 The Movies channel with the Theaters option selected.

Figure 24 Select a theater to display a list of what's playing there.

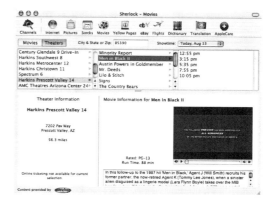

Figure 25 Select a movie to display showtimes and movie information.

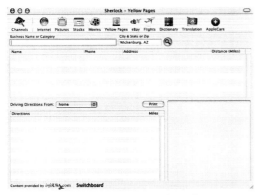

Figure 26 Sherlock's Yellow Pages channel.

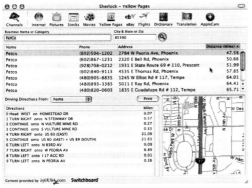

Figure 27 Select a business to display driving directions and a map. (And yes, those directions are from my house—although they're not exactly right. Sherlock gets your address from your Address Book record.)

The Yellow Pages Channel

The Yellow Pages channel (**Figure 26**) is a great way to find local businesses and get the directions you need to find them.

To search for a business listing

1. Open the Yellow Pages channel (**Figure 26**).

2. Enter a city and state or zip code in the City & State or Zip box.

3. Enter a business name or category in the Business Name or Category box in the top left of the window.

4. Click the magnifying glass button to begin the search.

5. After a moment, search results begin to appear. The topmost (closest) business is automatically selected; driving directions and a map appear in the bottom half of the window (**Figure 27**).

6. Select a listing to view driving directions and a map for it.

✔ Tips

- If you're looking for a specific business, you're more likely to find it if you enter the business name rather than category. For example, when I entered *pets* in the Business Name or Category box, neither PetSmart nor PetCo, the two biggest pet store chains in this area, were included in the list.

- In many instances, Internet driving directions are for the shortest route, which may not be the quickest or most convenient. If I followed the driving directions in **Figure 27**, for example, I'd hit at least 50 traffic lights; I know a slightly longer but quicker route with only three traffic lights. Which do you think I'd take?

The eBay Channel

The eBay channel (**Figure 28**) enables you to search for items available for sale on eBay, an online auction Web site. You enter search criteria and Sherlock retrieves a list of found items from eBay. You can then track the auction within Sherlock or visit the auction's Web page, where you can bid on it.

To search for items on eBay

1. Open the eBay channel and make sure the Search button is selected (**Figure 28**).

2. Enter search criteria in the top part of the window, right beneath the toolbar.

3. Click the magnifying glass button to start the search.

4. After a moment, search results begin to appear. The first item is selected and information about it appears in the bottom half of the window (**Figure 29**).

5. To see information about another item in the list, click it to select it.

6. To get more information about an item, double-click it. Your Web browser launches and displays the item's page on eBay (**Figure 30**).

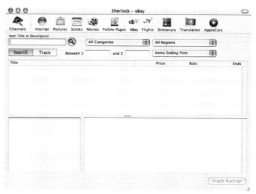

Figure 28 Sherlock's eBay channel.

Figure 29 Search results for an eBay search include basic listing info, as well as auction details and a photo.

Figure 30 Double-clicking an item in Sherlock's window diplays its Web page on eBay.

Figure 31 Clicking the Track button at the top of Sherlock's eBay channel displays a list of the auctions you are tracking.

To track an eBay auction item

1. Select the item you want to track in the list of found items (**Figure 29**).

2. Click the Track Auction button.

3. The item is added to the Track list in the eBay channel; click the Track button near the top of the window to see it (**Figure 31**).

✔ Tip

- Items you track on eBay remain in the Track list (**Figure 31**) until the auction is over.

To bid on an eBay item

1. Double-click the item you want to bid on in the list of found items (**Figure 29**) or the list of items you are tracking (**Figure 31**) to display its Web page (**Figure 30**).

2. Read the information on the page carefully.

3. Enter your bid in the form near the bottom of the page.

✔ Tip

- You must have an account on eBay to bid on items. Setting up an account is free. Follow the instructions on the eBay Web site to learn more.

TRACKING & BIDDING ON EBAY ITEMS

The Flights Channel

The Flights channel (**Figure** 32) enables you to get departure and arrival information for airline flights. Enter search criteria in the top of the window and Sherlock displays results from a database of flights. This is handy for checking the status of a flight you think might be delayed—it could prevent you from waiting longer than you need to at the airport!

✔ Tip

- The Flights channel provides information about current day flights only.

To search for flight information

1. Open the Flights channel (**Figure** 32).

2. Enter search criteria in the top part of the window, right beneath the toolbar.

3. Click the magnifying glass button to start the search.

4. After a moment, search results begin to appear. Click a flight to get information about it (**Figure** 33).

✔ Tip

- In step 4, if a check mark appears in the Chart column for a flight, a graphic of the flight's position and weather appears in the bottom right of the window (**Figure** 33). Is this cool or what?

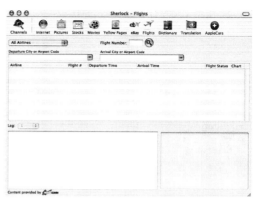

Figure 32 Sherlock's Flights channel.

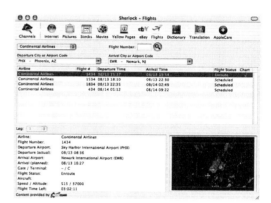

Figure 33 Sherlock displays information about a flight when you select it.

Figure 34 Sherlock's Dictionary channel.

Figure 35 Sherlock looks up a word and displays its definition and synonyms.

Figure 36
Can't spell? Not a problem. Sherlock displays a list of words it thinks you might have been trying to spell.

The Dictionary Channel

The Dictionary channel (**Figure 34**) enables you to get definitions and synonyms for words and acronyms. Enter the word you want to learn about and let Sherlock look it up on two online resources: American Heritage Dictionary and Roget's II Thesaurus.

To define a word

1. Open the Dictionary channel (**Figure 34**).

2. Enter the word or acryonym you want to define in the Word to Define box.

3. Click the magnifying glass button to look up the word.

4. Wait while Sherlock looks up the word. After a moment, search results appear in the window (**Figure 35**):

   ▲ The Dictionary list displays words that either exactly match what you entered or are related to what you entered. Select the word to see a definition in the box beside it.

   ▲ The Thesaurus list displays synonyms for the word you selected in the list above it. Select a synonym to see more information and synonyms.

✔ Tips

■ To look up one of the words in the Dictionary or Thesarus list, double-click it.

■ If Sherlock can't find the word because you misspelled it (heck, I did it twice while experimenting!), the Spelling Suggestions list appears in place of the Dictionary list (**Figure 36**). Double-click a word in the list to look it up.

The Translation Channel

Sherlock's Translation channel (**Figure 37**) uses online software tools to translate words and phrases between several languages, including: English, Chinese (Simplified and Traditional), Dutch, French, German, Greek, Italian, Japanese, Korean, Portuguese, Russian, and Spanish. Type in what you want to translate, click a button, and let Sherlock do the rest.

✔ Tip

- Because translations are handled by software tools and not by human translators, they should not be relied upon for complete accuracy.

To translate a word or phrase

1. Open the Translation channel (**Figure 37**).

2. Enter the word or phrase you want to translate in the Original Text box.

3. Select a translation option from the pop-up menu.

4. Click the Translate button between the top and bottom halves of the Translation window. The translation and a fine-print disclaimer appear in the bottom half of the window (**Figure 38**).

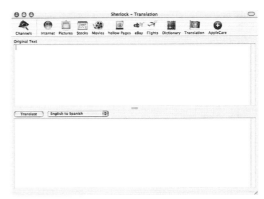

Figure 37 Sherlock's Translation channel.

Figure 38 A completed translation. I wonder how accurate this is?

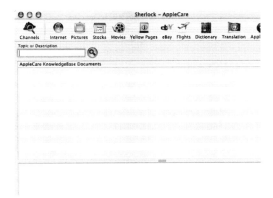

Figure 39 Sherlock's AppleCare channel.

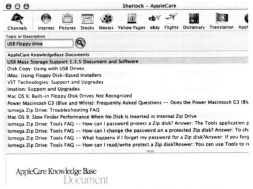

Figure 40 Sherlock displays a list of KnowledgeBase documents in the window. Click a document name to display it in the bottom half of the window.

The AppleCare Channel

Sherlock's AppleCare channel (**Figure 39**) is your direct connection to Apple's Knowledge-Base of information about Macintosh computers and software. It's a great place to learn more about your hardware and the Mac OS.

To search the AppleCare KnowledgeBase

1. Open the AppleCare channel (**Figure 39**).

2. Enter a search word or phrase in the Topic or Description box near the top of the window.

3. Click the magnifying glass button to start the search.

4. After a moment, search results begin to appear. Click an item in the list to display its document in the bottom half of the window (**Figure 40**).

Using Mac OS i-Applications

Using Mac OS X i-Applications

Desperate for a short chapter title, I use the term *i-Applications* (or *i-Apps*) to apply to a number of additional applications that are available to Mac OS X users:

◆ **iTunes** enables you to play CDs, record music from a CD to your hard disk, burn music CDs, or download music to an iPod or other MP3 player.

◆ **iPhoto** enables you to store, organize, and share digital photos.

◆ **iMovie** enables you to create your own movies, complete with transitional effects, subtitles, and voiceovers, from digital video clips.

◆ **iDVD** enables you to take movies created with iMovie and burn DVDs.

This chapter covers the basics of each of these applications—just enough information to help you explore them on your own.

✔ Tips

■ Unfortunately, iCal and iSync, two new Apple i-Applications, were not yet available when this book went to press. Check the companion Web site for this book, www.marialanger.com/booksites/macosx.html, after September 30 to download additional book pages that cover these applications.

■ Peachpit Press offers a number of titles in its *Visual QuickStart Guide* series that cover each of these programs. To get the most out of a specific application, I highly recommend that you obtain one of these books. You can learn more on the Peachpit Press Web site, www.peachpit.com.

Obtaining the Latest Versions

Most of the i-Apps—for example, iTunes, iPhoto, and iMovie—are installed automatically as part of a Mac OS X installation. Others must be downloaded from the Apple Web site. Either way, it's a good idea to make sure you have the latest version.

✔ Tip

- You need an Internet connection to update or download the applications covered in this chapter.

To update using Software Update

1. Choose Apple > System Preferences (**Figure 1**) or click the System Preferences button in the Dock to display the System Preferences window.

2. Click the Software Update icon in the System row to display the Software Update pane. If necessary, click the Update Software tab to display its options (**Figure 2**).

3. Click Check Now. Software Update connects to the Internet and checks for available updates.

   If Software Update finds updates, it displays them in a window like the one in **Figure 3**. Continue following instructions with step 4.

   or

   If Software Update does not find updates, it tells you. Choose System Preferences > Quit System Preferences or press ⌃⌘Q to dismiss the Software Update pane. Skip the remaining steps below.

4. Turn on the check box beside each update you want to download (**Figure 3**).

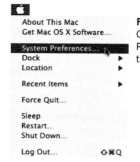

Figure 1
Choose System Preferences from the Apple menu.

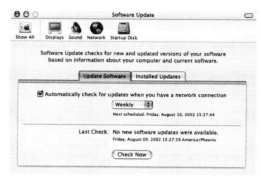

Figure 2 The Software Update pane.

Figure 3 Software Update lists the updates available for your computer. In this illustration, it wants to update the version of iDVD that's installed on my iMac.

5. Click Install. Software Update downloads the updater files you selected and installs them.

6. If Software Update prompts you to restart your computer, do so.

or

Choose Software Update > Quit Software Update or press ⌘ Q to quit the Software Update application. Then choose System Preferences > Quit System Preferences or press ⌘ Q to quit System Preferences.

✔ Tips

■ Software Update only updates Apple and related software that is already installed on your computer. For example, I have iDVD installed on my iMac, but not on my iBook. Software Update offered to update iDVD on my iMac (**Figure 3**), but never listed the update in the Software Update window on my iBook.

■ Software Update may offer to download updates you don't need, including foreign language updates. You can safely quit Software Update without installing unnecessary updates.

■ In step 5, if an Authenticate dialog appears, enter an administrator name and password and click OK.

■ In step 5, if a software license agreement appears, click Agree to continue.

■ It's a good idea to run Software Update regularly and download updates to Mac OS X and its applications. I tell you more about Software Update in *Mac OS X Advanced: Visual QuickStart Guide*.

To download the latest version of other i-Apps

1. Launch Internet Explorer or your preferred Web browser and use it to view one of the following URLs:

   ▲ **iTunes:** www.apple.com/itunes/ (**Figure 4**)

   ▲ **iPhoto:** www.apple.com/iphoto/

   ▲ **iMovie:** www.apple.com/imovie/

   ▲ **iDVD:** www.apple.com/idvd/ (**Figure 5**)

   ▲ **iCal:** www.apple.com/ical/

   ▲ **iSync:** www.apple.com/isync/

2. Follow the links on the page to download the latest version of the software you need. Follow any instructions that appear in the Web browser window. You may be prompted to enter information, including your name and e-mail address before you can download software.

3. When you are finished downloading software, choose Explorer > Quit Explorer or press ⌘Q.

✔ Tips

- I explain how to use Internet Explorer in **Chapter 9**.

- After step 2, you can watch the progress of the download in the Download Manager window (**Figure 6**). In Internet Explorer, choose Window > Download Manager to view this window if it does not appear automatically.

- The Web site for a specific application can provide additional information about the program's use and hardware compatibility. It's a good idea to read the information on an application's Web site, especially if you have trouble using the application with your hardware.

Figures 4 & 5 Here's the home page for iTunes (above) and iDVD (below). Both offer links for downloading software.

Figure 6 The Download Manager window displays the progress of downloads from Web sites.

Figures 7 & 8 A downloaded file can appear as a disk image file (left) which is mounted as a disk (right) when you double-click it.

iTunes3.pkg

Figure 9 Your goal is to find the installer file, which may look like this.

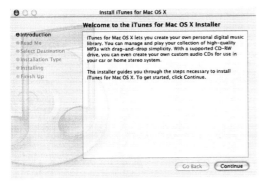

Figure 10 The main installer window guides you through the installation process.

To install downloaded software

1. Double-click the icon for the downloaded software. One of three things will happen:

   ▲ If the icon is for an installer (**Figure 9**), the installer launches. Skip ahead to step 5.

   ▲ If the icon is for a disk image file (**Figure 7**), Mac OS X launches Disk-Copy. Skip ahead to step 3.

   ▲ If the icon is for a compressed file, Mac OS X launches StuffIt Expander to open the file. Continue following instructions with step 2.

2. StuffIt Expander decompresses the file and displays its icon with the down-loaded file's icon. Double-click the icon. One of two things will happen:

   ▲ If the icon is for an installer (**Figure 9**), the installer launches. Skip ahead to step 5.

   ▲ If the icon is for a folder, the folder opens. Skip ahead to step 4.

   ▲ If the icon is for a disk image file (**Figure 7**), Mac OS X launches Disk-Copy to mount the image as a file on disk. Continue following instructions with step 3.

3. DiskCopy mounts the image file as a disk. Its icon appears on the desktop (**Figure 8**). Double-click it to open it.

4. In the Finder window, locate the installer icon for the software. (You may have to open multiple folders to find it.) Double-click the installer icon (**Figure 9**) to launch it.

5. In the main installer window (**Figure 10**), read the instructions that appear onscreen and click the Continue button to step through the installation process.

Continued on next page...

Continued from previous page.

6. At the end of the installation process, the installer tells you it has finished. Click Restart (**Figure 11**) to restart your computer or Close (if displayed) to quit the installer.

✔ Tips

■ By default, your Web browser should be configured to download software to the desktop. If you have changed this configuration to a different folder on disk, you must look for the downloaded files in that location. I explain how to change Web settings, including file download location, in **Chapter 9**.

■ You may be prompted to agree to a license agreement somewhere in the installation process. If you do not click Agree, you cannot install the software.

■ If you need an administrator password to install the software, you'll either be notified in the main installer window (**Figure 12**) or by the appearance of an Authenticate dialog (**Figure 13**). If the message appears in the main installer window, click the lock icon near the bottom of the window (**Figure 12**) to display the Authenticate dialog (**Figure 13**). Then enter an administrator name and password and click OK.

■ The installer varies from one application to another, so it's impossible to cover all variables here. The process, however, is relatively self-explanatory and easy to complete.

■ You can delete the downloaded file after the application has been successfully installed.

■ An application's installer normally installs Mac OS X software into the Applications folder on your hard disk.

Figure 11 The Installer tells you when it's finished working.

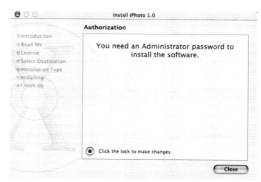

Figure 12 When you first launch the installer, it may tell you that you need an adminstrator password to install the software. It'll either display a message like this in the installer window...

Figure 13 ...or just display the Authenticate dialog.

Figure 14
The iTunes icon.

iTunes

Figure 15 The first screen of the iTunes Setup Assistant.

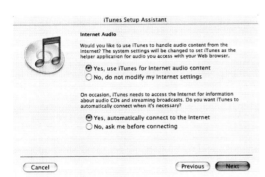

Figure 16 Set options for Internet playback in this screen.

iTunes

iTunes is a computer-based "jukebox" that enables you to do several things:

◆ Play MP3 format audio files.

◆ Record music from audio CDs on your Macintosh as MP3 files.

◆ Create custom CDs of your favorite music.

◆ Save MP3 files to an iPod or other MP3 player.

◆ Listen to Internet-based radio stations.

The next few pages explain how you can use iTunes to record and play MP3 music, copy MP3 files to an iPod, and burn audio CDs.

✔ Tips

■ MP3 is a standard format for audio files.

■ Your computer must have a CD-R drive or SuperDrive to burn CDs.

To set up iTunes

1. Double-click the iTunes icon (**Figure 14**).

2. If a license agreement window appears, click Accept.

3. The iTunes Setup Assistant window appears (**Figure 15**). Read the welcome message and click Next.

4. In the Internet Audio window (**Figure 16**), set options as desired:

   ▲ Select an Internet audio content option. **Yes, use iTunes for Internet audio content** instructs your computer to set your Web browser helper settings to use iTunes for all Internet audio playback. **No, do not modify my Internet settings** does not change your Web browser's helper settings.

Continued on next page...

Continued from previous page.

▲ Select an Internet connection option. **Yes, automatically connect to the Internet** tells iTunes that it's okay to connect to the Internet anytime it needs to. **No, ask me before connecting** tells iTunes to display a dialog that asks your permission before connecting to the Internet.

5. Click Next.

6. In the Find MP3 files window (**Figure 17**), select an option:

   ▲ **Yes, find any MP3 files I have on my hard disk(s)** tells iTunes to search your hard disk for MP3 files and add them to you music library.

   ▲ **No, I'll add them myself later** tells iTunes not to look for MP3 files.

7. Click Done.

   iTunes completes its configuration and displays the iTunes main window. If you instructed iTunes to find MP3 files and it found some, those files are displayed in the window (**Figure 18**).

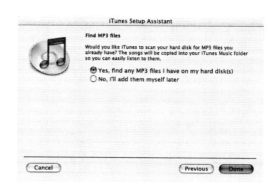

Figure 17 The Find MP3 files window.

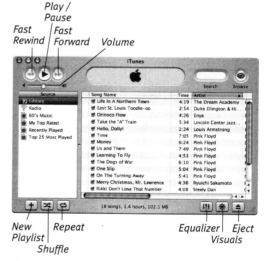

Figure 18 iTunes' main window. (This is the kind of music an oldtimer like me listens to.)

SETTING UP ITUNES

Import button

Figure 19 When you insert a CD, it appears in the Source list.

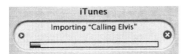

Figure 20 iTunes shows import progress at the top of its window.

To add songs from an audio CD to the Library

1. Insert an audio CD in your CD drive. After a moment, the CD's name appears in the Source list and a list of the tracks on it appears in the Song list (**Figure 19**).

2. Turn on the check box beside each song you want to add to the Library. (They should already all be turned on.)

3. Click the Import button. iTunes begins importing the first song. The status area provides progress information (**Figure 20**). The song may play while it is imported.

✔ Tips

■ Sometime during step 1, iTunes may ask your permission to connect to the Internet. It must do this to retrieve information about the songs on the CD.

■ You can specify whether a song plays while it is imported by setting iTunes preferences. Choose iTunes > Preferences to get started.

■ When iTunes is finished importing songs, it plays a sound. In most cases, iTunes will finish importing songs from a CD before it finishes playing them.

ADDING SONGS FROM A CD

To import MP3 files on disk to the Library

Drag the icon for the MP3 file from the Desktop or a Finder window to the iTunes window (**Figure 21**).

After a moment, the song appears in the Library window (**Figure 22**).

✔ Tips

- You can use this technique to add a bunch of MP3 files at once. Simply select their icons and drag any one of them into the window. I explain how to select multiple icons in the Finder in **Chapter 2**.

- You could also use the Add to Library command on the File menu, but I think this technique is quicker and easier.

To export songs from the iTunes Library as MP3 files

Drag the name of the song you want to export from the iTunes Library window to the Desktop or a Finder window (**Figure 23**).

After a moment, an MP3 icon for the exported song appears in the Finder (**Figure 24**).

✔ Tip

- You can use this technique to export a bunch of MP3 files at once. Simply hold down ⌘ while clicking each song you want to select. Then drag any one of them into the Finder window.

Figure 21 Importing an MP3 file on disk is as easy as dragging it into the iTunes window.

Figure 22 The song you dragged in appears in the iTunes Library window.

Figure 23 Exporting a song as an MP3 is as easy as dragging it from the iTunes window to a Finder window.

Figure 24 An icon for the exported MP3 file appears where the song was dragged.

To play music from iTunes

1. Select the Library or playlist in the Source list that includes the song(s) you want to play.

2. If you want to play a specific song, select the song you want to play.

3. Click the Play button (**Figure 18**), choose Controls > Play, or press [Spacebar]. The songs in the playlist or the song you selected plays.

✔ Tips

- In step 2, you can select multiple songs by holding down [⌥ ⌘] while selecting each song. Then, when you click Play, the songs you selected are played first.

- If you selected one or more specific songs, when the songs are finished playing, the next song in the list automatically begins playing.

- You can use the Shuffle and Repeat buttons or Controls menu commands to play songs in random order or repeat songs.

- If you often play music from iTunes while you work (as I do), I highly recommend connecting stereo speakers to your Macintosh. The sound out of the built-in speakers of some Mac models (like my old Strawberry iMac) can be worse than the sound out of an old AM radio with weak batteries.

To pause play

Click the Pause button, choose Controls > Pause, or press [Spacebar].

PLAYING MUSIC

To create a playlist

1. Click the New Playlist button (**Figure 18**), choose File > New Playlist, or press ⌃⌘N.

2. A new untitled playlist appears in the Source list (**Figure 25**). Type a name for the playlist, and press Enter (**Figure 26**).

To add songs to a playlist

1. If necessary, select Library in the source window to display all MP3 files.

2. Drag a song you want to include in the new playlist from the Song list to the new playlist name in the Source list (**Figure 27**).

3. Repeat step 2 for each song you want to add to the playlist.

4. When you're finished adding songs, click the playlist name. The songs appear in the list. You can play them by following the above instructions.

✔ Tips

■ In step 2, you can select and drag multiple songs. Hold down ⌃⌘ while selecting songs to select more than one, then drag any one of them.

■ You can change the order of songs in a playlist by dragging them up or down.

■ You can sort songs in a playlist by clicking a column heading. Clicking once sorts in ascending order; clicking twice sorts in descending order.

To remove a song from a playlist

1. Select the song you want to remove.

2. Press Delete. The song is removed from the playlist.

✔ Tip

■ Removing a song from a playlist does not remove it from the iTunes Library.

Figure 25
Clicking the New Playlist button creates a new, untitled playlist.

Figure 26
To give the playlist a name, simply type it in and press Enter.

Figure 27 To add songs to a playlist, drag them from the Song list to the playlist name.

Figure 28 The Simple tab of the Smart Playlist dialog.

Figure 29 iTunes found these songs for the smart play-list settings in **Figure 28**.

To create a smart playlist

1. Choose File > New Smart Playlist or press Option ⌃ ⌘N to display the Smart Playlist dialog (**Figure 28**).

2. To choose songs based on Artist, Composer, or Genre, turn on the first check box, choose an option from the pop-up menu, and enter matching criteria in the large text box.

3. To limit the size of the play list by time, file size, or number of songs, turn on the second check box, choose an option from the pop-up menu, and enter a value in the small text box. You can also use the other pop-up menu in that line to specify how songs should be chosen: randomly or by artist, last played, most played, or song name.

4. To automatically update the playlist each time songs are added or removed from the Library, turn on the Live updating check box.

5. Click OK.

6. A new smart playlist appears in the Source list with a suggested name based on what you entered. If desired, type a different name for the list, and press Enter.

✔ Tips

■ The smart playlist feature of iTunes, which was introduced in iTunes version 3.0, is extremely powerful. Explore the Advanced tab of the Smart Playlist window on your own to see additional options for creating smart playlists.

■ You can see what songs iTunes included in a smart playlist by clicking the name of the playlist (**Figure 29**).

To copy songs to an iPod or other MP3 player

1. Using the USB or Firewire cable that came with your iPod or other MP3 player, connect it to your Macintosh and, if necessary, turn it on.

2. If iTunes is not already running or does not automaticallly open, launch it. After a moment, the MP3 player should appear in the Source list (**Figure 30**).

3. Drag the song(s) you want to copy to the iPod or MP3 player from the Song list to the iPod or MP3 player in the Source list (**Figure 31**). The status area indicates that the song is being copied.

4. Repeat step 3 for each song you want to copy.

5. When you are finished copying songs, you can select the iPod or MP3 player in the Source list and click the Eject button to unmount it. You can then disconnect it from your Macintosh.

✔ Tips

- If iTunes was already running when you connected your MP3 player and it did not list the MP3 player in the Source list, quit iTunes and relaunch it. If it still doesn't appear, your MP3 player may not be compatible with iTunes. Check the iTunes Web site for assistance: www.apple.com/itunes/.

- In step 3, you can select and drag multiple songs. Hold down ⌘ while selecting songs to select more than one, then drag any one of them.

- The number of songs you can copy to an iPod or MP3 player is limited by the amount of memory in the player and the size of the songs. My 5 GB iPod has over 800 songs in it and room for more.

Figure 30
Your iPod or MP3 player should appear in the Source list, like my iPod, which I named "Pack of Tunes," does.

Figure 31 Drag the song from the Song list to the iPod or MP3 player.

COPYING SONGS TO AN iPOD OR MP3 PLAYER

Figure 32 This illustration shows the playlists (in the Source list) and the songs (in the Song list) copied to an iPod.

Display options for player

Figure 33 You can use the iPod Preferences dialog to set automatic update options for your iPod.

To copy playlists to an iPod

1. Using the USB or Firewire cable that came with your iPod, connect it to your Macintosh. If iTunes is not already running, it launches, and the iPod appears in the Source list (**Figure 30**).

2. Drag the playlist you want to copy to the iPod from the Song list to the iPod name in the Source list. The playlist appears indented beneath the iPod icon (**Figure 32**).

3. Repeat step 2 for each playlist you want to copy.

4. When you are finished copying songs, you can select the iPod name in the Source disk and click the Eject button to unmount it. You can then disconnect it from your Macintosh.

✔ Tips

- You can only copy one playlist at a time.

- When you copy a playlist, any songs in the playlist that are not already on the iPod are also copied.

- You can set up your iPod to automatically update songs and playlists when you connect. Click the Display options for player button that appears at the bottom of the iTunes window when your iPod is selected in the Source list (**Figure 32**), and set options in the iPod Preferences dialog that appears (**Figure 33**).

COPYING PLAYLISTS TO AN IPOD

285

To burn an audio CD

1. Create a playlist that contains the songs you want to include on the CD and select it (**Figure 34**).

2. Click the Burn CD button.

3. When prompted, insert a blank CD in your computer's CD-R drive or Super-Drive and close the drive.

4. When prompted, click the Burn CD button, which is now black and yellow (**Figure 35**) again.

5. Wait while iTunes prepares and burns the CD. This could take a while; the progress appears in the status window at the top of the iTunes window. You can switch to and work with other applications while you wait.

6. When iTunes is finished burning the CD, it makes a sound. The icon for the CD appears on your desktop.

✔ Tips

■ Your computer must have a compatible CD-R drive or SuperDrive to burn audio CDs. You can find a list of compatible devices on the iTunes Web site, www.apple.com/itunes/.

■ I explain how to create a playlist earlier in this section.

■ If the playlist you have selected will not fit on an audio CD, iTunes displays a dialog like the one in **Figure 36**, offering to create an MP3 CD. Choose this option only if you know your CD player can play MP3 CDs.

■ Do not cancel the disc burning process after it has begun. Doing so can render the CD unusable.

Figure 34 Select the Playlist you want to burn to CD and click the Burn CD button.

Figure 35 iTunes prompts you to click the Burn CD button again.

Figure 36 This dialog appears if you try to put too many songs on an audio CD.

iPhoto

iPhoto is a computer-based photo storage system that enables you to do several things:

◆ Import photos from a digital camera or disk.

◆ Organize photos by name, keywords, and other criteria.

◆ Edit photos to crop them and remove red-eye.

◆ Create a book full of photos.

◆ Share photos with others by printing, exporting, or building Web pages.

The next few pages explain the basics of using iPhoto to import, organize, and share photos.

✔ Tips

■ To import photos from a digital camera, you must have a digital camera that is compatible with iPhoto. You can learn about camera compatibility on the iPhoto Web site, www.apple.com/iphoto/.

■ You can also use Image Capture to import photos from a digital camera. I tell you about Image Capture in **Chapter 6**.

■ iPhoto can only import still pictures. To import video (AVI) pictures from a digital camera, use Image Capture, which is covered in **Chapter 6**. To import movies from a digital video camera, use iMovie, which is covered later in this chapter.

To launch iPhoto

Double-click the iPhoto icon (**Figure 37**) in your Applications folder. iPhoto's main window appears (**Figure 38**).

✔ Tip

■ The first time you launch iPhoto, a dialog like the one in **Figure 39** appears. Click Yes to set iPhoto so it automatically launches when you connect a camera.

To import photos from a camera

1. Using the USB or Firewire cable that came with your digital camera, connect the camera to your Macintosh and turn on the camera.

2. If iPhoto does not automatically launch, open it as discussed on the previous page. Make sure the Import button near the bottom of the window is selected.

3. iPhoto "sees" your camera and displays information about it in the lower-left corner of the window (**Figure 40**). Click the Import button at the lower-right corner of the window.

   iPhoto imports the photos. Its progress appears in the bottom of the window (**Figure 41**). When it's finished, thumbnails of the images appear in the iPhoto window (**Figure 42**).

✔ Tips

■ If iPhoto does not "see" your camera, it may not be compatible with iPhoto. Check Apple's iPhoto Web site for more information, www.apple.com/iphoto/.

■ To have iPhoto automatically erase all photos it downloads, turn on the Erase Camera after transfer check box.

Figure 37
The iPhoto icon.

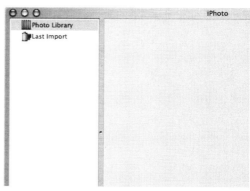
Figure 38 iPhoto's main window.

Figure 39 The first time you open iPhoto, it asks if you want to automatically launch it when you connect a camera.

Figure 40 iPhoto "sees" your camera and tells you how many pictures are on it.

Figure 41 iPhoto reports its progress at the bottom of the window.

■ When the import is complete, you can disconnect and turn off your camera.

■ iPhoto also recognizes photo CDs, including Kodak PictureCD discs, and will also automatically launch when you insert a photo CD. Follow step 3 above to import the images.

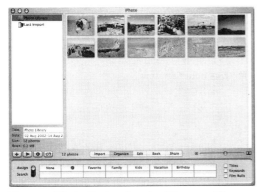

Figure 42 iPhoto displays thumbnail images of the photos it has imported.

Figure 43 The Import Photos dialog.

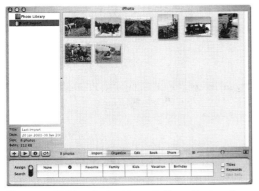

Figure 44 Clicking the Last Import album displays the most recently imported images.

To import images from disk

1. Choose File > Import.

2. Use the Import Photos dialog that appears (**Figure 43**) to locate the photo(s) you want to import.

3. To import only one photo, select the name of the photo and click Import.

   or

   To import multiple photos, hold down ⌃⌘ while selecting the name of each photo you want to import. Then click Import.

   or

   To import all photos in a folder, select the name of the folder and click Import.

   iPhoto imports the photo(s). It displays its progress in the bottom of its window. When it's finished, the photos appear in the main window.

✔ Tip

■ You may find this technique useful to add scanned photos and images to iPhoto.

To review the most recently imported files

Click Last Import in the album list. The most recently imported images appear as thumbnails in the main window (**Figure 44**).

To create an album

1. Click the New Album button at the bottom of the album list (**Figure 45**).

   or

   Choose File > New Album, or press ⌘Ⓝ.

2. Enter a name for the album in the New Album dialog (**Figure 46**).

3. Click OK.

   The album appears in the album list (**Figure 47**).

To add photos to an album

1. In the album list, select Photo Library or the name of the album containing the photos you want to add.

2. Drag the thumbnail image from the main window to the name of the photo album you want to add the image to (**Figure 48**). When you release the mouse button, the image is added to the album.

✔ Tip

■ You can select and drag multiple images at once. Hold down ⌘ while selecting each image, then drag any one image to the album name. All selected images are added to the album.

To remove photos from an album

1. Select the thumbnail for the image you want to remove.

2. Press ⒹⒺⓁⒺⓉⒺ. The photo disappears.

✖ Warning!

■ If you try to remove a photo from the Photo Library or Last Import album, a dialog like the one in **Figure 49** appears. Clicking OK *permanently* deletes the photo from iPhoto and your hard drive.

New Album   Show/Hide Info

Slide show   Rotate

Figure 45 Buttons at the bottom of the album list.

Figure 46 The New Album dialog.

Figure 47
The new album is added to the album list.

Figure 48 Drag a thumbnail image to the photo album.

Figure 49 Clicking OK in this dialog removes the photo from your computer.

CREATING & MODIFYING A PHOTO ALBUM

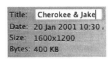

Figure 50
Enter a title for the photo in the Title box.

Figure 51 Click as many keywords as you like to assign them to the selected photo.

Figure 52 You can edit keywords by making changes to the keywords at the bottom of the window.

To enter a title for a photo

1. If necessary, click the Organize button near the bottom of the iPhoto window.

2. Select the album containing the photo you want to enter a title for.

3. Select the thumbnail for the photo.

4. Enter a title for the photo in the Title box beneath the album list (**Figure 50**) and press ⏎ Enter .

✔ Tips

■ If the Title box does not appear beneath the album list, click the Show/Hide Info button (**Figure 45**) until it does.

■ If desired, you can give two or more photos in the same album the same title.

To assign keywords to a photo

1. If necessary, click the Organize button near the bottom of the iPhoto window.

2. Make sure the Assign/Search switch in the bottom-left corner is set to Assign.

3. Select the album containing the photo you want to assign keywords to.

4. Select the thumbnail for the photo.

5. Click the keywords you want to assign to the photo (**Figure 51**). You can assign as many as you like.

✔ Tips

■ To edit keywords, choose Edit > Edit Keywords or press ⌃ ⌘ K , and make changes in the keyword boxes at the bottom of the window (**Figure 52**). When you are finished, choose Edit > Done Editing Keywords or or press ⌃ ⌘ K .

■ To remove keywords from a photo, follow the above steps, but in step 5, click the None keyword.

ASSIGNING TITLES & KEYWORDS TO PHOTOS

291

To change the size of thumbnail images

Move the size slider to the left or right:

◆ Move the slider to the left to make the thumbnails smaller.

◆ Move the slider to the right to make the thumbnails larger (**Figure 53**).

✔ Tip

■ Changes to the thumbnail size affect all albums, not just the one that is selected when you make the change.

To show titles or keywords with thumbnails

To display photo titles beneath thumbnails (**Figure 54**), turn on the Titles check box in the bottom-right corner of the window.

or

To display photo keywords to the right of thumbnails (**Figure 54**), turn on the Keywords check box in the bottom-right corner of the window.

✔ Tips

■ As shown in **Figure 54**, you can display both titles and keywords for photos.

■ Changes to the Titles and Keywords check boxes affect all albums, not just the one that is selected when you make the change.

Size slider

Figure 53 Drag the size slider to the right to make the thumbnails larger.

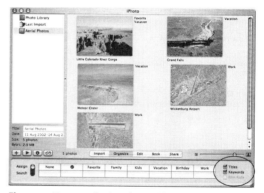

Figure 54 You can display photo titles and keywords for each thumbnail image.

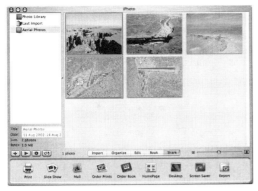

Figure 55 Select the photos you want to print.

Figure 56 The Print dialog with the default Style option—Full Page—chosen.

Contact Sheet
✓ Full Page
Greeting Card
Standard Prints

Figure 57
The Style
pop-up menu.

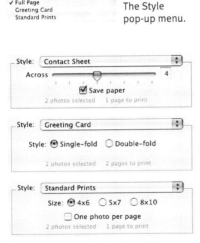

Figures 58, 59, & 60 The Print dialog offers different options for the Contact Sheet (top), Greeting Card (middle), and Standard Prints (bottom) styles.

To print photos

1. If necessary, click the Share button near the bottom of the iPhoto window.

2. Select the photos you want to print. To select more than one photo (**Figure 55**), hold down ⌃ ⌘ while clicking each photo.

3. Click the Print button at the bottom of the window, choose File > Print, or press ⌃ ⌘ P to display the Print dialog (**Figure 56**).

4. Choose the printer you want to use from the Printer pop-up menu.

5. Choose a style from the Style pop-up menu (**Figure 57**):

   ▲ **Contact Sheet** prints multiple photos on each page. With this option chosen, the slider changes the number of photos across each page, thus changing the size of each photo (**Figure 58**).

   ▲ **Full Page** prints one photo on each page. With this option chosen, the slider adjusts the size of the page's margins (**Figure 57**).

   ▲ **Greeting Card** prints one photo on each page. With this option chosen, you can use radio buttons to specify whether you want a single-fold or double-fold card (**Figure 59**).

   ▲ **Standard Prints** prints one photo on each page. With this option chosen, you can specify whether you want 4x6, 5x7, or 8x10 prints (**Figure 60**).

6. Click Print. The photos are printed to your specifications.

✔ Tips

■ The Preview area of the Print dialog changes when you change Style settings.

■ I tell you more about printing in **Chapter 8**.

To display a slide show

1. If necessary, click the Share button near the bottom of the iPhoto window to display buttons for the sharing options (**Figure 61**).

2. Select the photos you want to include in the slide show. To select multiple photos, hold down ⌃⌘ while clicking each one.

3. Click the Slide Show button to display the Slide Show Settings dialog (**Figure 62**).

4. Enter a value in the Play each slide for box to determine how long each slide should appear onscreen.

5. Toggle the Repeat slide show check box to indicate whether the slide show should repeat after all photos have been displayed once.

6. Choose an option from the Music pop-up menu (**Figure 63**). None puts the slide show in silent mode.

7. Click OK.

   If you selected music for the slide show, the music begins. The first photo fades in, remains onscreen, then fades out to be replaced with the next photo.

8. To end the slide show, press Esc.

✔ Tips

- You can display a slide show quickly using the default settings by clicking the Slide Show button at the bottom of the album list (**Figure 55**).

- If any of your photos have vertical (or portrait) orientation use the Rotate button at the bottom of the album list (**Figure 55**) to correct its orientation before including it in a slide show. (Unless, of course, you prefer to tilt your head when that photo appears.)

Figure 61 When you click the Share button, buttons for iPhoto's sharing features appear.

Figure 62 The Slide Show Settings dialog.

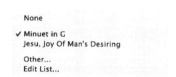

Figure 63 The Music pop-up menu enables you to select a tune or omit music.

iMovie

iMovie is a like a director's editing studio right inside your Mac. You can use it to do several things:

- ◆ Import movie clips from a digital video camera into your computer.

- ◆ Edit clips for length and content.

- ◆ Add titles, special transitional effects, music, and voiceovers.

- ◆ Combine the clips to make a movie.

- ◆ Export the completed movie to a file on disk or to a video camera.

The next few pages provide some basic information about using iMovie to import, edit, and combine movie clips, as well as how to save a finished movie as a QuickTime movie.

✔ Tip

- ■ To import movie clips from a digital video camera, you must have a video camera that can be connected to your computer via Firewire cable and is compatible with iMovie. You can learn more about camera compatibility at Apple's iMovie Web site, www.apple.com/imovie/.

iMOVIE

To launch iMovie

1. Double-click the iMovie icon (**Figure 64**) in your Applications folder.

   If you have already used iMovie to work with movie clips, it opens and displays its windows for the last movie you worked on. Skip the remaining steps.

2. If this is the first time you're running iMovie, an intro window like the one in **Figure 65** appears. Click New Project.

3. Use the Create New Project window that appears (**Figure 66**) to enter a name and select a location for your movie files. Then click Create.

   iMovie's empty windows appear (**Figure 67**).

✔ Tips

- iMovie documents are called *movie projects*. A movie project contains all the information necessary to create your movie.

- When you create a movie project, iMovie creates a folder that contains all of the movie clips and other files for that project.

- If you have already created a movie project and want to start a new one, choose File > New Project, or press ⌃ ⌘ N. Then follow step 3 above to name and save your new project.

- To work with an existing movie project, either click Open Project in the intro window (**Figure 65**), or choose File > Open Project. Then use the dialog that appears to locate and open your movie project file.

Figure 64
The iMovie application icon.

Figure 65 This iMovie introduction screen appears when you first launch iMovie.

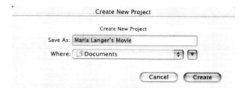

Figure 66 Use this dialog to enter a name and select a disk location for your movie project.

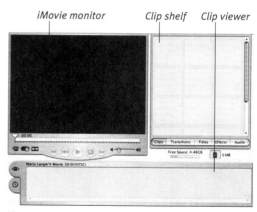

iMovie monitor   Clip shelf   Clip viewer

Figure 67 iMovie's interface includes three main windows.

LAUNCHING iMOVIE

DV
button
Rewind
Pause
Play
Stop
Fast Forward

Figure 68 When iMovie "sees" your digital video camera, it tells you.

Figure 69 iMovie begins importing clips.

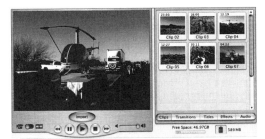

Figure 70 Each clip appears in the clip shelf.

To import movie clips

1. Using a Firewire cable, connect your digital video camera to your Macintosh and turn the camera on. If necessary, set the camera to its VCR or Play mode and rewind to the beginning of the first clip you want to import.

2. If you haven't already done so, launch iMovie.

3. Click the DV button at the bottom of the iMovie monitor. The iMovie monitor turns blue and the words *Camera Connected* appear (**Figure 68**).

4. Click the Import button. iMovie starts the camera and begins importing movie clips. The video for each clip appears in the iMovie monitor while each clip appears in the clip shelf (**Figures 69** and **70**).

5. When you're finished importing clips, click the Stop button at the bottom of the iMovie monitor window. The camera stops.

✔ Tips

■ If iMovie does not "see" your camera (**Figure 68**), it may not be compatible. You can learn more at www.apple.com/imovie/.

■ iMovie can separate clips based on when the camera was stopped or paused during recording. It calculates the total time for each clip and displays it with the clip in the clip shelf (**Figure 70**).

■ The free space indicator beneath the clip shelf shows how the video import consumes your hard disk space (**Figures 69** and **70**).

■ When you're finished importing clips, you can disconnect and turn off your camera.

To review & edit movie clips

1. In the clip shelf, click to select the clip you want to review and edit. The first frame of the clip appears in the iMovie monitor (**Figure 71**).

2. To play the clip, click the Play button at the bottom of the iMovie monitor (**Figure 72**). As the movie plays, the playhead triangle moves along the blue scrubber bar to track the play progress. You can also manually drag the playhead to view a specific frame.

3. To select a portion of the movie, drag the playhead to the beginning of the portion you want to select, hold down Shift, and drag the playhead to the end of the portion you want to select. The scrubber bar turns yellow between beginning and ending points (**Figure 73**).

4. Edit the clip using commands on the Edit menu (**Figure 74**):

   ▲ To cut or copy a clip selection, choose Edit > Cut (⌃ ⌘ X) or Edit > Copy (⌃ ⌘ C).

   ▲ To paste a clip selection from the clipboard into the clip at the playhead point, choose Edit > Paste (⌃ ⌘ V).

   ▲ To remove all of the clip except the selection, choose Edit > Crop (⌃ ⌘ K).

   ▲ To cut the clip into two separate clips split at the playhead, choose Edit > Split Video Clip at Playhead (⌃ ⌘ T).

   ▲ To create a still video clip of the image in the iMovie monitor, choose Edit > Create Still Clip (Shift ⌃ ⌘ S).

✔ Tip

■ You can use other controls at the bottom of the iMovie monitor (**Figure 72**) to control movie play. Experiment with them on your own.

Figure 71 Select the clip you want to edit. (This is John.)

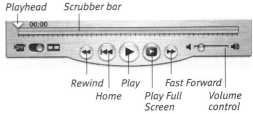

Playhead   Scrubber bar

Rewind | Play | Fast Forward
Home | Play Full Screen | Volume control

Figure 72 The controls at the bottom of the iMovie monitor when a clip is selected for playing or editing.

Figure 73 The scrubber bar turns yellow to indicate the portion of the clip that is selected.

Figure 74 iMovie's Edit menu when a portion of a clip is selected.

Figure 75 Drag a clip from the clip shelf to the clip viewer.

Figure 76 The clip you moved from the clip shelf appears in the clip viewer.

Figure 77 Multiple clips in the clip viewer.

To delete a clip

1. In the clip shelf, click to select the clip you want to delete.

2. Press (Delete). The clip is removed from the movie project.

✔ Tip

- When you delete a clip, it is deleted from your computer's hard disk and no longer available for use in the movie project.

To add clips to a movie

1. Drag the clip you want to add from the clip shelf to the clip viewer (**Figure 75**) When you release the mouse button, the clip appears in the clip viewer (**Figure 76**).

2. Repeat step 1 until all clips you want to include in the movie have been added to the clip viewer (**Figure 77**).

✔ Tip

- To remove a clip from the clip viewer without deleting it from the movie project, drag it back to the clip shelf.

DELETING CLIPS, ADDING CLIPS TO MOVIES

To add transitions between clips

1. Click the Transitions button at the bottom of the clip shelf to display the Transitions pane (**Figure 78**).

2. Click to select the transition you want to use. A preview of the transition appears in the Preview area at the top of the Transitions pane (**Figure 79**).

3. Use the slider to set the speed of the transition. The Preview area shows the results of your change.

4. Drag the transition into position in the clip viewer (**Figure 80**). When you release the mouse button, it appears in the clip viewer (**Figure 81**).

5. Repeat steps 2 through 4 for each transition you want to add. **Figure 82** shows what the clip viewer window might look like with several transitions added.

✔ Tip

- Transition effects enable you to make smoother changes from one movie scene to another.

To preview a movie

1. Choose Edit > Select None (**Figure 74**), or press ⌘ ⌘ D.

2. Click the Play button at the bottom of the the iMovie monitor (**Figure 72**).

   The movie plays in the iMovie monitor window, from the beginning to the end.

✔ Tip

- To play only part of a movie, in the clip viewer, select the clips and transitions you want to play. You can hold down ⌘ ⌘ while clicking each item to select more than one. Then click the Play button.

Figure 78
The Transitions pane.

Figure 79
When you select a transition, you can watch a preview in the top of the Transitions pane.

Figure 80 Drag the transition into position in the clip viewer.

Figure 81 The transition appears as a tiny icon in the clip viewer.

Figure 82 Here's an example with several transitions added to the clip viewer.

Adding Transitions, Previewing Movies

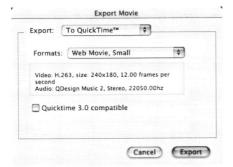

✓ To Camera
  To QuickTime™
  For iDVD

Figure 83
The Export pop-up menu offers three options.

Figure 84 The Export Movie dialog with Quick-Time export options displayed.

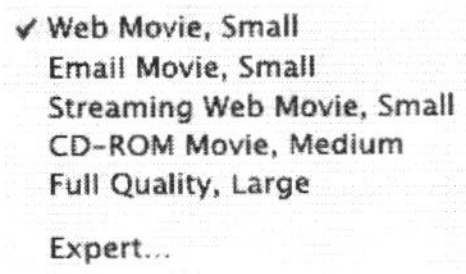

✓ Web Movie, Small
  Email Movie, Small
  Streaming Web Movie, Small
  CD-ROM Movie, Medium
  Full Quality, Large

  Expert...

Figure 85
The Formats pop-up menu enables you to choose a format appropriate for how you plan to use the movie.

Figure 86 Use this dialog to save the movie.

Figure 87 A Progress dialog like this one appears while the movie is being exported.

Figure 88
A movie viewed with QuickTime Player.

To export a movie project as a QuickTime movie

1. Choose File > Export Movie, or press ⌃ ⌘ E.

2. In the Export Movie dialog that appears, choose To QuickTime™ from the Export pop-up menu (**Figure 83**) to display QuickTime export options (**Figure 84**).

3. Choose an appropriate option from the Formats pop-up menu (**Figure 85**).

4. To make the movie compatible with QuickTime version 3, turn on the Quick-Time 3.0 compatible check box.

5. Click Export.

6. Use the Export QuickTime™ Movie dialog that appears (**Figure 86**) to enter a name and select a disk location for the movie. Then click Save.

   iMovie exports the movie. As it works, a Progress dialog like the one in **Figure 87** appears. When the Progress dialog disappears, the export is finished.

✔ Tip

■ Once you have exported your movie project as a QuickTime movie, you can open and view it in QuickTime Player (**Figure 88**). Simply double-click the movie's icon. I tell you more about QuickTime Player in **Chapter 6**.

To export a movie project for use with iDVD

1. Choose File > Export Movie, or press ⌃⌘E.

2. In the Export Movie dialog that appears, choose For iDVD from the Export pop-up menu (**Figure 83**) to display iDVD export settings (**Figure 89**).

3. Click Export.

4. Use the Export QuickTime™ Movie dialog that appears (**Figure 86**) to enter a name and select a disk location for the movie. Then click Save.

   iMovie exports the movie. As it works, a Progress dialog like the one in **Figure 87** appears. When the Progress dialog disappears, the export is finished.

✔ Tip

■ Movies exported for iDVD are exported as QuickTime movies with specific settings that work with iDVD.

Figure 89 The Export Movie dialog with For iDVD chosen from the Export pop-up menu.

iDVD

iDVD gives you the ability to create DVD discs. It enables you to do the following:

◆ Add movies created with iMovie.

◆ Add slide shows of still pictures, with or without a soundtrack.

◆ Create professional-looking menus that include motion and sound.

◆ Preview and burn a DVD.

On the next few pages, I explain how to get started using iDVD, including how to choose a menu theme, add movies and slide shows, preview your DVD, and burn a DVD disc.

✔ Tips

■ To use iDVD and burn DVD discs, your Macintosh must have a SuperDrive or be connected to compatible DVD writer hardware.

■ You can learn more about the system requirements for iDVD at Apple's iDVD Web site, www.apple.com/idvd/.

iDVD

To prepare & organize media for use with iDVD

1. In the Finder, create a folder to store all media that will be used in your DVD.

2. Drag or save media files to the folder you created.

✔ Tips

- iDVD can work with the following types of media:

  ▲ **Movies** should be saved as digital video movies in QuickTime format. You can use iMovie's export command to save movies for iDVD as discussed earlier in this chapter.

  ▲ **Pictures** should be sized at 640 x 480 pixels and saved in JPEG (.jpg) or TIFF (.tif or .tiff) format. iPhoto can export to both of these formats.

  ▲ **Sounds** should be saved in Quick-Time, AIFF, or MP3 format. iTunes can save music in MP3 format, as discussed earlier in this chapter.

- Although you don't have to organize iDVD media in advance, it'll make creating your DVD easier if you do.

- You can further organize your iDVD media by including folders within the folders. **Figure 90** shows an example.

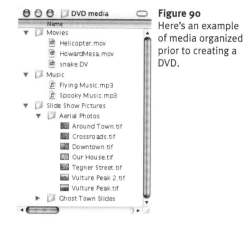

Figure 90
Here's an example of media organized prior to creating a DVD.

Figure 91
The iDVD application icon.

Figure 92 iDVD's intro window.

Figure 93 Use this dialog to name and save your iDVD project.

Figure 94 iDVD's default menu window displays a theme.

To launch iDVD

1. Double-click the iDVD icon (**Figure 91**) in your Applications folder. (It may be inside the iDVD 2 folder.)

   If you have already used iDVD, it opens and displays its windows for the last DVD you worked on. Skip the remaining steps.

2. If this is the first time you're running iDVD, an intro window like the one in **Figure 92** appears. Click New Project.

3. Use the Save New Project As window that appears (**Figure 93**) to enter a name and select a location for your iDVD project file. Then click Save.

   iDVD's menu window appears (**Figure 94**).

✔ Tips

- iDVD documents are called *iDVD projects*.

- If you have already created an iDVD project and want to start a new one, choose File > New Project, or press ⌘N. Then follow step 3 above to name and save your new project.

- To work with an existing iDVD project, either click Open Project in the intro window (**Figure 92**) or choose File > Open Project. Then use the dialog that appears to locate and open your iDVD project file.

To choose a theme

1. Click the Theme button at the bottom of the iDVD window (**Figure 94**) to slide out the Theme drawer.

2. If necessary, click the Theme tab to display its options (**Figure 95**).

3. Click the preview for the theme you want to use for your DVD. The menu window changes to display your selected theme (**Figure 96**).

✔ Tip

■ Some themes include animation and sound. If you find this distracting as you work, click the motion button at the bottom of the menu window to quiet things down.

To rename the main menu

1. Select the main menu text (**Figure 97**).

2. Enter the text you want to appear in the main menu (**Figure 98**) and press (Return).

✔ Tip

■ You can use this technique to change any menu text, including the text that appears under buttons.

Figure 95 When you click the Theme button, the Theme drawer slides out.

Figure 96 The theme you select is applied to the menu window.

Figure 97 & 98 Editing menu text is as simple as selecting it (above), typing in new text (below), and pressing (Return).

CHOOSING A THEME, RENAMING THE MENU

Figure 99 Drag the icon for the movie you want to add from the Finder window to iDVD's menu window.

Figure 100 A button for the movie appears.

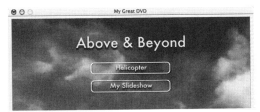

Figure 101 When you click the Slideshow button, a button for your slide show appears in the menu window.

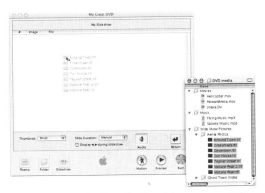

Figure 102 Drag the icons for the pictures you want in your slide show from the Finder window to iDVD's slide show window.

To add a movie

Drag the icon for the movie from the Finder window to iDVD's menu window (**Figure 99**).

When you release the mouse button, the movie appears as a button in the menu window (**Figure 100**).

To add a slide show

1. Click the Slideshow button at the bottom of the menu window.

2. A slide show button appears in the menu window (**Figure 101**). Double-click it to open the slide show window.

3. Drag the icons for the pictures you want to include in the slide show from the Finder window to iDVD's slide show window (**Figure 102**).

   When you release the mouse button, thumbnails of the images appear in the slide show window (**Figure 103**).

4. Click the Return button to return to the main menu window.

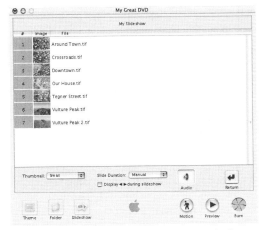

Figure 103 Thumbnails for the images appear in the slide show window.

To customize the appearance of buttons

1. If the Themes drawer is not already showing, click the Themes button to display it.

2. Click the Customize tab to display its options (**Figure 104**).

3. Make changes to settings in the Button area as desired:

   ▲ Choose a shape from the button shape pop-up menu (**Figure 105**).

   ▲ Choose a text position from the Position pop-up menu (**Figure 106**).

   ▲ Choose a text typeface from the Font pop-up menu. (This menu lists all of the fonts properly installed in your system.)

   ▲ Choose a text color from the Color pop-up menu (**Figure 107**).

   ▲ Use the slider to change the size of the text.

   Your changes take effect immediately (**Figure 112**).

To rename a button

1. Select the button text.

2. Enter the text you want to appear in the button and press Return.

To move buttons

1. Display the Customize tab of the Themes drawer (**Figure 104**) as instructed above.

2. Select the Free Position radio button.

3. Use your mouse pointer to drag the buttons into their desired positions in the menu window (**Figure 112**).

Figure 104
The Customize tab of the Themes drawer.

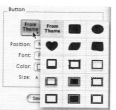

Figure 105
You can choose a button shape from this pop-up menu.

Figures 106 & 107
The Position (left) and Color (right) pop-up menus.

Figures 108 & 109 Select the movie's button to display the slider (left), then slide the tab until the image you want to appear is displayed (right).

Figure 110 Drag the image from the Finder window to the button on which you want it to appear.

Figure 111
The image appears on the button.

Figure 112 Here's an example of a menu customized using techniques on these two pages.

To display a specific frame on a movie button

1. If necessary, follow the instructions on the previous page to choose a button shape that displays an image.

2. Click the movie's button. A slider appears above it (**Figure 108**).

3. Drag the slider until the frame you want to appear is displayed (**Figures 109** and **112**).

✔ Tip

■ To display a still image rather than a looping animation from the movie, turn off the Movie checkbox (**Figure 108** or **109**).

To display a specific image on a slide show button

1. If necessary, follow the instructions on the previous page to choose a button shape that displays an image.

2. Drag the icon for the picture you want to display on the button from the Finder window to the button (**Figure 110**).

   When you release the mouse button, the picture appears on the button (**Figures 111** and **112**).

To add music to a slide show

1. Double-click the button for the slide show to which you want to add music to open the slide show window.

2. Drag the icon for the music file from the Finder window to the Audio well in the slide show window (**Figure 113**).

   When you release the mouse button, the icon for the audio file appears in the Audio well and the Slide Duration pop-up menu is set to Fit To Audio (**Figure 114**).

3. Click the Return button to return to the menu window.

To preview the DVD

1. Click the Preview button at the bottom of the menu window.

2. A DVD player control appears and one of the buttons becomes selected (**Figure 115**). Click buttons on the control to simulate running the DVD from a DVD player.

3. When you are finished trying out the DVD, click the Preview button again to return to editing mode.

✔ Tip

■ You can also use the arrow keys and (Return) to select and choose DVD menu items while previewing a DVD.

Figure 113 Drag the audio file from the Finder window to the Audio well in the slide show window.

Figure 114 An icon for the audio file appears in the Audio well.

Figure 115 The Preview feature simulates a DVD player.

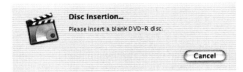

Figure 116 A dialog like this prompts you to insert a blank DVD-R disc.

To burn a DVD disc

1. If you disabled the Motion feature while you worked with iDVD, click the Motion button to enable it.

2. Click the Burn button at the bottom of the menu window.

3. The Burn button pulsates black and yellow. Click it again.

4. A dialog appears, telling you to insert a blank DVD-R disc (**Figure 116**). Insert the disc and close the disc tray.

5. After a moment, the dialog is replaced with a progress dialog. It tells you what iDVD is doing and how much time the operation will take. Wait until the disc burning process is complete.

6. When the process is complete, the DVD disc is ejected. A dialog appears, telling you to insert a blank DVD-R disc if you want to create another DVD. Click Done.

✔ Tip

■ If you cancel the disc burning process before it is finished, the disc may be rendered unusable.

BURNING A DVD DISC

AppleScript Basics

AppleScript

AppleScript is the scripting language that comes with Mac OS X. It enables you to automate tasks and extend the functionality of Mac OS X.

You use AppleScript's Script Editor application to write small programs or *scripts* that include specially worded *statements*. When you run a script, the script can send instructions to the operating system or applications and receive messages in return.

For example, say that at the end of each working day, you back up the contents of a specific folder to a network disk before you shut down your computer. The folder is large and the network can be slow, so you often have to wait ten minutes or more to shut down the computer when the backup is finished. You can write a script that mounts the network drive, backs up the folder, and shuts down your computer automatically. You simply run the script, turn out the lights, and go home. AppleScript does the rest.

As with most programming languages, AppleScript can be extremely complex—far too complex to fully cover in this book. In this chapter, I'll provide some basic information about using Script Editor and examining the example scripts that come with Mac OS X. This introduction should be enough to help you decide whether you want to fully explore the world of AppleScript programming.

✔ Tips

■ AppleScript statements are converted by Mac OS into *Apple events*—messages that can be understood by the operating system and applications.

■ You can find a lot more information about AppleScript, including tutorials, sample scripts, and a reference manual, at Apple's AppleScript Web site, www.apple.com/applescript/.

■ Peachpit Press offers a number of books that cover AppleScript. Check its Web site, www.peachpit.com, for a complete list of titles.

AppleScript Files

There are three types of AppleScript files (**Figure 1**):

Mount Disk Mount Disk Applet Mount Disk Script

Figure 1 An AppleScript file as a script text file (left), an applet (middle) and a compiled script (right).

◆ **Script text files** are text files containing AppleScript statements. They can be opened with Script Editor or any text editor application and can be run from within Script Editor. Double-clicking a script text file icon launches Script Editor or the text editing application in which it was created.

◆ **Compiled scripts** are completed scripts that can be launched from an application's script menu or from the script menu. Double-clicking a compiled script icon launches Script Editor.

◆ **Applets** or **script applications** are full-fledged applications that can be launched by double-clicking their icons.

✔ Tip

■ In most cases, you will create compiled scripts.

Figure 2 The contents of the AppleScript folder.

Figure 3 A new, untitled Script Editor window.

Figure 4 An extremely simple script in a Script Editor window.

Script Editor

Script Editor is an application you can use to write AppleScript scripts. It has a number of features that make it an extremely useful tool for script writing:

◆ The Script Editor window can automatically format script statements so they're easy to read.

◆ The syntax checker can examine your script statements and identify any syntax errors that would prevent the script from running or compiling.

◆ The Open Dictionary command makes it possible to view an application's dictionary of AppleScript commands and classes.

◆ The record script feature (when it works) can record actions as script steps.

◆ The Save and Save As commands enable you to save scripts as script text files, compiled scripts, and applets.

✔ Tip

■ As this book went to press, AppleScript 1.9 did not support recording scripts in the Mac OS X 10.2 Finder. In fact, I couldn't find any application it would work with.

To launch Script Editor

Open the Script Editor icon in the Apple-Script folder in your Applications folder (**Figure 2**). An untitled Script Editor window appears (**Figure 3**).

or

Open the icon for a compiled script (**Figure 1**, right). The script appears in a Script Editor window (**Figure 4**).

To write a script

1. If necessary, choose File > New Script (**Figure 5**) or press ⌘ ⌘ N to open an empty Script Editor window (**Figure 3**).

2. If desired, type a description for the script in the Description box.

3. Type the script steps in the bottom half of the window. Be sure to press Return after each line. **Figure 6** shows an example of another simple script.

To check the syntax for a script

Click the Check Syntax button in the script window (**Figure 6**).

If your script's syntax is error-free, Script Editor formats and color-codes your statements (**Figure 7**).

or

If Script Editor finds a problem with your script, it displays a dialog that describes the problem and indicates where it is in the script by selecting it (**Figure 8**). Click Cancel to dismiss the dialog and fix the problem.

✔ Tips

- The syntax checker attempts to *compile* the script, which translates it into *code* that can be read and understood by your computer. (Compiled code does not appear onscreen.) If the script cannot be compiled, a syntax error results.

- Unfortunately, even if you write a script without any syntax errors, the script is not guaranteed to work. The only way to make sure a script works is to run it.

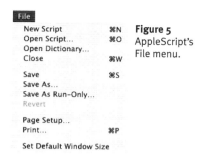

Figure 5
AppleScript's File menu.

Figure 6 Another simple script.

Figure 7 If your script's syntax is okay, Script Editor formats it for you, making it easier to read.

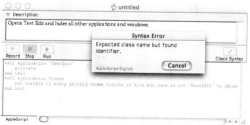

Figure 8 If your script's syntax has a problem, Script Editor displays a cryptic note to explain what it is. In this example, Script Editor had a problem with the word *process* in the second to last line. But the problem was a direct result of me removing the double quote characters from around the word *Finder* in the previous line. As you can imagine, writing and debugging scripts requires a good knowledge of AppleScript!

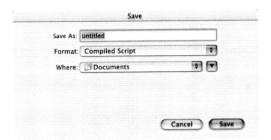

Figure 9 The Save dialog includes a menu you can use to set the format of the file you are saving.

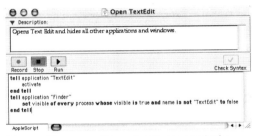

Figure 10
The Format
pop-up menu.

Figure 11 The name of the script file appears in the title bar.

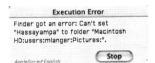

Figure 12 An example of an error message.

To save a script

1. Choose File > Save or press ⌃⌘S to display the Save dialog (**Figure 9**).

2. Enter a script name in the Save As box.

3. Choose a file format from the Format pop-up menu (**Figure 10**).

4. Use the Where part of the dialog to select a location in which to save the file.

5. Click Save. The file is saved on disk. The script name appears in the title bar of the Script Editor window (**Figure 11**).

✔ Tips

■ You cannot save a script if it will not compile. Check the script syntax before attempting to save the file; I explain how on the previous page.

■ If you're not sure what to choose in step 3, choose Compiled Script.

■ It's a good idea to save a script before trying to run it for the first time.

■ Using the Save dialog is covered in **Chapter 5**.

To run a script

Do one of the following:

◆ To run a compiled script from within Script Editor, click the Run button in the Script Editor window (**Figure 11**).

◆ To run an applet from the Finder, double-click the icon for the applet (**Figure 1**, middle).

If the script is valid, it performs all script commands.

or

If the script is not valid, an error message appears (**Figure 12**). Click Stop to stop the script.

AppleScript Dictionaries

Scriptable applications include *AppleScript dictionaries*, which list and provide syntax information for valid AppleScript commands and classes. These dictionaries are a valuable reference for anyone who wants to write scripts.

An AppleScript dictionary is organized into *suites*. Each suite includes a number of related *commands* and *classes*. Commands are like verbs—they tell an application to do something. Classes are types of objects that a command can be performed on. For example, in TextEdit's Standard Suite, *close* is a command that can be performed on an object such as *window*.

Figures 14 and 15 show examples of Apple-Script Dictionaries for two applications: Finder and TextEdit. In each illustration, the first suite is selected to display all commands and classes in that suite. On the left side of the window, suite names appear in bold text, commands appear in normal text, and classes appear in italic text.

✔ Tip

■ Although dictionaries are helpful for learning valid AppleScript commands, they are not sufficient for teaching a beginner how to write scripts.

To consult an application's AppleScript dictionary

1. Choose File > Open Dictionary.

2. In the Open Dictionary dialog that appears (**Figure 13**), select a dictionary and click Open. The dictionary opens in its own window (**Figures 14** and **15**).

3. Click the name of a suite, command, or class to display its information in the right side of the window.

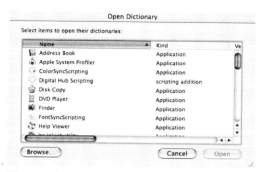

Figure 13 The Open Dictionary dialog.

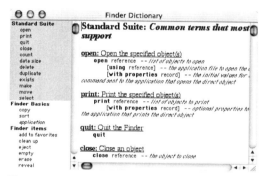

Figures 14 & 15 The AppleScript Dictionaries for Finder (above) and TextEdit (below).

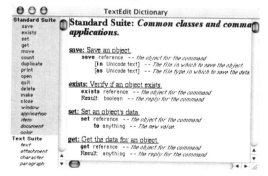

Figure 16 Double-clicking the Example Scripts alias icon in the AppleScript folder opens the Scripts folder.

Figure 17 Some scripts can be simple, like this one to open a folder, ...

Figure 18 ...while others can be complex, like this one, which accesses the Internet to get the current temperature at your location. (A thermometer outside your window would be simpler.)

Example Scripts

The AppleScript folder within your Applications folder (**Figure 2**) includes an alias called Example Scripts. Double-clicking this alias opens the Scripts folder (**Figure 16**) inside the Library folder. This is where you can find example scripts that you can explore to learn more about scripting. You can also use many of these scripts as they are or modify them for your own use.

To examine an example script

Double-click the example script file's icon to open it in Script Editor (**Figures 17** and **18**).

✔ Tips

- You can modify and experiment with these example scripts as desired.

- If you make changes to an example script, I highly recommend that you use the Save As command to save the revised script with a different name or in a different location. Doing so will keep the original example intact, in case you want to consult it again.

- You can download additional sample scripts from Apple's AppleScript Web site, www.apple.com/applescript/.

Script Menu.menu

Script Menu.menu is an application that puts a script menu in the menu bar (**Figure 19**). Click the menu's icon to display a menu with submenus of compiled scripts (**Figure 20**). This makes it easy to run compiled scripts without launching Script Editor.

Figure 19 A script menu icon appears on the menu bar.

✔ Tip

■ Do the submenu names in the script menu (**Figure 20**) look familiar? They should. They correspond to the folder names in the Scripts folder (**Figure 16**). And the scripts on each submenu correspond to the scripts within each folder.

Figure 20 Clicking the script menu's icon displays a menu with submenus full of scripts.

To install Script Menu

Open the Script Menu.menu icon in the AppleScript folder in your Applications folder (**Figure 2**). The menu appears (**Figure 19**).

To run a script from the script menu

Choose the name of the script you want to run from the appropriate submenu on the script menu (**Figure 20**).

To add a script to the script menu

Move or copy the file icon for a compiled script into the appropriate folder within the Scripts folder (**Figure 16**) in the Library folder.

✔ Tips

■ You can quickly open the Scripts folder by choosing Open Scripts Folder from the script menu (**Figure 20**).

■ You can create submenus within the script menu by adding folders to the Scripts folder (**Figure 16**).

Getting Help

Getting Help

Mac OS offers two basic ways to get additional information and answers to questions as you work with your computer:

◆ **Help Tags** identify screen items as you point to them. This help feature is supported by many (but not all) applications.

◆ **Mac Help** uses the Help Viewer application to provide information about using Mac OS and Mac OS X applications. This Help feature, which is accessible through commands on the Help menu, is searchable and includes clickable links to information.

This chapter explains how to get help when you need it.

✔ Tip

■ Balloon Help and Guide Help, which were available in Mac OS 9.x and earlier, are no longer available in Mac OS X. You can still find them in applications running in the Classic environment.

Help Tags

Help Tags identify screen elements that you point to by providing information in small yellow boxes (**Figures 1**, **2**, and **3**).

✔ Tips

- Help Tags replace the Balloon Help feature available in Mac OS 9.x and earlier versions of Mac OS.

- Help Tags are especially useful when first starting out with a new software application. Pointing at various interface elements and reading Help Tags is a great way to start learning about how a program works.

To use Help Tags

Point to an item for which you want more information. If a Help Tag is available for the item, it appears after a moment (**Figures 1**, **2**, and **3**).

Figure 1 A Help Tag in the Address book main window, ...

Figure 2 ...in the TextEdit Preferences window, ...

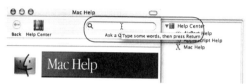

Figure 3 ...and in the Mac Help window.

Mac Help

Mac Help uses the Help Viewer application to display information about Mac OS or a specific application. It includes several features that enable you to find information—and use it—quickly:

◆ **Questions** (**Figures 6a** and **6b**) offers links to answers for frequently asked questions.

◆ **Search feature** enables you to search for topics containing specific words or phrases.

◆ **Links to related information** enable you to move from one topic to a related topic.

◆ **Links to applications** enable you to open an application referenced by a help topic.

◆ **Links to online information** enable you to get the latest information from Apple's Web site.

✔ Tips

■ Although this feature's generic name is Mac Help, help windows may display the name of the application that help is displayed for.

■ You can find additional support for Mac OS, as well as Apple hardware and software, on Apple's Support Web site, www.apple.com/support/ or through the AppleCare channel of Sherlock. I tell you about the Internet in **Chapter 9** and about Sherlock in **Chapter 10**.

To open Mac Help

Choose Help > *Application Name* Help
(**Figures 4a**, **4b**, and **4c**), or press ⌃⌘⌥.

or

Choose Help from a contextual menu
(**Figure 5**).

or

Click the Help button in a window or dialog
in which it appears.

The main Help window (**Figures 6a** and **6b**)
or help topic (**Figure 6c**) appears.

✔ Tips

- Using contextual menus is covered in
  Chapter 2.

- Clicking the Help Center button in the
  toolbar toggles the display of a drawer
  with Mac Help topics (**Figure 7**). Clicking
  one of the topics opens the main window
  for that topic. The topics that appear in
  the Help Center vary depending on the
  applications for which you have viewed
  Mac Help.

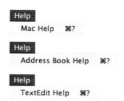

Figures 4a, 4b, & 4c
The Help command on
Help menus for the Finder
(top), Address Book
(middle), and TextEdit
(bottom).

Figure 5
The Help command
can also be found
on some contextual
menus.

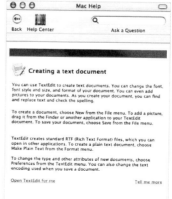

Figures 6a, 6b, & 6c These are the main Help windows for the Finder (left) and Address Book (middle). TextEdit's main Help window (right) is also a help topic, providing information in addition to links.

OPENING MAC HELP

Figure 7 The Help Center is a drawer full of main Help topics that cover a variety of Mac OS X applications.

Figure 8 Enter a search word or phrase in the field at the top of the Help window.

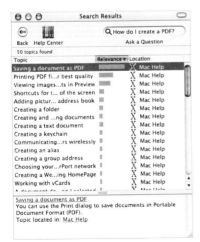

Figure 9 When you click Ask, a list of topics matching the search criteria appears.

To search Help

1. Enter a search word, phrase, or question in the entry field at the top of the Help window (**Figure 8**) and press Return.

2. After a moment, the Help window fills with a list of search results. Click a topic to display information about it in the bottom of the window (**Figure 9**).

3. Double-click a topic in the search results list or click the topic's name in the bottom of the window. The topic's information appears in the window (**Figure 10**).

✔ Tips

- The bars in the Relevance column in the Search Results list indicate how well the topics match your search word, phrase, or question. The bigger the bar, the more relevant the item.

- You can click the Back button (**Figures 9 and 10**) to view previously viewed Help windows.

Figure 10 Clicking a link displays information as a Help topic.

SEARCHING HELP

Application Help

Many applications include extensive online help. The help features of various applications may look and work differently, so it's impossible to cover them in detail here. Most online help features, however, are easy to use.

✔ Tips

■ Some applications, such as the Microsoft Office suite of products, include an entire online manual that is searchable and printable.

■ Not all applications include online help. If you can't locate an online help feature for an application, check the documentation that came with the application to see if it has one and how you can access it.

To access an application's online help

Choose a command from the Help menu within that application (**Figure 11**).

or

Click a Help button within a dialog.

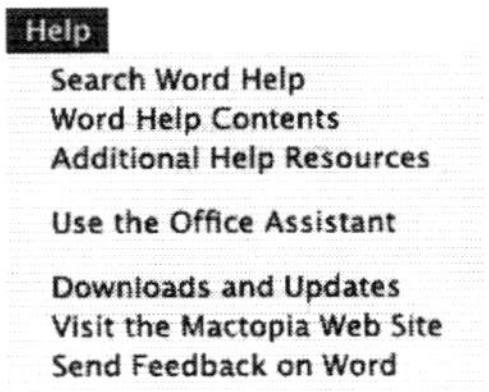

Help

Search Word Help
Word Help Contents
Additional Help Resources

Use the Office Assistant

Downloads and Updates
Visit the Mactopia Web Site
Send Feedback on Word

Figure 11
The Help menu in Microsoft Word X offers a number of commands for getting onscreen help from within Microsoft Office or on the Microsoft Web site.

Help & Troubleshooting Advice

Here's some advice for getting help with and troubleshooting problems.

- **Join a Macintosh user group.** Joining a user group and attending meetings is probably the most cost-effective way to learn about your computer and get help. You can find a users' group near you by consulting the Apple User Group Web site, www.apple.com/usergroups/.

- **Visit Apple's Web site.** If you have access to the Web, you can find a wealth of information about your computer online. Start at www.apple.com/support/ and search for the information you need.

- **Visit the Web sites for the companies that develop the applications you use most.** A regular visit to these sites can keep you up to date on updates and upgrades to keep your software running smoothly. These sites can also provide technical support for problems you encounter while using the software. Learn the URLs for these sites by consulting the documentation that came with the software.

- **Visit Web sites that offer troubleshooting information.** MacFixIt (www.macfixit.com) and MacInTouch (www.macintouch.com) are two excellent resources.

- **Read Macintosh magazines.** A number of magazines, each geared toward a different level of user, can help you learn about your computer: *Macworld*, *Mac Addict*, and *Mac Home Journal* are the most popular. Stay away from PC-centric magazines; the majority of the information they provide will not apply to your Macintosh and may confuse you.

Continued on next page...

Continued from previous page.

◆ **Buy a good troubleshooting guide.**
I highly recommend *Mac OS X Disaster Relief,* a Peachpit Press book by Ted Landau. I'm not recommending this book because Peachpit or Ted asked me to. I'm recommending it because I think it's the best Mac OS X troubleshooting book around. It's the book I use when Mac OS X starts acting up on my computers.

HELP & TROUBLESHOOTING ADVICE

Menus & Keyboard Equivalents

A

Menus & Keyboard Equivalents

This appendix illustrates all of Mac OS X's Finder menus and provides a list of corresponding keyboard equivalents.

To use a keyboard equivalent, hold down the modifier key (usually ⌘) while pressing the keyboard key for the command.

Menus and keyboard commands are discussed in detail in **Chapter 2**.

Apple Menu

| Shift ⌘ Q | Log Out |
| Option ⌘ D | Dock > Turn Hiding On/Off |

Finder Menu

Shift ⌘ Delete	Empty Trash
Shift ⌘ Y	Services > New Sticky Note
⌘ H	Hide Finder
Option ⌘ H	Hide Others

File Menu

⌘N	New Finder Window
Shift ⌘N	New Folder
⌘O	Open
⌘W	Close Window
Option ⌘W	Close All
⌘I	Get Info
Option ⌘I	Show Inspector
⌘D	Duplicate
⌘L	Make Alias
⌘R	Show Original
⌘T	Add to Favorites
⌘Delete	Move To Trash
⌘E	Eject
⌘F	Find

```
File
 New Finder Window    ⌘N
 New Folder          ⇧⌘N
 Open                 ⌘O
 Open With             ▶
 Close Window         ⌘W

 Get Info             ⌘I

 Duplicate            ⌘D
 Make Alias           ⌘L
 Show Original        ⌘R
 Add to Favorites     ⌘T

 Move to Trash       ⌘⌫
 Eject                ⌘E
 Burn Disc...

 Find...              ⌘F
```

Edit Menu

⌘Z	Undo
⌘X	Cut
⌘C	Copy
⌘V	Paste
⌘A	Select All

```
Edit
 Can't Undo           ⌘Z

 Cut                  ⌘X
 Copy                 ⌘C
 Paste                ⌘V
 Select All           ⌘A
 Show Clipboard
```

View Menu

⌘1	as Icons
⌘2	as List
⌘3	as Columns
⌘B	Show/Hide Toolbar
⌘J	Show/Hide View Options

```
View
 ✓ as Icons           ⌘1
   as List            ⌘2
   as Columns         ⌘3

 Clean Up
 Arrange               ▶

 Hide Toolbar         ⌘B
 Customize Toolbar...
 Hide Status Bar

 Show View Options    ⌘J
```

Go Menu

⌘[	Back
⌘]	Forward
Shift ⌘C	Computer
Shift ⌘H	Home
Shift ⌘I	iDisk
Shift ⌘A	Applications
Shift ⌘F	Favorites
Shift ⌘G	Go to Folder
⌘K	Connect to Server

Window Menu

| ⌘M | Minimize Window |

Help Menu

| ⌘? | Mac Help |

Getting Started with .Mac

Figure 1 This version of the .Mac Home page appears if you are not logged in to .Mac.

.Mac

Although this book concentrates on the software that comes with Mac OS X, it wouldn't be complete without at least a brief mention of .Mac.

Apple's new online service, .Mac (pronounced *dot-Mac*), offers a variety of Internet-based services that work with Mac OS:

◆ **Email** (referred to as *Webmail* when accessed via the Web) gives you an e-mail address in the .mac domain that can be accessed via Apple's Mail software, any other e-mail client software, or a Web browser.

◆ **iDisk** gives you 100 MB of hard disk space on Apple's server for saving or sharing files.

◆ **HomePage** lets you create and publish a custom Web site hosted on Apple's Web server, using easy-to-use, online Web authoring tools.

◆ **Backup** enables you to perform manual or automatic backups to iDisk, CD, or DVD.

◆ **Anti-Virus** is McAfee Virex software, which protects your computer from viruses, "Trojan horses," worms, and other computer infections.

Continued on next page...

.MAC

Continued from previous page.

◆ **Support** enables you to access a variety of Web-based support services and features, including the AppleCare KnowledgeBase, and a member-only support forum.

◆ **iCards** enables you to send custom greeting cards to anyone with an e-mail address.

The next two pages explain how to sign up for and log in to .Mac.

✔ Tips

■ .Mac replaces iTools, which was discontinued in July 2002.

■ The Internet is covered in detail in **Chapter 9**.

■ You can learn more about .Mac at www.mac.com (**Figure 1**).

■ .Mac features are relatively easy to use, with step-by-step instructions and lots of online help.

■ .Mac features are discussed in detail in *Mac OS X Advanced: Visual QuickPro Guide*.

.MAC

Figure 2 To join .Mac, start by filling out the Sign Up form.

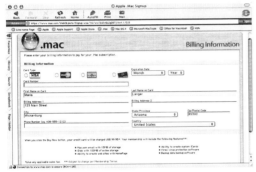

Figure 3 Use the Billing Information form to enter credit card information to pay for your membership.

Figure 4 When your membership has been processed, all of your membership information appears on a page like this.

Joining .Mac

Apple offers two kinds of .Mac memberships:

- ◆ **Trial Membership** enables you to try a limited version of most features for free for two months.

- ◆ **Full Membership** gives you full access to all .Mac features for a year. As this book went to press, the annual fee was $99.95.

These instructions explain how to join with a full membership.

✔ Tip

- You must be 13 years of age or older to join .Mac.

To join .Mac

1. Use your Web browser to view the .Mac home page at www.mac.com (**Figure 1**).

2. Click a Join Now button.

3. Fill in the Sign Up form that appears in your Web browser window (**Figure 2**).

4. Click the Continue button at the bottom of the form.

5. Fill in the Billing Information form that appears (**Figure 3**).

6. Click the Buy Now button at the bottom of the form.

7. When your account has been set up, a Print your information page like the one in **Figure 4** appears. Click your browser's Print button and use the dialog that appears to print the information for future reference.

8. Click Continue.

Continued on next page...

JOINING .MAC

Continued from previous page.

9. A Thank You page appears next (**Figure 5**). It summarizes the features of .Mac. Click the Start Using .Mac button at the bottom of the page to go to the .Mac Home page, where you're already logged in (**Figure 6**).

✔ Tips

■ After step 6, if the Member name you selected is already in use, you'll be prompted to enter a different member name. Follow the instructions that appear to continue.

■ You'll need the e-mail address and server information that appears in the Print your information window to set up your .Mac e-mail account in Mail or another e-mail client software program.

To log into .Mac

1. Use your Web browser to view the .Mac Home page at www.mac.com (**Figure 1**).

2. Click the Log In link.

3. Enter your member name and password in the appropriate boxes of the log in form (**Figure 7**) and click Enter. The .Mac Home page appears (**Figure 6**).

✔ Tips

■ The .Mac Web site saves your member name and password on your computer, so you don't have to log in every time you want to use .Mac features. If your member name appears on the .Mac Home page when you access it (**Figure 6**), you're already logged in.

■ If you did not completely log out the last time you used .Mac, your member name will automatically be entered in the Log In form (**Figure 7**).

Figure 5 Another page summarizes the .Mac features.

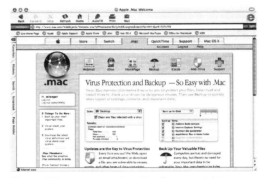

Figure 6 You can start using .Mac features right away.

Figure 7 Fill in this form and click Enter to log into .Mac.

To log out

.Mac offers two log out options:

◆ To log out so your browser remembers your member name but not your password, click the Log Out link on the .Mac Home page or the Log Out button at the top of any .Mac page.

◆ To log out so your browser does not remember eithe ryour member name or password, click the Log Out Completely link on the .Mac Home page.

✔ Tip

■ It is not necessary to log out of .Mac. However, if you do not log out, anyone using your computer will have access to your .Mac account. It's a good idea to log out after using .Mac when you're working on a computer that is shared by others.

LOGGING OUT

Setting Up Mac OS to Use Your .Mac Account

Several .Mac features work from within Mac OS X. To make the most of this, it's a good idea to enter your .Mac account information in Mac OS X.

✔ Tip

- If you entered information about your .Mac account when you first configured Mac OS X as discussed in **Chapter 1**, you can skip this section. Mac OS X already has all the information it needs to use .Mac.

To enter .Mac information in the Internet preferences pane

1. Choose Apple > System Preferences or click the System Preferences icon on the Dock.

2. In the System Preferences window that appears (**Figure 8**), click the Internet icon.

3. In the Internet preferences pane, click the .Mac tab to display its options (**Figure 9**).

4. Enter your .Mac member name and password in the appropriate boxes.

5. Choose System Preferences > Quit System Preferences.

✔ Tips

- You can click the iDisk tab of the Internet preferences pane to get information about your iDisk storage space and set options for your iDisk Public folder (**Figure 10**).

- System Preferences are covered in detail in *Mac OS X Advanced: Visual QuickPro Guide*.

Figure 8 The System Preferences window.

Figure 9 Enter your member name and password in the .Mac tab of the Internet preferences pane.

Figure 10 You can also use the Internet preferences pane to check on the status of iDisk.

SETTING UP MAC OS X FOR .MAC

Index

INDEX

INDEX

INDEX

INDEX

OS X

Watch for these titles:

The Little Mac OS X Book

By Robin Williams
ISBN: 0-201-74866-5
824 pages • $29.99

Mac OS X Advanced: Visual QuickPro Guide

By Maria Langer
ISBN: 0-201-74577-1
312 pages • $24.99

Mac 911

By Chris Breen
ISBN: 0-201-77339-2
352 pages • $29.99

Mac OS X Disaster Relief

By Ted Landau
ISBN: 0-201-78869-1
624 pages • $34.99

The Macintosh Bible, 8th Edition

By Clifford Colby and
Marty Cortinas
ISBN: 0-201-70899-X
984 pages • $34.99

iMovie 2 for Macintosh: Visual QuickStart Guide

By Jeff Carlson
ISBN: 0-201-78788-1
216 pages • $19.99

AppleScript for Applications: Visual QuickStart Guide

By Ethan Wilde
ISBN: 0-201-71613-5
480 pages • $21.99

Real World Mac OS X Server

By John Welch
ISBN: 0-201-78264-2
800 pages • $44.99

Look for updated editions of your favorite books at
www.peachpit.com

WWW.PEACHPIT.COM

Quality How-to Computer Books

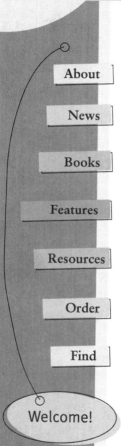

Visit Peachpit Press on the Web at www.peachpit.com

- Check out new feature articles each Monday: excerpts, interviews, tips, and plenty of how-tos

- Find any Peachpit book by title, series, author, or topic on the Books page

- See what our authors are up to on the News page: signings, chats, appearances, and more

- Meet the Peachpit staff and authors in the About section: bios, profiles, and candid shots

- Use Resources to reach our academic, sales, customer service, and tech support areas and find out how to become a Peachpit author

Peachpit.com is also the place to:

- Chat with our authors online
- Take advantage of special Web-only offers
- Get the latest info on new books